AS
EMPIRES
FELL

The ISEAS – Yusof Ishak Institute (formerly Institute of Southeast Asian Studies) is an autonomous organization established in 1968. It is a regional centre dedicated to the study of socio-political, security, and economic trends and developments in Southeast Asia and its wider geostrategic and economic environment. The Institute's research programmes are grouped under Regional Economic Studies (RES), Regional Strategic and Political Studies (RSPS), and Regional Social and Cultural Studies (RSCS). The Institute is also home to the ASEAN Studies Centre (ASC), the Temasek History Research Centre (THRC), and the Singapore APEC Study Centre.

ISEAS Publishing, an established academic press, has issued more than 2,000 books and journals. It is the largest scholarly publisher of research about Southeast Asia from within the region. ISEAS Publishing works with many other academic and trade publishers and distributors to disseminate important research and analyses from and about Southeast Asia to the rest of the world.

AS EMPIRES FELL

The Life and Times of Lee Hau-Shik,
the First Finance Minister of Malaya

OOI KEE BENG

YUSOF ISHAK INSTITUTE

First published in Singapore in 2020 by
ISEAS Publishing
30 Heng Mui Keng Terrace
Singapore 119614

E-mail: publish@iseas.edu.sg
Website: <http://bookshop.iseas.edu.sg>

All rights reserved. No part of this publication may be reproduced, stored in a retrieval system, or transmitted in any form or by any means, electronic, mechanical, photocopying, recording or otherwise, without the prior permission of the ISEAS – Yusof Ishak Institute.

© 2020 ISEAS – Yusof Ishak Institute, Singapore

The responsibility for facts and opinions in this publication rests exclusively with the author and his interpretations do not necessarily reflect the views or the policy of the publisher or its supporters.

ISEAS Library Cataloguing-in-Publication Data

Name: Ooi, Kee Beng, 1955-
Title: As Empires Fell: the life and times of Lee Hau-Shik, the First Finance Minister of Malaya / by Ooi Kee Beng.
Description: Singapore : ISEAS – Yusof Ishak Institute, 2020. | Includes bibliographical references.
Identifiers: ISBN 978-981-4881-44-9 (paperback) | ISBN 978-981-4881-45-6 (pdf)
Subjects: LCSH: Lee, Hau Shik, Tun Colonel Sir, 1900-1998—Biography. | Chinese—Malaysia—Biography. | Politicians—Malaysia—Biography. | Statesmen—Malaysia—Biography. | Businessmen—Malaysia—Biography. | Malaya—History.
Classification: LCC DS597.15 L47O59

Typeset by Stallion Press (S) Pte Ltd

CONTENTS

Preface vii
Acknowledgement ix
Introduction xi

Part One: 1901–42 1
Chapter 1 Colonial Life Between the Wars 3
Chapter 2 Times of Opportunity 31

Part Two: 1942–45 57
Chapter 3 Political Awakening Amid Global Wars 59
Chapter 4 Finding Refuge in India 80

Part Three: 1945–59 115
Chapter 5 Politics in a Messy New World 117
Chapter 6 Moving Towards Merdeka 141

Epilogue: After 1959 200
Appendix 207
Bibliography 209
Index 221
About the Author 235

PREFACE

This book is first of all written for Malaysians so that they may know themselves and their past more profoundly. It is a story about one of the country's founding fathers. Not only did Lee Hau-Shik help found many important institutions, foremost of which was the Malayan Chinese Association, his is the only non-Malay signature on the Declaration of Independence signed in February 1956 in London. If one further considers the fact that he was not even born in Malaya, a supremely race-conscious country, then one has to be curious about who this remarkable person was, and what the times he lived in actually were like.

This Chinese community leader who ignited Malaya's hugely successful independence movement that we remember as the Alliance; this owner of tin mines on whose head the invading Japanese army put a high price; this civilian who became a colonel in both the British army and the Chinese army; this stern person of extremely short physique who, when he withdrew from politics at the age of 58, carried the title of "Sir" and of "Tun", the latter the highest honorific one can attain in Malaya; this migrant who became Minister of Finance and to whom much credit for the founding of the Central Bank of Malaya is given—how is one not to be curious about this man, about his life and times and how this capitalist came to play such a central role in the anti-colonial movement?

Colonel Henry Lee Hau-Shik and Dr Ismail Abdul Rahman were the two people Tunku Abdul Rahman chose to sit on the colonial Executive Council in 1953 to project the interests of the emerging nation of Malaya. It is my hope that this biography of Hau-Shik, read together with my earlier book on Ismail, *The Reluctant Politician* (2006), will provide future generations of Malaysians with an easy yet steady grasp of how their country came into being, and encourage a deeper understanding about the expediencies of the age.

ACKNOWLEDGEMENT

Due to changes in employment and in country of residence while I was working on this book, the final product took much longer than had been planned. For this I am truly sorry to all those who had waited eagerly for it to see the light of day. In truth, this was a project that was in some ways bounced my way while I was Deputy Director at the Institute of Southeast Asian Studies (ISEAS, now ISEAS—Yusof Ishak Institute). I thought it too important a subject to be ignored any further, but other book projects came in the way which for various reasons I had to prioritize. But be that as it may, the book being completed after 9 May 2018, when a new government took power in Malaysia, has meant that a new significance is now given to the life and times of Lee Hau-Shik. Lessons that can be learned from reading about him are definitely relevant to the search for new and less divisive narratives being embarked upon by Malaysianists and Malaysians. The H.S. Lee Papers now kept so competently at ISEAS Library are a rich source of information about the man, and equally importantly, also about the chaotic times in which he lived. Nothing beats browsing through original texts for providing an author with inspiration and insight about a time that is not his own. And so, working on this project has been a humbling experience.

Most importantly, the book is full of reminders about how difficult a peaceful and progressive governance of a multicultural democracy can be, and how easily things can go off the rails in terms of economic progress, fair distribution of wealth and opportunities, and harmony between disparate communities. The historical context is always decisive in a scholar's search for deeper relevance and broader meanings, be it in the study of a man or of his times.

I must first of all thank the family of Lee Hau-Shik, especially Thomas Lee, whose patience I tested to the limit through my delays, and ISEAS – Yusof Ishak Institute, especially the directors under whom I served, Mr K. Kesavapany and Mr Tan Chin Tiong, and the librarians whose help was easily available and warmly given, especially Mr Pitt Kuan Wah and Ms Liang Shuang.

Many others were helpful along the way, and I remember warmly their assistance in the completion of this book, even if I have to leave their names unmentioned here because they are so many, and I do not wish to leave any one person out.

Needless to say, all mistakes and factual errors found herein—and they are bound to be numerous given the volume of material I had to plough through—are my responsibility, and mine alone.

INTRODUCTION

Seldom does one get a chance to write a biography of a historically important personality based on that person's own private papers. Exactly such an opportunity was given to me in 2005 when the Tun Dr Ismail Abdul Rahman papers were offered for safekeeping at ISEAS Library. Over the following few years, three books came out of that heap of papers.[1]

Another such chance was offered to me again a few years later when the family of Lee Hau-Shik—the first finance minister of the Federation of Malaya, one of the founders of the Malayan Chinese Association, and also one of the persons responsible for the highly successful innovation of fielding a coalition of race-based parties back in 1952 in Kuala Lumpur—decided after years of hesitation to also place the man's private papers at ISEAS Library.

While the Ismail papers came in five or six plastic bags, the Lee Hau-Shik papers arrived in over 50 full boxes. Having too few sources hampers a researcher, no doubt, but having too much can be an even greater problem. The documents and pictures reflected the many periods of Hau-Shik's life, but often, they merely provided bits of information stretched over time, multilayered the ways life is played out for each of us, in essence.

However, since the main threads of Hau-Shik's life are known, conjuring a narrative out of the material was in itself not all that difficult. But in order to inject the right historical significance into his story, and to tell a tale that holds lessons for the present time and retains the attention of the modern reader, I decided that it was necessary to contextualize his life into objective periods. After all, the history of Southeast Asia in the first half of the twentieth century was such a tumultous one, and if important dynamics were not highlighted, then the details of his life would lose potency and appear interesting only to those personally involved in some fashion.

What we end up with here, then, is a unique kind of biography. In effect, I must admit that I am opportunistically using the life of Lee Hau-Shik as a telescopic lens through which larger stories can be told within which his private one is played out in—here passively or as a supporting actor perhaps, but there definitely as the lead making up his own lines as he went along.

The book comes in three parts, and ends with an epilogue in which loose ends are collected and his story brought to a close.

Part One is concerned with the first four decades of the twentieth century. Chapter 1 describes the complex socio-political and socio-economic situation of the population of Malaya, where the tongue of land separating the seas fringing the Pacific Ocean meets those flowing in from the Indian Ocean; to which huge numbers of migrants from East Asia and South Asia, and from within Southeast Asia itself came, many to make a living, and some to seek fortunes. Long concerned with controlling key ports, the British had by the late nineteenth century felt it necessary to extend its influence into the peninsula itself. Maintaining the reliability of the supply lines for tin, and then for rubber and other crops and primary goods demanded that. India being a British colony, the transferring of Indian labour to work the mines, the plantations, the civil service and the transport system was a straight forward matter in itself. However, the influx of Chinese migrants to Southeast Asia, most fleeing the chaos plaguing the slow fall of the Qing Dynasty, brought a more complicated set of dynamics to British Malaya.

However, Hau-Shik was not typical of those Chinese. Coming from a wealthy and influential family, his migration to Kuala Lumpur was as an investor interested in tin and several other businesses, an early Chinese capitalist competing with a few others of his kind and with the British capitalist class.

Chapter 2 is about his early life, stretching till the time the Japanese Imperial Army arrived in 1942 to secure supply routes for goods and primary material for themselves. His days are played out not only against the backdrop of Malayan demographics but also on the larger stage of convulsive time and space—between his Chinese homeland and the British world into which he was drawn by education, by interest, and even by marriage. The social movements and the economic possibilites of the times drew him on—out of China, though never fully, into regions where civilizations combined and competed, and cultures conflated and conflicted. There was much a young man of means and imagination could do to make a bigger name for himself and a larger fortune for his family.

It was indeed a time when civilizations were playing their endgame, and falling like bowling pins to leave space for ... well, what would be left and what would come were what Hau-Shik's struggles in politics were about.

Part Two also contains two chapters, the first of which, Chapter 3, focuses on the struggle between Japan, China and the European powers culminating in the creation of the "Greater East Asian Co-Prosperity Sphere" by the Japanese and their push into Southeast Asia as far to the south as Australia and to the east as India. The attacks on Southeast Asia began at the same time as the bombing of Pearl Harbour, and the advance made by the Japanese Imperial Army was indeed a blitzkrieg, occupying as they did all the lands that today make up the ASEAN member states. Malaya fell faster than anticipated, with Penang falling without a fight and the fortress that was Singapore surrendering surprisingly easily.

On hindsight, we see that great risks were being taken by the Japanese armed forces. There was a great probability that their navy would be defeated in the Pacific, which would leave their home islands undefended, which did happen; but at the same time, there was a chance that the Axis forces pushing through Egypt and the Middle East would cut the British empire into two to leave the whole of East and South Asia ripe for occupation by the Japanese forces, which did not happen.

Having the economic means and the political connections, and being on the wanted list of the advancing Japanese, Hau-Shik and his family managed to evacuate out of Kuala Lumpur and then out of Singapore, to head for Chungking, the capital of Kuomintang-held parts of China. Forced to head for Calcutta when news that Rangoon, from whence they were to travel into China, had fallen, they began life as somewhat privileged war refugees in India. There they stayed for four years, most of the time fearful that an invasion was coming. This is the story told in Chapter 4.

The elbowing for imperial space that had gone on in East Asia since the late nineteenth century culminated in what is often called the Pacific War. To be sure, this war between Japan and America and Europe came as accompaniment to the one between a rising Japan and a transforming China that had been going on for much longer. But all these came to a sudden end with a bang—two big bangs in fact, Hiroshima and Nagasaki. The fear that Japanese forces throughout the region would not choose to surrender but would instead fight to the bitter end thus proved unfounded. The atomic bombs changed all that.

But warfare in the region—and in the world—did not really end. An uneasy period of war by proxy and localized fighting would begin. This Cold War would end only in 1991. In the direct aftermath of the Japanese emperor's surrender, however, the colonialists went into a period of damage control and defensive colonialism. The age of nationalism had arrived, and many more Asian nations would soon appear to become members in the United Nations Organization. But to get there, wars of stubborn colonial retreat had to be fought, most notably in Vietnam, where the anti-colonial war fought against the French quickly became an anti-communist war fought by the Americans.

Seen in that context, Malaya was in fact a happy country. Though bloody, the guerilla warfare fought on the peninsula was much more contained in casualty and damage than in all the other major countries in the region. The British were practically the only colonialists who could come back to reclaim their lost territories without having to fight for it. This also allowed them the luxury of planning their retreat over the coming 25 years, While Chapter 5 narrates the general conditions of recolonization after 1945, Chapter 6 describes Malaya's struggle to become an independent country. And it is here in time and space that the experiences, the connections and the stature of Lee Hau-Shik placed him in a historically crucial position. His role was a central one—in Malaya's gaining of independence, and in the form in which it did that.

Not only was it born a strange federation of sultanates, it was governed by a coalition made up of race-based parties each championing its own constituency. How this unfolded holds lessons for those who wish to reform and rectify the system today, and who wish for Malaysia "to live up to its promise"—a common aspiration heard among Malaysians settled the world over.

The Epilogue is added to provide some final remarks about the man and his role in history. The details of Hau-Shik's life as a banker and a financier shall be left for a researcher of a more appropriate academic persuasion than I hold to do. In that endeavour, there is much in the Lee Hau-Shik papers for him to discover and uncover.

NOTE

1. Tun Dr Ismail was a key player in the independence process of Malaya, and held many important positions in the government including Minister of Home Affairs and occasionally took on the role of Acting Prime Minister. In fact, when he passed away of a massive heart attack in 1973, he was holding that position. The three books published by ISEAS Publishing, based on his private papers are: *The Reluctant Politician: Tun Dr Ismail and His Time* (2006); *Malaya's First Year at the United Nations as Reflected in Dr Ismail's Reports Home to Tunku Abdul Rahman* (2009); and *Drifting into Politics: The Unfinished Biography of Tun Dr Ismail* (2015).

PART ONE
1901–42

PART ONE

1901-42

Chapter 1

COLONIAL LIFE BETWEEN THE WARS

> In Malaya, improved transport was introduced to meet international rather than domestic needs. The economy was geared to the extraction of tin and the cultivation of rubber for export, neither of which provided a stimulus for the establishment of domestic heavy industry. The railways were essentially part of a system of colonial economic penetration; connected to Europe by way of the ports, they made possible the rapid carriage of goods. Thus they had practically no multiplier effect on the local economy; almost all the materials, skills, and labor (and to some extent the fuel) necessary for railway construction and operation were imported from abroad.
>
> —Amarjit Kaur[1]

THE LOT OF the labour immigrant is seldom a happy one, today or a century ago. For many of those who travelled from China and India to work in the tin mines or rubber estates in British Malaya, life was far from easy in the period between the two world wars.

To be sure, the whole peninsula underwent tremendous changes in political, economic, demographic and ethnic dimensions during those years. The tin industry that had brought so many to Malaya's shores with its promises of wealth experienced its share of booms and busts, as did the rubber industry. As a whole, the urban population in Malaya grew from 22.7 per cent before the First World War to 35.1 per cent after the Second. This made it the most urbanized place in Asia outside of Japan.[2]

ORGANIZING LABOUR

While British interest in the Malay Peninsula had been strategic in the beginning, by the twentieth century, use of land for rubber production and the mining of tin had become their major economic concerns. These industries formed the basis of the colonial Malayan economy, governed by an administrative system created to provide it with stability and profit. Where labour was concerned, adjustability to shifts in demand as well as sustained low and stable wages were key considerations for the authorities as well as the employers.

The indentured labour system that had been the fate of migrant labourers was abolished by 1914, and it was amidst pressure from the British government in India and from London for improved working conditions for labourers that the Labour Code was established in 1912. Revisions after the First World War introduced new provisions such as the free repatriation of labourers, nurseries and schools for children of labourers, prohibition of child labour, prescription of standard wages, and maternity allowances for women labourers.

However, from the start, the heterogeneity of the labour force and the two main sources of labour supply led to a duality that reflected the plural-societal nature of the Malayan economy. With the Government of India's Indian Emigration Act of 1922, an agent was appointed to oversee the working conditions of

Indian labourers in Malaya, concerned mainly with labour conditions and standard wages. This was a further consequence, for better or worse, of the strong official attention focused—and control exercised—upon this group. Employers of Indian labourers were obliged to provide them with accommodation within the estates.

In many ways, therefore, Indian workers experienced a life quite different from that of their Chinese counterparts. With no pressure from China, colonial authorities in Malaya, in the form of officials of the Chinese Protectorate, had simply incorporated customary practices into their labour regulating activities. The Protectorate which was formed in 1877, had always had to adapt to age-old secret society practices, and its responsibilities were taken over by the Labour Department when this latter body was formed in 1911.

Labour movement activities thus came to develop more concertedly among the Chinese than among the Indians. This was obvious already in the early 1920s, stirred as the Chinese population was by profound political events in China.

Guilds based on sector and dialect group had until the 1920s been the organizational form in which both employers and employees were members and through which work conditions and wage terms were regulated. These tended to function each within its own physical territory as well. But as more industrial means of production came into being, and as Chinese living overseas were drawn into the struggles taking place back home in China, the cohering role of the guilds was quickly overshadowed by more aggressive forces.

In 1924–28, labour unions appeared in Malaya which did not arise from the ranks of the workers as labour organizations had formerly done, but now did so under the influence of the Kuomintang and the Chinese Communist Party. These two, for that short period of time before they became blood enemies, were working in alliance in China. In order to mobilize the Malayan Chinese and to egg on their sense of patriotism, as many as 62 night schools teaching *Guoyu* (Mandarin) were set up in Malaya during those years, 30 of which were in Singapore alone. The rest were spread over the urban centres on the peninsula.

The Hainanese seemed to have been most actively involved in the labour movement at this time, and general labour unions appeared first in the state of Perak, and then throughout the Federated Malay States.[3]

In the years before the Great Depression, Malaya lived through relative peace and prosperity, run by English officials during a period when relations between the races appeared a model of harmony. All around the region, however, the political and economic situation was distressing indeed; and so the colony stood out as a tremendous success.

But with the collapse of the world economy by 1931, spending in both the public and private sectors slowed radically. The drop in labour demands in the mines and estates reversed the immigration flows sharply back to China and India. In 1929, the year stocks plunged in New York, Malaya's products headed for the United States made up 42 per cent of all her exports, and of these exports to the United States as much as 95 per cent came from the tin and rubber industries. The United Kingdom's share of Malayan exports that year, in contrast, was only 14.3 per cent. More interestingly, while 13.7 per cent of imports into Malaya in 1931 came from the United Kingdom, and 2.5 per cent from the United States, as much as 38.1 per cent came from the Dutch East Indies. These simple facts show how the Malayan economy was already more connected to the world than to Britain.[4] What made Malaya so valuable to its colonial masters was therefore not the products in themselves, but the ownership pattern of the key industries.

Global competition was tough during the Great Depression, and preferential duties and tariff schedules began to be implemented from 1932 onwards. In 1934, import quotas on cotton and rayons were introduced in British colonies specifically against Japanese imports. Indeed, the proportion of British and Japanese exports of cotton into Malaya, which was five to two in 1929, turned dramatically by 1933 to one to four. With preferential duties and import quotas in place, British share of imports into Malaya increased successively after 1934.[5]

In 1930–32, over 75,000 Chinese were repatriated to China, half as decrepit men. In the same period, as many as 190,352 Indians were sent home from Malaya as well. Such readjustments of the labour force saw unemployment among migrants drop drastically by 1933, and remaining relief camps were closed.[6] Between 1929 and 1932, estate employees fell from 206,000 to 104,000; and mine workers from 100,000 to 40,000. At the same time, wages for both the skilled and the unskilled labourers dropped progressively.[7]

The introduction of new industries required new ways of supplying labour, and consequently, the unpredictability of employment brought social changes as well. Of great significance to later political developments was the movement of unemployed workers into vegetable garden farming. Given the fluctuations of the rubber and tin markets, this economic activity—and lifestyle—functioned well as an ad hoc solution to temporary unemployment. This development did not seem to have reached significant proportions until the Great Depression set in.[8] Recommendations were made officially to encourage the farming of land by unemployed Chinese, disseminated through the vernacular press.

As a result of this official stimulus and coupled with the massive unemployment situation, low wages and the influx of Chinese female immigrants, it was inevitable that many labourers turned to the cultivation of land as a form of subsistence activity from which they made a rapid transition to cash crop cultivation.[9]

The agricultural sector as a whole on the Malay Peninsula had been slow in developing. The economies of the Malay kingdoms had mainly been based on trade and small-scale tin mining on the west coast; and farming was mainly subsistence in nature. Only in Kedah, opposite the thriving port of Penang, did it form part of the export economy in the form of rice cultivation. Spices like nutmeg and cloves were opportunistically transplanted by the English to Penang from the Dutch-controlled Banda Islands before the end of the Napoleonic Wars. Crops such as pepper and gambier were the first to be planted on a large scale, however, and this occurred largely in the south of the peninsula, while sugar cane became a major crop grown in Province Wellesley and Perak in the latter half of the nineteenth century. All these were often overshadowed by rubber, which supplied the world economy. The oil palm was introduced only in the 1920s, and would gain full prominence only in the 1980s.[10]

Social changes among the Chinese in Malaya stemmed also from the fact that many labourers had by the 1930s worked off their debt to contractors, and were treated with more caution by contractors. They were also more aware of their rights. The huge immigration of women had also started creating a more family-centred workforce, and cooking and marketing for daily needs were now handled by the family structure, and not through contractors. The use of opium was reduced, and supplies could be obtained from government shops. This also sidelined the contractors who had previously managed this function.

This growing independence from contractors was enhanced by employers preferring direct employment to reliance on contractors for the supply of labourers.[11]

In short, the contract labour system, which saw contractors exercising disproportionate power over labourers on most matters, had begun to unravel.

With war impending by the second half of the 1930s, and the attendant fear of insufficient food supply, an experimental scheme for rice cultivation was started on 5,000 acres of land in Perak.[12] Garden farming had over time become a significant occupation, and by 1939, as much as 8,529 acres were under such cultivation in the Federated Malay States, and this was probably without including illegally farmed land. These settlements tended to be considered to be more permanent by the settlers than officialdom had assumed, given how it provided not only good income but also security. Thus, some farmers chose not to return to mine or estate work when the tin and rubber markets began booming again. Such a change in relation to the land itself undoubtedly led to a change in attitude among the farmers in their relation to the politics and economics surrounding them. This stirred up union activities and enhanced the role so far played by political parties and community organizations.[13]

The Communist Party of Malaya (CPM) came into being in 1930 in the middle of the Great Depression. Its initial lack of influence was recognized by the government then to be the result of "poor organisation, lack of funds and effective police action".[14] Indeed, its labour front, the Malayan General Labour Union (MGLU), was simply an amalgamation of small trade unions. In its 1931 membership register, 60 per cent of its members were Hainanese, 30 per cent were Cantonese, while the remainder were Hakkas, Hokkiens and Indians. In the first years of its existence, the CPM kept to classical proletarian ideology which led it on the one hand to censure the Chinese guilds for their clannishness, narrow goals, and close ties with employers, and on the other to criticize workers for their lack of class consciousness and for their deep association with secret societies. Its attempt in the early 1930s at creating a multiracial front never took off, and was largely weighed down by bad finances and ineffectual leaders; by its institutional recruitment from the Chinese community; and by its strong connection to the struggle in China, where the Chinese Communist Party was fighting for its life against the Kuomintang.[15]

In the latter half of the 1930s, labour unrest on the peninsula drew the CPM's attention northwards from Singapore. Top cadres were transferred north to set up a branch in Selangor to take advantage of the grievances of coal miners in Batu Arang and rubber tappers in Kajang. In Kajang, the majority of estate workers were women drawn from the surrounding squatter settlements. Vocational unions were also being established, such as the Pineapple Cutters Benevolent Association. Nationalist fervour also grew tremendously among the Chinese in Malaya with the outbreak of the Sino-Japanese war in July 1937. United in their opposition to the Japanese invasion of China, Chinese organizations in Malaya formed relief fund committees to collect donations for China's defence. Soon, practically all urban trades had formed organizations, and along traditional guild lines. In the meantime, the wave of labour activism and patriotism also saw the CPM gaining ground through the Anti-Enemy Backing-Up Society, which by 1939 was boasting a membership of 30,000.[16]

With the end of the Great Depression, the Malayan economy had begun to enjoy relative prosperity, with demand for both tin and rubber reaching new heights. By 1937, after it was clear that the British-Japanese Alliance had become null and void, the British announced plans to build a naval facility in Singapore to contain any Japanese incursions into Malaya. This led to speculation in commodities in Malaya, strengthening trade figures even further.[17]

Wages were, however, kept low despite the increased demand for labour, and even as the cost of living in booming times climbed substantially. This led to the first major industrial conflict in Malaya.

Chinese unemployment had reappeared in January 1938, following an increase in immigration in the wake of high rubber prices the year before.[18]

At the same time, reduced tin production in accordance with a lower tin quota worsened the situation, leading the government to expand relief public works to absorb the excess labour. Within a year, as many as 40,000 of the 100,000 workers normally employed in the Malayan mines had lost their jobs.[19] In Perak in May 1939, for example, 28,000 were without work, 95 per cent of whom were Chinese.

TIN IN THE TWENTIETH CENTURY

Arab writings from the ninth century had reported tin being mined in Malaya, but it was in the nineteenth century that this industry matured. First, the tin plate industry had come into being in Great Britain and the United States, while the American Civil War boosted the canning industry as well as the production of the oil barrel. Second, this sudden demand for tin attracted Chinese labourers fleeing famine back home. By 1879, more than 40,000 Chinese were working in the Larut Valley in Perak, while others were settled around Kuala Lumpur in Selangor. The bitter and persistent struggles between Chinese clans and secret societies aroused enough anxiety among businessmen and investors in the British Straits Settlements for them to lobby for British officers to be attached to the sultans of the states where the tin industry was prominent. There was also fear that some other European power—most probably Germany—would take advantage of the chaos in the tin mining areas.[20] And so, from 1874 onwards, British Residents were placed in the states of Perak, Selangor, Negri Sembilan and Pahang.[21] By 1880, tin production on the peninsula had jumped to 20,000 tons from perhaps 6,000 tons in 1874. The discovery of tin in the Kinta Valley in 1880 saw the Chinese population in Perak reaching 80,000 by the late 1880s. The work was tough and the pay was low, and as many as 95 per cent of the mine labourers were Chinese.[22] In the nineteenth century, the success of the tin mining industry was totally dependent on these Chinese coolies. As Frank Swettenham noted, "It is their work, the taxation of the luxuries they enjoy, which has provided something like nine-tenths of (British Malaya's) revenue."[23]

The introduction to Malaya of the bucket dredge, which had been used successfully in the gold mines of Alaska and Australia at the end of the nineteenth century, was delayed by the First World War. But once it came to the valleys of the peninsula, it brought another round of transformation to the industry. By 1928, as many as 100 of these machines were in use, and these were responsible for as much as 30 per cent of total production. The Chinese, however, lacking experience of large-scale enterprise and access to huge financing and to the technical knowledge needed for assembly, maintenance and operation of such dredges, found themselves being left behind. By 1937, European-owned mines were responsible for two-thirds of the tin produced on the peninsula.[24]

The tin industry thus underwent a steady capture by the Europeans away from the hands of the Chinese. While Chinese mines managed to produce 78 per cent of total ore output in 1910, by 1938, it was European companies that were producing two-thirds of total production. As mentioned, this shift was possible due to the introduction of dredges in 1912, which went on to become the major form of technology used in tin mines. The Europeans exercised total control over this innovation, and tin dredges were soon responsible for as much as 45 per cent of total output.

Export figures for both tin and rubber reveal how dominant these products were to the colonial economy. In 1937, these two constituted 73.4 per cent of the export value of the Malayan economy. As much as 44.5 per cent of exports went to the United States, with payments being made in London and these were a crucial source of foreign exchange for the British, especially after the war with Adolf Hitler began in 1939.[25] The Japanese invasion in 1942, however, put an end to this huge benefit.

The control over natural rubber exercised by the Atlantic powers was formidable. In 1940, 77 per cent of the world's production of the commodity came from British Malaya and the Dutch East Indies. In fact, the western countries were responsible for as much as 93 per cent of the world's production of natural rubber that year. In the 1930s therefore, much effort was made by Adolf Hitler to multiply the production of synthetic rubber in Germany. Interestingly, Japanese capture of the British and Dutch colonies in Southeast Asia in 1942 did not ease the Nazis' hunger for rubber. The Japanese had other priorities and lacked the management skills needed to put rubber production on a footing that would have benefitted their allies in Europe. The Allied blockade was too complete to start with and the rubber plantations were left untouched throughout the war.[26]

As a constant backdrop to the profitable industry, the toll taken on rubber plantation workers could often be quite high. In 1910, 5 per cent of the 100,000 Tamil workers died of malaria, dysentery and diarrhoea. In places with the worst records, the death rate would, as in the case of an estate in Negri Sembilan, reach as high as 9.92 per cent; and in Hendra Estate in Perak, there were 85 deaths per thousand workers.[27]

Significantly, the local economy to which they now contributed was a narrow one, based on the two global industries that British colonialism had earmarked for the peninsula. In fact, as some would strongly claim, "the rubber industry was entirely a British invention".[28]

URBANITY AND UNEMPLOYMENT

What is rather unique and should be properly noted is that Malayan cities did not grow through domestic migration from rural to urban areas. In fact, urbanization in the first half of the twentieth century did not affect much of the social and economic life of the rural Malay community. The cities grew through direct and indirect immigration from China (and India); with the usual accompanying social and psychological strain being amplified if one keeps in mind that the urbanization was achieved, as is always the case, by rural peoples moving to cities—but this flow into urbanity—and this creating of urbanity—occurred in a distant land. Significantly, all minor ports on the western coast of the peninsula began as immigrant settlements. The major ports—Penang and Singapore—are both on off-shore islands, and were grounded by the British. At the same time, the Malays, though not urban dwellers, had been a coastal people and thus the newly-urban Chinese and the maritime Malay generally lived in geographical proximity to each other.

The Indians were not especially urban, making up only 11 per cent of Malaya's urban population in 1947. It was the Chinese more than any other group who comprised the city dwellers.

Although only every other Chinese who had moved to Malaya lived in an urban setting, they made up 68 per cent of the urban population by 1947. This also meant that every other Chinese was living in a rural setting just after the war. Many had over the decades of economic downturns occupied unused land to grow food and care for poultry.[29] This population of squatters and smallholders held strong implications for the guerrilla war that was just breaking out between the colonial masters and the Malayan Communist Party and its People's Movement (*Min Yuan*), which supplied the guerrillas with food, funds, information and other necessities.

While only one in five Chinese—22 per cent to be exact—living in Malaya in 1921 was born there; by 1947, that figure had climbed to 62.5 per cent, i.e. more than three in five. For the Indians, the rise was from 12.4 per cent to 49.8 per cent.[30]

As a rule, during periods of unemployment, labourers would seek work either in public works or in plantations. In 1896, some 5,000 unemployed Chinese mine workers found work constructing the trunk road joining Selangor to Pahang.[31] Workers discharged from the mines seemed to have augmented the supply of labour to the plantations. During a slump in tin prices in 1908 and 1909, European planters discharged significant numbers of tin miners.

In response to the slump caused by the declaration of war in Europe in August 1914, immigration to Malaya was stopped and over the following six months, labourers who were willing to be repatriated were sent back to their homelands. The situation turned worse after the war. The rubber slump of 1920–21 saw the estate labour force being reduced by 25 per cent. Of the 60,000 labourers affected, about 40,000 were South Indians. Temporary camps for unemployed Indians were started in Kuala Lumpur, and a permanent one in Penang.[32]

Temporary camps for unemployed Chinese labourers were set up in Perak, Selangor and Negri Sembilan, at equal cost to the Federated Malay States government and private Chinese charities. Substantive supplementary aid to these camps came from Chinese guilds and other organizations. The long-term use of migrant labour was showing its downside. As the Secretary of Chinese Affairs for the Federated Malay States stated in the government's annual report of 1923:

> Immigrants, who then came here as boys and have spent their lives in toil, but through illness or misfortune have not succeeded in making themselves independent, are now past the age when they can any longer support themselves; and, as their long absence from their native places has cut them off from their families, some provision had become inevitable.

With the coming of the world depression, some relief camps for unemployed Chinese workers were set up again by 1930, funded by Chinese guilds and other organizations, and the government. Many took to hawking to survive. A Hakka district association took upon itself to feed the unemployed who came to them, and from all communities.[33]

The depression of the 1930s forced many Chinese to turn to crop cultivation, and a majority did this on land to which they did not have legal titles. This followed the Amendment of the Malay Reservations Act of 1933, which placed stringent rules on land ownership by non-Malays. Illegal squatters had, therefore, by 1940 reached as many as 140,000, and would increase further during the Japanese Occupation to reach half a million by 1945. The food crisis that followed the war would further lead the British Military Administration to encourage the continuation of squatter agriculture.[34]

COLONIALISM'S PLURAL SOCIETY

In his 1937 classic *Malaysia*, the American professor Rupert Emerson noted key differences in the socio-economic consciousness of the three main migrated groups on the peninsula—the Chinese, the British and the Indians. These divulge clearly the basic character of the plural society that was Malaya. To start with, the Malays were largely peasants, fishermen or civil servants.

> [The British], despite considerable differences in class origins at home, form in Malaya as in all colonies, only a single upper class. The functions of the white man in a colony are limited to ruling, owning and managing. Any other form of occupation is degrading and damaging to the white prestige on which the whole system rests. [...] Even national lines, so bitterly held at home, have a way of softening down as against the overwhelming numbers of the colored races: all who are of the white race are Europeans and stand potentially together in the face of the enemy who is being ruled and exploited.[35]

Of significant interest is the separation of ownership from management:

> The great rubber plantations, tin mines, mercantile house, banks, and shipping lines of Malaya and the Netherlands Indies are for the most part owned in Great Britain and Holland or elsewhere in Europe or America, and the Europeans connected with them in the colonies are there as managers, agents, technical experts.

Chinese enterprises, by contrast, tended to be smaller in scale and were locally owned.[36]

While the Malayan Chinese population was obviously a very mixed bunch where class differences were concerned, recognition of these was limited "because of the fluidity of the society, the migratory character of the community, and the division along linguistic lines".

> Divided on clan and linguistic lines, they still in a sense form a complete community within Malaya. The huge array of coolies sweating out their lives in back-breaking labor of all varieties is balanced in a proportion more or less equal to that existing elsewhere by a large middle class of shopkeepers, merchants, artisans, and government employees, and by a small group of capitalists who have ruthlessly fought their way up to head banks, big mercantile houses, mines, and plantations. In addition there is a considerable group of small-holders earning a bare living on agricultural projects of one sort or another.[37]

"The Chinese problem" was already viewed in the 1930s as "the most serious one Malaya faces". At the same time, the Indians were simply "an imported labouring class which has thrust no roots into the local soil". As many as five-sixths of Indians in Malaya were from Madras and were engaged either in the rubber plantations or on government or private jobs. Compared to the Chinese, Indian labourers were very closely supervised "under a large mass of legislation governing all details of their treatment". According to Emerson, the Chinese functioned more like a homogenous community than did the Indians. This was despite—some would say, because of—the extremely high level of social mobility among the former, which saw the most successful business-suited capitalist coming from the same kin as the half-naked labourer on the streets.[38]

FEMALE MIGRATION

Family life was a luxury not all that common among migrants in Malaya. Even in 1931, this was a fate enjoyed only by every other adult Chinese male. This was not strange since the female-male ratio then for Chinese living in the peninsula was only one to four. The overall sex ratio that year for the whole colony was about six to ten. This improved to eight females to ten males after the Second World War, which brought it just shy of the general average. Indian men had a much harder time finding a wife, and their women-to-men ratio reached six to ten only in 1947.[39]

Estimates show that Chinese female immigration into the peninsula, though not absent, was not significant until after the First World War. Indeed, a ban on female emigration was in effect in China until 1910, just before the Qing Empire fell. In the 1930s, when Chinese women made up as many as 25 per cent of the community, they overtook for the first time the corresponding figure for Indian immigrants, which had remained steadily around 10–15 per cent since the 1860s. For the period when statistics were kept, i.e. 1916–40, net Chinese immigration reached 1,553,047 persons. Interestingly, while net Chinese immigration to Malaya for the 1920s reached 1,229,014, this dropped sharply in the 1930s to only 28,899. This was the direct result of a quota on Chinese immigration finally being imposed on 1 August 1930 by the colonial authorities. Three years later, the Aliens Ordinance was passed to limit male immigrants to 1,000 per month. This sex-biased restriction led immediately to a jump in Chinese female migrants instead. From 1933 to 1938, therefore, as many as 190,000 women between 18 and 40 years old migrated to Malaya, an unexpected and unwanted situation that led in 1938 to the rewording of the Ordinance's quota to include women. Push factors for this outflow of women from China included the displacement of the hitherto healthy silk industry in Guangzhou by cheap textile imports from Europe. Furthermore, by this late period, dependence of many families on remittances sent from overseas had become endemic, and the new ruling in Malaya forced households to release their daughters as temporary migrants to faraway lands in place of their sons.[40]

Interestingly, during the Great Depression, repatriation of women immigrants was not allowed although in 1930–32, as many as 75,000 Chinese were actually sent home at government expense. Accompanying women had to pay their own way, which led Chinese organizations to argue that at least old and decrepit women should have their home trip paid for by the government. The colonial policy was aimed at retaining as many women as possible on the peninsula, in the hope that it would lessen asocial behaviour amongst male Chinese, and also limit the influence of secret societies.[41] These societies, though already in existence back in China, gained exaggerated influence over the predominantly male population in Malaya, where activities outside of work revolved around gambling, opium use and brothel visits. Control over such activities was the point of contention between the government and secret societies. The latter, however, seemed slowly to have been replaced, at least in the Straits Settlements, by businessmen of some respectability by 1889 when the government set up the Chinese Advisory Board representing different dialect groups. In the few years preceding this, branches of the Po Leung Kuk, a welfare organization first established in Hong Kong in 1878 to stop the kidnapping of women and children, was set up by businessmen in Singapore, Malacca and Penang. In the Straits Settlements, the aim was mainly to provide refuge and rehabilitation for victims of women trafficking.

Significantly, the Chinese Chamber of Commerce was established in 1900. By 1910, the government had succeeded in holding a monopoly on gambling, opium farms and smoke houses. Together with drinking and prostitution, these were the major revenue for the government. Needless to say, venereal diseases took their toll on the population. When brothels—but not prostitution—were proscribed in 1927, many had no option but to move into "sly" prostitution.[42,43]

This certainly eased the marriage prospects of male Chinese already living in Malaya, and resulted in a sharp increase in working class families. The proportion of Malaya-born persons among the Chinese jumped—from 22 per cent in 1921 to as many as 62 per cent in 1947. Most significantly, by that year, as many as 44.3 per cent of the 5,899,660 inhabitants in Malaya were Chinese, actually surpassing the group titled "Malays" by 1.2 per cent.

The lot of the female Chinese migrants had traditionally been a disheartening one. By cultural definition, her respectability was in question. Given the heavily male-dominated environments in migrant communities, importing prostitutes was a lucrative business that was tolerated by the colonial authorities, as were associated enterprises like gambling and opium smoking. Women ending up as prostitutes seemed common in the early period. Among the 1,000 or so brothel workers recorded in Penang in 1891, about 900 were Chinese and the rest were from India.[44] Prostitution was not illegal as long as the women entered the trade "on their own free will". As many as 80 per cent of young girls who came to Singapore in the 1870s were destined for the brothels. In 1884, 2,000 of 6,600 Chinese women in Singapore were prostitutes, and most of these were between 13 and 16 years of age.[45]

> Female prostitution in colonial Malaya can be considered a form of labor, one of the limited options available to women at that time. While the records are not totally clear on this, it also appears that much of this labor may have been coerced.

Given historical conditions, however, it is not surprising that prostitution was among the first main areas of work for female immigrants.[46]

Prostitutes could be divided into three groups. The first group comprised of the "sold" ones who were virtually slaves owned by brothels. The second group was made up of "pawned" prostitutes who had to work off personal or family debts. Such a process was not an easy one, given how they also had to pay protection money to secret societies. The third group, which was relatively small in earlier times, operated independently only in a direct sense, and usually had to pay for protection, rents and other costs.[47] Whichever group they belonged to, the majority lived under "a mixture of fear, intimidation and filial obedience".[48]

The need for domestic labour was met in Chinese households before 1930 through the employment of men from Hainan, and through the *mui tsai* system. For domestic work, young women were preferred to men since the latter tended to be organized in some sense and could bargain for better conditions. The employer's control over women was often stronger. Just as importantly, a system with young women could fulfil other functions as well, such as being potential concubines or wives. There was also the push factor back home in China, which had been suffering poverty and chaos for decades, and daughters were easily acquired from traffickers and impoverished families. Registration of these domestic helpers became compulsory in 1933 and their official number was 3,004. Most of these were found in Singapore and the main towns on the peninsula. By 1936, the figure had dropped to 2,109.[49]

Pressure from various quarters on the government of the Straits Settlements to take action against cruelty within the *mui tsai* system had led to the Female Domestic Servants Bill of 1925 which forbid the employment of girls younger than 10 years old. Proving age was quite impossible in many cases though, and in 1933, the Mui Tsai Bill came into being to administer the system. This latter Bill "was aimed at making the mui tsai 'free' workers who would be paid wages for their domestic services and who could leave their employers if they wished". Its effects were deemed minimal though, and even drove the system underground. In this respect, the Po Leung Kuk organization played a much more effective role, keeping those girls who were not adopted until they were 18 when they found work on their own or got married.[50]

By the late 1930s and clearly after the Second World War, as many as 85 per cent of Chinese women in the workforce were in paid domestic service. Some worked in the light industries found in Malaya under colonialism, and replaced male workers during the Japanese Occupation.[51]

Women participation in the tin and rubber industries was also substantive. In 1931 already, 10,168 (11.3 per cent) of the 89,618 involved in mining and quarrying were women, most of whom were Chinese using the pan-washing method of ore retrieval. Over time, given the fluctuations that affected the industry, women functioned to a significant extent as reserve labour. In the late 1940s, the tin industry provided the third largest source of employment for women, after rubber cultivation and services.[52]

In the rubber estates, women and children made up a third of the labour force in 1933, and increased to 45 per cent after the war. Chinese women made up 9 per cent and 25.5 per cent of these respectively. In fact, by 1947, almost every other Chinese working in the estates was female, drawn from the squatter population now found throughout the countryside. This population had grown over time due to unemployment during the tin and rubber slumps of the 1910s and 1930s, enhanced further by dislocations during the war and after. The wages paid to Chinese women were lower than those given to Chinese men (70 cents to 90 cents per day), but equal to those paid to South Indian, Javanese and Malay male workers. Women of these latter groups were offered 55 cents per day.[53]

Another interesting aspect of Chinese migration in Malaya was how education for their children was arranged. As the community became less transient, the British practice of non-interference was successively abandoned, a process egged on by how the 1911 Revolution in China had politicized the Chinese in their colonies. New schools were constantly established to garner support from Chinese living overseas for the new republic.

> For many years the Southern Republican Party (better known as the Kuo Min Tang or Nationalistic Party) has pursued a definite political and educational policy in Malaya. It aims at establishing a close connection between the Chinese immigrants in Malaya and the Republican Government of China, commercially and politically through local Chambers of Commerce and branches of the Kuo Min Tang, educationally through schools under the control of the General Education Association. In pursuit of this policy, the Southern Republican Party frequently sends representatives from Canton to Malaya who hold commissions from the Military Government and who explain its aims to the Chinese settled here. Its propaganda is circulated everywhere through the medium of the Shu Po She (Reading Rooms), the school and the Chinese newspaper.[54]

The Kuomintang was significantly of southern origin, and allowed for a stronger emotional bond to the Nanyang Chinese. Understandably, the British feared that these new developments would allow the instability already felt in their domains on the Chinese coastline to spread to Southeast Asia. In 1920, the

Registration of Schools Enactment came into effect to curtail the influence of China-trained teachers among Malayan Chinese. It was enforced in the face of strong opposition, and the effort to stem the flow of revolution was followed in 1923 by an attempt to suppress the Kuomintang in Malaya and by the suggestion to begin funding Chinese education in order to control it. The latter gained support from the Colonial Office, and the Director of Education, R.O. Winstedt, who strangely added the condition that funds would be given only to those using dialects—and not Mandarin—as the medium of instruction. The ban on the Kuomintang went into implementation, with limited effect no doubt, only in 1929. Following that, teachers had to be born in Malaya, and schools using Mandarin were included for funding. Some measures were taken to encourage Chinese families to enrol their children in English schools as well.

The fact that the Chinese government considered all Chinese as Chinese nationals did not help matters, and it was only as late as in 1955, at the Bandung Conference held in Bali, that Beijing, then under the Communist Party, declared an end to that traditional attitude.

In 1931, about 17 per cent of Chinese children between the ages of five and 15 were in Chinese schools, and 7 per cent of them studied in English schools. As many as 900 school teachers were from the mainland. Literacy among Chinese above 15 years of age was around 41 per cent in Chinese, and 3.7 per cent in English. It was becoming clear that earlier measures were not having much effect, which led to a change in tactics by the mid-1930s. A 1934 memorandum from A.B. Jordan, the Secretary for Chinese Affairs, pointed out the urgent need for concerted actions, and out of four options, one was chosen by the government by the end of 1935, namely, to "pursue a policy which could assist significantly the financing of Chinese education to enable constructive innovations to be undertaken under the supervision of the Education Department".[55]

In his study of education policies in Malaya before the war, Philip Loh came to the following conclusion where the Chinese school system was concerned:

> The Chinese school, trapped in an intricate web of partisan Chinese politics and Chinese chauvinism, tended to lose sight of its educational objectives. The schools suffered from inadequate finance, poor management and a lack of trained teachers. More significantly the schools were plagued by recurring attempts of the reformists and radicals posing as teachers to subvert their pupils from any sense of belonging to the country of their residence and a respect for established authority. Encouraged to confront established authority, it was not too long before pupils began to show scant respect for their teachers. The seeds of student unrest and student alienation in the Chinese schools were sown during this period.[56]

Another significant piece of information on the socio-economic situation in Malaya is that, just after the Second World War, literacy was highest among the Indians, with 401 per thousand of them being able to read and write. The Chinese ranked slightly lower at 354, with the Malays last, at 253. In Singapore alone, however, where Indian literacy was at 590 per thousand; the Malays, at 374 per thousand, outranked the Chinese, who achieved 339 per thousand. The Malays, however, fared worse in health issues such as mortality, infant mortality and maternal mortality.[57] The economic well-being of the Malays is harder to ascertain or define, living as many of them did on subsistence agriculture and fishing, and being outside the wage system.

A look at the causes of death in the Straits Settlements, for which there is substantial data, is revealing. The main killer was malaria at the beginning of the twentieth century, but this had dropped to a much less significant position by the late 1930s, from 30 per cent of deaths in 1900 to 2.8 per cent by 1934. During the same period, tuberculosis fell from causing 10.9 per cent of deaths to 8.2 per cent. The trends were assumed to be similar in the rest of the peninsula, and all in all, epidemics were rare.[58]

The above description of the condition of the immigrant labourers in the colonial economy of Malaya before the Second World War is admittedly sketchy, but here, it serves as a poignant backdrop with which to begin our story about an extraordinary man—Lee Hau-Shik. His economic stature and his social background placed him distant from that of the common labourer; but he would come to play a key role in the political consolidation of the Malayan Chinese community at large—and of Malaya as a whole.

NOTES

1. Amarjit Kaur, "The Impact of Railroads on the Malayan Economy, 1874–1941", *Journal of Asian Studies* 39, no. 4 (August 1980): 696.
2. K.G. Tregonning, "Straits Tin: A Brief Account of the First Seventy-five Years of The Straits Trading Company, Limited", *Journal of the Malayan Branch of the Royal Asiatic Society* 36, no. 1 (201) (May 1963): 81–83.
3. Leong Yee Fong, *Labour and Trade Unionism in Colonial Malaya: A Study of the Socio-Economic and Political Bases of the Malayan Labour Movement, 1930–1957* (Penang: Penerbit Universiti Sains Malaysia, 1999), pp. 13–31.
4. Rupert Emerson, *Malaysia: A Study of Direct and Indirect Rule* (Kuala Lumpur: University of Malaya Press, (1970) 1937), pp. 312, 364–65.
5. Ibid., pp. 366–73.

6. J. Norman Parmer, *Colonial Labor Policy and Administration: A History of Labor in the Rubber Plantation Industry in Malaya, c. 1910–1941* (New York: Association of Asian Studies, 1960), pp. 247–48.
7. Leong (1999), p. 33.
8. Ibid., pp. 38–40.
9. Ibid., p. 33.
10. Tan Pek Leng, *Land to Till: The Chinese in the Agricultural Economy of Malaysia* (Kuala Lumpur: Centre for Malaysian Studies, 2008), p. 21.
11. Leong (1999), pp. 41–42.
12. Parmer (1960), pp. 247–48.
13. Leong (1999), pp. 39–40.
14. Parmer (1960), pp. 242–46.
15. Leong (1999), pp. 48–54.
16. Ibid., pp. 52–54.
17. Douglas Ford, *Britain's Secret War against Japan, 1937–1945* (Oxford: Routledge, 2006), pp. 17–18.
18. Parmer (1960), p. 247.
19. Ibid., pp. 247–48.
20. Tregonning (1963), pp. 81–83.
21. R.O. Winstedt, *A History of Malaya* (Singapore and Kuala Lumpur: Maricans & Sons, 1935), pp. 222–36.
22. Tregonning (1963), pp. 81–83.
23. Frank Swettenham, *British Malaya* (London, 1906), p. 31, cited in Ho Tak Ming, *Ipoh: When Tin was King* (Ipoh: Perak Academy, 2009).
24. Tregonning (1963), pp. 118–20.
25. Goh Keng Swee, *The Economic Front from a Malayan Point of View* (Singapore: Singapore Authority, 1940), pp. 25–26.
26. John Tully, *The Devil's Milk: A Social History of Rubber* (New York: Monthly Review Press, 2011), pp. 293–94.
27. Ibid., pp. 250–51.
28. Victor Purcell, "Malaya under the British", *World Affairs* 108, no. 1 (March 1945): 33–38.
29. Parmer (1960), p. 230.

30. Eunice Cooper, "Urbanization in Malaya", *Population Studies* 5, no. 2 (1951): 117–31.
31. *Malay Mail* (Kuala Lumpur), 23 November 1897, p. 3, cited in Parmer (1960), pp. 222–23.
32. *Annual Report*, Chief Secretary, Federated Malay States, 1921, p. 14, cited in Parmer (1960), pp. 226–28.
33. Parmer (1960), pp. 229, 241.
34. Heng Pek Koon, *Chinese Politics in Malaysia: A History of the Malaysian Chinese Association* (Singapore: Oxford University Press, 1988), pp. 101–2.
35. Emerson (1937), p. 29.
36. Ibid., pp. 29–33.
37. Ibid., p. 29.
38. Ibid., pp. 33–34.
39. Cooper (1951), pp. 126–30.
40. Sharon M. Lee, "Female Immigrants and Labor in Colonial Malaya: 1860–1947", *International Migration Review* 23, no. 2 (Summer 1989): 310, 314–18.
41. Parmer (1960), p. 242.
42. Lai Ah Eng, *Peasants, Proletarians and Prostitutes: A Preliminary Investigation into the Work of Chinese Women in Colonial Malaya*, Research Notes and Discussion Paper no. 59 (Singapore: Institute of Southeast Asian Studies, 1986), pp. 13, 38.
43. Neil Khor Jin Keong and Khoo Keat Siew, *The Penang Po Leung Kuk: Chinese Women, Prostitution and a Welfare Organisation* (Malayan Branch of the Royal Asiatic Society, Monograph no. 37, 2004), pp. 55, 165.
44. Lee (1989), pp. 309–31.
45. Lai (1986), p. 28.
46. Lee (1989), p. 319.
47. Khor and Khoo (2004), pp. 39–40.
48. Lai (1986), pp. 31–32.
49. Ibid., p. 46.
50. Ibid., pp. 50–52.

51. Ibid., pp. 90–91.
52. Ibid., pp. 56–57.
53. Ibid., pp. 64–71.
54. A.M. Goodman, "Memorandum on Chinese Education", in CO 717, vol. 13, cited in Philip Loh Fook Seng, *Seeds of Separatism: Educational Policy in Malaya 1874–1940*, East Asian Social Science Monographs (Kuala Lumpur: Oxford University Press, 1975), pp. 94–95.
55. Loh (1975), pp. 95–101.
56. Ibid., p. 124.
57. Cooper (1951), pp. 126–30.
58. Lenore Manderson, *Sickness and the State: Health and Illness in Colonial Malaya 1870–1940* (Cambridge: Cambridge University Press, 2002), pp. 62–63.

Chapter 2

TIMES OF OPPORTUNITY

> In neither the Malay States nor the Colony do the British seem at any point to have prejudiced the continuance of their autocratic control by promises of a future independence toward which their present efforts might be seen as leading. The practical commitments as far as the Colony is concerned point in fact in the other direction since it is grossly unlikely that the Singapore Naval Base and the fortifications which, according to recent report, are to be erected at Penang will be peacefully handed over in any foreseeable future to the heterogenous populace of the Straits.
>
> —Rupert Emerson 1937[1]

THE PRECEDING chapter presented with some alacrity what conditions were like for migrant workers who took the risk of moving to the Malayan Peninsula from China and from British India. In many ways, British Malaya was a pioneer territory for them. Originally run for strategic and logistical reasons to facilitate the global trading ambitions of the East India Company, Malaya under the British soon became the supplier of two of the world's most important products in the latter half of the nineteenth century and the first half of the twentieth.

Working the tin mines or the rubber estates were the major draw for migrant workers. Both these commodities were essential to the early industrial world. Where the capitalists were concerned, competition was between Europeans and Asian upper classes whose business sense encouraged them to look to the region and to its emerging economic trends.

Tin and rubber were still infant industries, and ownership conditions, technological innovations, and market control were hotly contested matters. The world was changing fervently, and the colonizing of East Asia in effect drew its peoples to participate in the globalizing economics of the times. They were not passive bystanders in their own history.

Polities were changing as well. Empires had fallen, or were falling, and new powers had appeared in their stead on the world stage. Germany was on the rise in the heart of Europe, just as Japan was doing at the eastern edge of Asia. The triumph of the United States of America in the First World War had given the world notice that it was an unstoppable future global power, while the October 1917 Revolution in Moscow was altering the foundations of political thought and conflict. China remained in the throes of the gradual but certain imperial decay that began with the Opium War in 1839–42.

Living in such times was no easy matter. Uncertainties, of course, also offered opportunities for those with the means, the insight and the foresight to put their ideas into practice. Against this unique historical backdrop, this present chapter introduces Lee Hau-Shik. He was not of the labouring class that flooded Malaya in the early twentieth century, whose members were simply seeking a living with the faint hope that there was a fortune waiting even for the likes of them somewhere in the near future and in this faraway place.

His was certainly a family of means, but the privileges and social position it enjoyed were grounded in the administrative structure of the Qing Dynasty, which had been dying a slow death and which totally disintegrated by 1911.

Even to knowledgeable Malaysians today, the name H.S. Lee seldom conjures any stronger association than that he was one of the founders of the Malayan Chinese Association; that he was among the tiny handful of Malayans who travelled to London to negotiate the terms of independence for the country; that he was the country's first finance minister; and that he was the founder of the Development & Commercial (D&C) Bank.

FORGOTTEN SIGNIFICANCE

He was certainly all those things, but how profoundly all those roles reflected the conditions of the times has seldom been probed. He was a major participant in the colony's politics for 20 years or so leading up to the formation of Malaya and beyond, and having an intense personality, his life and struggles took place right in the thick of events. The fact that his signature was the only Chinese one on the declaration of Independence signed in London should arouse curiosity among scholars today about H.S. Lee's role and significance in the two decades before colonialism ended in Malaya, not only where political dynamics were concerned, but also in the socio-economics of the times.

Let us step into his family life with a three-paragraph-long matter-of-fact note that he wrote on 25 July 1986—two years before his own death—about his father:

LEE KWAI LIM, the fourth son of LEE HOK KOH was born on 6th May 1877. After passing the Governmental Official

Examinations, he joined the Civil Service and was stationed in Peking, Manchuria and other Provinces during the Qing Dynasty. After some years, he resigned from the Civil Service and took up business in Hong Kong where he associated with Dr. Sun Yat Sen and his party to become involved in the revolution against the Manchus. When the [Republic of China] was formed, he was elected a member of the 1st Provincial Assembly of the Kwang Tung Province. He was appointed Advisor to the Government of Canton and was sent to Malaya to make a report on the Chinese and their well-being in Malaya. He came to Malaya and started [a] remittance business in various parts of Malaya to enable the Chinese to remit money back to China. Branches and lodging homes were established in Kuala Lumpur, Ipoh, Seremban, Singapore, Hong Kong, Shun Yee (Xinyi), Ko Chow (Gao Zhou) and Zhang Jiang, all known as "Kam Lun Tai".

He also assisted the Chinese to come to Malaya to seek employment by negotiating with the shipping companies for reduced fares. Due to his frequent visits to Malaya, he became friendly with the Chinese in Malaya who looked upon him as the leader for advice on their undertakings. He was also interested in tin mining, and started mines in Salak South. Because of his knowledge, he was invited by the Kwangsi Provincial Government to investigate the possibilities of tin mining in Kwangsi Province.

During [a trip] in Kwangsi, his motor car went off the road. [His] driver died and he suffered a broken spine. [He] was brought back to Hong Kong for medical treatment. However, he did not recover from his motor car injury and died about a month later on 3rd July 1936 in Hong Kong. He left his wife, Madam Kam Kho Chun, three sons namely Hau Shik Lee, Hau Mo Lee, and Hau Wai Lee, and two daughters namely Oi Sim and Yue Wai. Madam Kam is the aunt of Samuel Kam.[2]

In turn, in his autobiography published when he was 96 years old, Samuel Kam had this to say about his first cousin:

> Henry, born in 1900 [sic, should be 1901], was 15 years my senior. We first met in Hong Kong when I was still in primary school. His mother, Kam Gu-chan [a.k.a. Kho Chun] was my aunt on my father's side. After obtaining a degree in law and economics from the prestigious Cambridge University, Henry joined his father, Lee Kwai Lam [Kwai Lim] over in Malaya. The Lee family had businesses in tin mining and inn-keeping in the Straits Settlements.
>
> Given his strong Cambridge ties, Henry later ventured into Malayan politics. I was told a story of young Henry when he was chairman of the Malayan Oxbridge Alumni Association. When a prince from the British royal family visited Singapore, Henry went with the Governor of the Straits Settlements to welcome His Royal Highness. To everyone's surprise, the prince, a former schoolmate of Henry at Cambridge, chose to take a ride in Henry's car instead of the governor's. The episode shot Henry to fame and it became the talk of the town for a long time.
>
> The second time I saw him was in 1935 when I was one of four best men at the wedding of his younger brother Lee Hau Mo. Hau Mo married the daughter of Malayan magnate Chan Wing; a grand wedding was held in Hong Kong. But Henry had another reason to be back. His father was in hospital with serious injuries following a car accident. Henry's father was the owner of the Guangxi Mining Company where my father was a shareholder as well as director. They were returning to Hong Kong in the same car after the directors' meeting in Guangxi when the accident happened. While my father miraculously escaped unhurt, my uncle suffered severe injuries and later succumbed to post-injury complications. After Henry had taken his father's remains back to the ancestral village in Xinyi for burial, he returned to Malaya.[3]

The Lee family was a distinguished one indeed. Based in Xinyi County in Gaozhou Prefecture in Guangdong Province, it had strong ties to the Qing government. Two members of the family are remembered to have passed the imperial exams during the Qianlong period (1736–95), and one of Hau-Shik's great grandfathers had served as a senior official under the Tongzhi Emperor (1856–75). His grandfather was an imperially titled personage, while a paternal uncle, Lee Wai Sheung, was secretary of the treasury in Guangdong Province, and a friend of General Chiang Kai-shek. Another relative was the Governor of Hubei Province.[4]

STALWARTS IN A DECAYING DYNASTY

How Hau-Shik's father, Lee Kwai Lim (a.k.a. Lee Chee Lin and Li Tou Kong), a viceroy in the decaying imperial service went into business; how he associated with the rebel leader Dr Sun Yat-sen; and how his business interests led him to Malaya, and then fatefully to mine for tin in Guangxi Province were all a powerful reflection of the regional politics of the times, both of its instability and its opportunities. In fact, one event of great salience in this context was the lifting of the official ban on emigration by the Qing government in 1893. Nationalism was yet to fire the imagination of most young Asians; and East and Southeast Asia were chaotically poised between an increasingly belligerent Japan, a painfully more conflicted China, and an array of European colonialists who were feeling less and less secure. The economics of the times stimulated the desperate, the hopeful and the adventurous to leave an impoverished China to partake of breaks offered by new and promising industries in territories in a Southeast Asia colonized by greedy powers based half a world away.

Besides owning a mercury and a sulphur mine, Kwai Lim founded Kam Lun Tai as a silk trading company with several branches spread over southern Guangdong. The firm expanded to Hong Kong in 1899, to a shop on Connaught Road Central. He and his wife moved there the following year, and by 1903, his company had evolved into a chain of lodging houses stretching across the seas to Singapore, Penang, Ipoh, Seremban and Kuala Lumpur as well, making it one of the first among the very few China-based companies of that period to venture into Southeast Asia.[5]

Given their privileged background, the Lee family could hardly be classed with normal immigrants leaving their homes in desperation and despair. Kwai Lim's business sense and social position allowed him to take advantage of opportunities that the fall of the Qing Empire presented. In fact, Kam Lun Tai simply rose to meet the demands of the times and offered a range of services that the mobile coastal population of the decaying China needed.

Chinese migrants heading for the cities, mines and plantations of Southeast Asia sought transport, lodging and contacts, not to mention monetary and remittance services. These were what the Lees could provide. It is the socio-economic background that explains the strong ties within the Chinese community, especially in the state of Selangor, that Hau-Shik had and could put to good use in the politics of late-colonial Malaya.

The Lees should thus be classified as—and with advantage perceived as—Chinese capitalists agilely functioning in the nascent regional economy posited by the fall of the Qing occurring in tandem with the struggle by modern nations such as Japan for power and resources in Asia. As noted by Victor Zheng et al.:

> Before 1914, Western banks were active in Asia. The outbreak of World War One in 1914 drove European capital quickly out

from Asia to finance the war in Europe. However, there was a great demand for money exchange and remittance services as more and more coolies [and] workers wanted to send money from Southeast Asia back to their home-town to support their families. The absence of government control in that business and the lack of formal organization to handle remittance between southern China and Southeast Asia before the 1930s also made well-established Chinese shops with extensive regional network ready agents in handling remittance.[6]

REGIONAL CAPITALISTS

After expanding to Malaya in 1903, Kam Lun Tai soon branched into the tin industry, forming a subsidiary company called Tai Yau in the process. Labour shortage was a constant problem for mine owners, and Kwai Lim could easily make use of his transport and lodging channels to recruit men from Gaozhou, which was suffering from heavy unemployment at this time. The Hong Kong office thus became the node in this network, recruiting workers from Guangdong for Malaya. Kam Lun Tai even provided loans to these men. It is estimated that all in all, the company supplied about 10,000 workers to the Malayan mines. Another source claims that figure to be 20,000.[7] The remittance service was, however, the major profit maker in this traffic.[8]

Hugely successful as an innovative entrepreneur, Kwai Lim was also directly implicated in the turbulent politics of the times. He donated to the revolutionary movement led by Dr Sun Yat-sen and was a member of the Tung Meng Hui, the predecessor to the Kuomintang. When the Republic of China was formed in 1911, he was appointed department secretary to the civil administration for Guangdong Province, advisor to the Guangzhou Municipality and member of the provincial assembly. However, the worsening political turmoil soon pushed him to leave his political offices for good.⁹

His business interests saw him going into partnerships to invest in tin mining in various regions in southern China, and even in cinnabar mining in 1932. The car accident in the winter of 1935 in Nanning proved fatal. He passed away on 3 July 1936 at the age of 59 in a Hong Kong hospital and his body was taken back to Xinyi for burial.¹⁰

Hau-Shik, Kwai Lim's eldest son, was born in Hong Kong on 19 November 1901, the year his parents moved there. In Beijing, the bizarre Boxer Rebellion had just been crushed by an assemblage of foreign and modern armies. The writing was on the wall that the Qing Empire was catching its last breath—the imperial system that had served China for millennia was in fact only a decade away from its final demise.

Hau-Shik's early schooling from the age of 11 was no doubt done at the Christian College in Guangzhou, but he was nevertheless brought up in a strict traditional manner, and was thus well-versed in Cantonese as well as English. After two years at the college, he was enrolled in Canton Secondary School. On receiving a scholarship from the Guangdong government, he then continued his schooling at Queen's College in Hong Kong.

It was in September 1916 that he left to study at St. John's College in Cambridge. There, he had as schoolmate Britain's Prince Albert—who would become King George VI in May 1937, following the abdication of his elder brother, Edward VIII. His headmaster at Queen's, Bartram Tanner, had this to say of him in Hau-Shik's leaving certificate:

> His conduct has been excellent. He has always given every satisfaction as a student and has passed all his class examination with much credit. He was Vernacular Prize-winner in Class 2,

and in the next half-yearly examination (matric's class) was placed at the top of the list in Chinese and fourth in English. We are sorry he should be leaving now, but consider him wise in proceeding to England to continue his studies there.[11]

Hau-Shik—also now known as Henry—graduated in Law and Economics at Cambridge, and was one of the first Chinese to be accepted as a Fellow by the Royal Economics Society.[12] In early 1923, he married Dawn Kathleen Glen. Their first son, Douglas, was born in Cambridge before the new family moved back to Hong Kong in 1924.

Yong Yung Tai, an uncle to Hau-Shik, was Governor of Guangdong Province then, and recommended that he worked as Commissioner for Customs on Hainan Island. The young man grew quickly disillusioned with the work conditions and the corruption there, however, and resigned to move back to Hong Kong to work for the P&O Bank. Hau-Shik progressed quickly within this prestigious institution, and soon became a personal assistant to the head of the foreign exchange department.

A second son, Vivian Leslie, was born to Hau-Shik and Dawn around this time, but their marriage soon broke down, apparently under great pressure from Hau-Shik's conservative mother, Kam Kwok-Chun. The couple separated in 1926 and Dawn, a woman with very modern English tastes, including cigarettes and sports cars, took Vivian back to England with her. The two brothers thus grew up in separate parts of the world and would not see each other again until both were in their old age, and finally arranged to meet up in London in 1998.

A heartbroken Hau-Shik took a much-needed vacation in Malaya around this time. His father asked that he took charge of his tin mining business there—in Ipoh, Seremban and Kepong, and it was from this early period that his romance with Malaya began. He could not in his wildest dreams have guessed at this time how deeply he would participate in the history of this emerging nation.

Affluent since birth and educated both in traditional Chinese fashion and in the English style, Hau-Shik was well equipped to manage the shifting expediencies of the times, and to occupy the unique space between East and West. His access to politicians back in China and Hong Kong was strengthened by almost immediate inclusion into the high society of British Malaya: "Very obviously, because of the outstanding educational achievement, great wealth and intertwined family connection, elitist emigrant families are usually identified as target groups that many host governments [would] like to absorb into the polity."

MAKING KUALA LUMPUR HOME

Hau-Shik married again. His second wife, Kwan Choi Lin, bore him seven children.[13] Being a thorough and principled individual, Hau-Shik could not but make an immediate and deep impression on the Chinese community in Malaya. Just three years after his arrival in Kuala Lumpur, he was already a member of the Kuala Lumpur Sanitary Board, a body that was in effect the town council.[14] In 1931, he was elected a committee member of the Miners' Association.

Hau-Shik had gained public attention when he opposed a levy that the government of the Federated Malay States tried to impose the year before. He was actively involved in the mining association's matters, and in 1933 became its president, a position he held until 1936. During this time, he was also the association's nominee to the FMS Mines Chamber of Commerce and the Selangor Chinese Chamber of Commerce (SCCC). He became the president of the latter in 1939 after becoming its vice-president in 1934. His social stature grew steadily just before the war, and he was made Justice of the Peace in 1941.

The SCCC was an extremely influential body for the Selangor Chinese. It had been established in 1904, and as with other chambers of commerce founded at that time throughout the region at the instigation of the Qing Court, its interests stretched beyond the economic. With the fall of the Manchu government in 1911, the sympathies of the SCCC switched to the Republic of China. Kam Lun Tai, under Hau-Shik's father, had apparently been an SCCC member since 1918.

> Being the chief spokesman for the Selangor Chinese, the SCCC had considerable success in harmonising various Chinese communities, promoting Chinese culture, negotiating with the British authorities on Chinese community affairs and fostering closer links between the Chinese community and the Chinese government.[15]

After Hau-Shik's father died on 3 July 1936 at the age of 59 from injuries suffered in the car accident in Guangxi, he, being the oldest son, took over the family's mining enterprises in Malaya. He renamed all six mines, numbering them H.S. Lee Mine No. 1 to No. 6. He went on to acquire more mines. Around Kuala Lumpur he bought mines in Salak South, Puchong and Ampang; and in Perak, he purchased one in Malim Nawar. The European dredges that had been so useful in earlier decades could retrieve ore only to a certain ground level; and Hau-Shik, through the use of open case mining, made it possible for his workers to dig at greater depths. That way, he could put mines that had been abandoned by European miners to good use again. Douglas Waring, who was chairman for the huge mining company Anglo-Oriental and who later became chairman of London Tin Corporation, and then of the Mining Association of Malaya, became a close associate, especially after Hau-Shik became chairman of the Chinese Mining Association.

Hau-Shik's son, Douglas oversaw the mines while the next two sons, George and Robert, were sent off to Camborne School of Mines in Cornwall to become mine engineers. The youngest sons, Thomas and Alex, would become lawyers.

Kam Lun Tai did not survive Kwai-Lim's death very well. Exactly a year after his demise, the Luguoqiao (Marco Polo Bridge) Incident of 7 July 1937 in Beijing began Japan's invasion of China proper. The flow of immigrants out of China slowed, cutting back patrons in need of Kam Lun Tai's lodgings and shrinking the remittances sent from abroad. At the same time, the government decided to take over the company's sulphur mines in China in support of the war effort.[16]

Hau-Shik's emotional ties at this time to the land of his birth were nowhere shown to be as strong as in his immediate commitment to raise funds in support of China's resistance to the Japanese invasion. The Selangor China Relief Fund was immediately started with him as president. Indeed, the sense of outrage was felt throughout the world among people of Chinese origin, but nowhere was more money raised for the China cause than in Malaya and Singapore.[17]

Kam Kwok-Chun, Hau-Shik's mother, passed away at the age of 58 on 26 July 1938, two years after her husband's demise.

Hau-Shik himself had not shown much interest in the family's traditional business, and seemed instead to have been quite captivated by the tin industry in Malaysia. His brother Hau Mo, also educated in Britain, showed scant interest too in the cultivating of family ties on which the business was traditionally based. The youngest brother, Hau Wai, was serving in the Kuomintang army (and would be killed by the People's

Liberation Army in Shanghai in 1948). What the case of the Lees suggests is that "entrepreneurship and personal network cannot be transmitted quickly, easily and systematically".[18]

And so, Kam Lun Tai was sold off. Part of the fascination the tin industry held for Hau-Shik seemed to be in the social and political contexts. In fact, he was involved in the setting up of quite a few organizations. The Gaozhou Association, for example, was a welfare body founded to aid new arrivals from the Gaozhou region. He also helped found the Selangor Guangdong Association. Both of these opened up branches in other Malayan urban centres. He also helped found and led the Chinese Miners' Association for many years, and also the Selangor Chinese Chamber of Commerce.[19]

In 1929, the Kuomintang had put into place laws to control the establishment of new chambers of commerce in the region. Since the SCCC was established for community protection long before this, "it remained to a considerable degree independent of the KMT's attempt to control it".[20] The Kuomintang under Chiang Kai-shek had unified China by 1927, but already in 1924, it had started systematizing what was known as the national salvation movement, and this extended beyond the boundaries of China to include Chinese communities in Southeast Asia. With the threat to China from Japan as evidenced by the Twenty One Demands from 1915 and the Japanese occupation of Manchuria in 1931, the passion for national salvation became intimately tied to anti-Japanese sentiments.[21]

HELPING THE MOTHERLAND

When the conflict between Japan and China broke into open war following the Marco Polo Bridge Incident on 7 July 1937, the anti-Japanese sentiment among Chinese communities in Southeast Asia increased greatly.

Yoji Akashi's *The Nanyang Chinese National Salvation Movement, 1937–1941*, describes three stages in the development of this movement. Between 1937 and 1938, the response from overseas Chinese to the war in Chinese was more localized and spontaneous, and so suffered from the lack of coordination. A systematic contribution and aid programme became possible between 1939 and late 1940 following the founding of a coordinating body. However, closer ties quickly strained relations between the Nanyang Chinese communities and the Kuomintang government, the latter being riddled with corruption and being given to excessive meddling. The movement ceased to be effective by 1941.[22]

A series of China Relief Fund Associations had thus come into being, the first in Johor, followed by another in Singapore led by Tan Kah Kee. The SCCC, led by Hau-Shik and Ang Cheng Chong, founded its own on 22 August 1937, covering the whole of Selangor state. Similar associations were established in quick succession in Penang, Malacca and in fact in all the Malayan states.[23]

Protests against stores that continued to deal in Japanese merchandise turned into rioting in Penang on 3–5 July 1938, the week before the first anniversary of the start of the Sino-Japanese war. This tested the patience of the British colonialists, who had been unable to stop funds from being channelled to China purportedly for refugee relief but most likely as support for the Kuomintang government. Worried and spurred by this, Tan Kah Kee, a prominent and politically active Hokkien businessman, quickly set about that year laying the foundations for a central coordinating body.

And so on China's National Day, 10 October 1938, with Kao Ling-pai, the Chinese Consul-General in Singapore present, 165 delegates from 45 Southeast Asian cities, including Hong Kong, met to found the Federation of China Relief Fund of the South

Seas. Its headquarters was at the Ee Hoe Ean Club on Bukit Pasoh Street in Singapore, and in representing overseas Chinese throughout the region, it replaced the Singapore Chinese Chamber of Commerce as the hub for China nationalism in Singapore.

There was no smooth sailing, however. Hau-Shik, head of Selangor China Relief Fund Association, together with Lau Pak Khuan, head of the Perak China Relief Fund Association, submitted certain points to be taken up for discussion, the most important of which was that states and not individuals be regarded as having voting rights in the executive committee. When they realized that none of their proposals had been included in the agenda, they called for a press conference to voice their grievances. Hau-Shik alleged that Tan Kah Kee had filled the committee with his own men. He also claimed that although many had voted for him, his name somehow appeared on the roster only after some delegates demanded a recount. Tan's reputation among Southeast Asian overseas Chinese was great, and it was probably the wish to limit the unavoidable dominance that Tan would exercise over the organization that the Selangor/Perak suggestions were raised.[24]

In the preface to his autobiography, Tan Kah Kee claimed that in 1939 alone, the Overseas Chinese remitted in various ways a total of $1.1 billion yuan back to China, seven-tenths of which came from Southeast Asia. This was a significant amount indeed, especially if one measures that against the $1.8 billion that the war cost the Kuomintang that same year.[25] As noted by Harvard professor Rupert Emerson in his acclaimed book from 1937:

> It is notorious that the overseas Chinese have furnished both much of the leadership and much of the financial support for the nationalist and Westernizing movements at home, and, on the reverse side, the Kuomintang and the National Government have made serious, if somewhat sporadic, efforts to come into

closer contact with and to exercise some degree of control over their brethren outside.²⁶

Despite the initial success of the Federation of China Relief Fund of the South Seas and its significant impact throughout the region, the difficulties it faced remained formidable. Not only did the communists compete with Kuomintang supporters for influence in the movement, communal factionalism was rife. The Hakkas, for example, held their own fund-raising drive under Aw Boon Haw, the Tiger Balm King, supported by his daily, *Sin Chew Jit Poh* and the Hakka Association.²⁷ It was a well-known fact that Tan and Aw did not get along, and personal prestige and influence were probably behind the rift between these two highly prominent characters.²⁸

When war finally broke out between Britain and Germany on 3 September 1939, the Kuomintang government of China was still on friendly terms with Japan's European Axis partner. Fearing that remittances back to China might soon be restricted, Tan Kah Kee quickly issued a declaration in the name of the Federation of China Relief Fund of the South Seas in support of the British in their European war. Thus, when the Colonial Office sought indications a month later on whether overseas Chinese under British rule were supportive of their colonial masters or not, the Singapore government had a concrete positive statement to send to London.²⁹

By the end of 1939, all Chinese coastal ports had fallen to the Japanese, and trips to and from China were possible only through Burma or Annam. Tan thought it necessary for a delegation of overseas Chinese to visit their brethren who were fighting the enemy, and to comfort war victims with their presence and promise of support. On 6 March 1940, over 30 members of what was called the Comfort Mission, set off from Singapore for

Chungking, the wartime capital, via Rangoon. More than a dozen others made their own way to Kunming and to Chungking for this purpose.[30]

This was indeed a show of broad support by the federation's members. However, by February 1941, disappointment over the inefficacy, incompetence and blatant corruption of the Kuomintang saw Tan Kah Kee resigning from all public offices connected with the Nationalist government.[31]

Indeed, the tensions evident among leaders of the communities of overseas Chinese act as a good reminder that these communities had complex internal dynamics of their own, and while the social and economic conditions of the overseas Chinese at large may have been diverse, they were symbiotic at the same time, having developed organically to changing economic, political and geographic conditions. Given the accelerated uncertainties of the times, however, any attempt to find common ground was immediately plagued by conflicts. To make matters worse, the Kuomintang in China itself was riddled with corruption, and its many branches and members in the South Seas were not any better.

All disunions were soon overwhelmed by the Japanese invasion of Malaya, which began on 8 December 1941, coordinated with their air strike on Pearl Harbour. The battleships Prince of Wales and Repulse were sunk two days later, and over the next few days, Kedah and Pahang fell. The taking of Penang, which the Japanese had thought would cause them some problems, was done without the loss of a single soldier.[32] The British had chosen to evacuate the island and had hastily sent all their men, women and children to Singapore. No one of any other ethnic background was included in this departure, however, and this caused great consternation and worry in Singapore, and put the government there in a desperate situation since it was also seeking a general mobilization of the Chinese to defend the island. As damage control, a general amnesty was thus quickly granted to all political prisoners locked up at Changi Gaol, including the communists.[33]

As the Japanese landed in Malaya, Hau-Shik was made Chief Air Raid Warden in Kuala Lumpur. This force at its peak had as many as 6,000 men.[34] With this position came the rank of "colonel" as well.[35]

In gathering all forces against the common enemy, the British also decided to give *de facto* recognition to the theretofore illegal Malayan Communist Party. In the meantime, the Chung Kuo Council for General Mobilization was formed on 31 December 1941 under a reluctant Tan Kah Kee, who felt that the job was beyond his capacity to perform well but who agreed under pressure from the government. Officials from various branches of government began training the Singapore population and refugees, who consisted of "labourers and students, middle-aged men and boys in their teens" and who were "destined to become the nucleus of the Malayan People's Anti-Japanese Army".

An affidavit from September 1940 composed by Hau-Shik for lawyers in Hong Kong handling his father's estate provides us with terse information about "immovable properties" that he, "a man of independent means", possessed in Kuala Lumpur just before the Japanese invaded. He owned ten houses on eight grants of land plus two unused plots at Golf View Road.[36]

Hau-Shik and his family soon had to leave all that behind. They fled Kuala Lumpur at the head of a large convoy, crossing into Singapore just ahead of the invading army. Hau-Shik, prominently known for his fund-raising and anti-Japanese activities, and apparently with a bounty of $60,000 placed on his head by the Japanese, was practically certain to be severely punished once the island fell. And so, he was among those who fled on a small British steamer for Rangoon.

This plan of escape had been conveyed to the British by the Chinese Consul General in Singapore, Gao Lingbai. All in all, 108 Chinese, 75 per cent of whom were women and children, were on board the ship. Hau-Shik was in charge of the evacuees committee formed to coordinate matters. On the way up the Bay of Bengal, however, it became clear to all on board that Rangoon—the last route into China—was about to fall to the Japanese as well, and so their boat was diverted to Madras instead, and then to Calcutta.[37]

Singapore fell on 15 February 1942. By March, the whole of Southeast Asia was under Japanese control, and the encirclement of China seemed all but completed. The two routes through which the Chinese army could be supplied after the Chinese coast was securely in Japanese hands were through Annam and Burma. These were now gone. With that, remittances back to China from the Overseas Chinese completely stopped.[38]

> Many units fought to the last soldier; a Chinese volunteer platoon made a gallant stand against the invaders in the north of Singapore until all perished. Others, including Tan Kah Kee, gave up the futile resistance. After sending to China the $13 million yuan that had been collected in a contribution campaign in early December (this drive terminated in late January 1942), Tan escaped from Singapore to Sumatra in a small ferry boat on the night of February 2.[39]

Rangoon did fall to the Japanese, but perhaps at a slower pace than many expected. It was only on 7 March that they marched in to take over a port that was burning from the scorched-earth withdrawal of the British forces.

An era was ending. The period to come would see the total retreat of colonial powers from the region and the swift emergence of nation states in Southeast Asia. The structure of power, political loyalties and the places the overseas Chinese would call home were all about to change.

Writing in 1937, on the eve of the formal outbreak of the Sino-Japanese war, Rupert Emerson noted the following about the Chinese in British Malaya:

> The growth of Chinese nationalism, the appearance of the Chinese Republic, and the rise to dominance of the Kuomintang have brought about a transformation of the political consciousness of the Chinese overseas which tends radically to alter their relations to the governments under which they live.[40]

Hau-Shik and his family—his party included eight children, aged two to 18, according to the registration form he filled in later in preparation for a trip to China—would stay in India for the rest of the Pacific War.[41] While Hau-Shik's fate would see him becoming a key player in the formation of a new nation to replace British Malaya after the war, Tan Kah Kee's destined him to return in 1950 to the land of his birth but now governed by a hopeful but insecure communist regime.

NOTES

1. Rupert Emerson, *Malaysia: A Study of Direct and Indirect Rule* (Kuala Lumpur: University of Malaya Press, (1970) 1937), p. 696. Original publisher: The Macmillan Company.
2. This brief note was supplied to the author by Thomas Lee, Hau-Shik's son. Hau-Shik and Samuel Kam were first cousins, Kam Kho Chun being the sister of Samuel Kam's father. The long-lived Samuel S.W. Kam (1915–) was an industrialist who as its CEO brought fame and success to Lam Soon Malaysia. This was a Singapore company that moved to Malaya under extreme pressure in 1957 from new taxes imposed on foreign companies by Hau-Shik after he became

Malaya's Finance Minister. See also Samuel W.S. Kam, *Through Wars and Peace: From the Gunfire of the Sino-Japanese War to the Golden Oil of Malaya. A Memoir by Samuel S.W. Kam at 96* (Hong Kong: Peace Book Company, 2011).

Samuel Kam is recognized as one of the key persons in the development of Malaysia's palm oil industry. See also *Business Circle*, "Pioneer in the Palm Oil Industry", undated, https://www.businesscircle.com.my/pioneer-in-the-palm-oil-industry-2/.

Guangdong was their home province. More exactly, their ancestral home was the village of Tai Lu Kai in Xinyi in Gaozhou Prefecture. Their consciousness of these ties ran deep, and despite their travels, the clan affiliation remained strong. Hau-Shik was founder-president of the Malaysian Kochow Clan Association until his death in 1988. He was succeeded by Samuel Kam. See Kam (2011), p. 298. Hau-Shik was knighted in 1957, see Kam (2011), p. 208.

3. Kam (2011), pp. 203–8. The prince in question was Albert, who would reluctantly be crowned Britain's George VI in 1936 following the abdication of his brother, King Edward VIII, who sat for but 11 months on the throne before stepping down to marry the American divorcee, Wallis Simpson.

4. In the 1990s, Hau-Shik's sons employed the services of Professor Joseph P. McDermott at the Faculty of Oriental Studies at Cambridge University to explore the genealogy of their family. A letter written by Professor D.L. McMullen on 30 December 1997, and sent as a preliminary report on the matter to Alex Lee (from Alex Lee's private papers [R-15/1/98], supplied by Thomas Lee in June 2019), carried some information of interest gleaned from available genealogies. In brief, a known ancestor, Li Dongshao, claimed in writing as his ancestor the famous Tang Dynasty general, Li Sheng (727–793), Prince of Xiping, "a man credited with having saved the dynasty, who was honoured in every possible way by the emperor". The professor added a word of caution that "The general scholarly opinion is that

such claims of ancestry when made by post-Song genealogies are unlikely to be verifiable."
5. Lee Kam Hing, "Lee Hau Shik: His Life and Times", in *Chinese Diaspora since Admiral Zheng He: With Special Reference to Maritime Asia*, by Leo Suryadinata (Singapore: Chinese Heritage Centre, 2007), p. 152. See also Victor Zheng, Wong Siu-lun, and Sun Wen-bin, "Beyond Family Enterprise: The Early Phase of H.S. Lee's Business and Political Career", Conference paper of *The 5th Conference of the International Society for the Study of Chinese Overseas*, 10 May 2004, http://hub.hku.hk/handle/10722/93554.
6. Zheng et al. (2004).
7. Tan Miau Ing, "Tun Sir Henry Lee Hau Shik and [the] Anti-Japanese Movement", unpublished, 2009.
8. Lee (2007), pp. 152–53.
9. Tan (2009).
10. H.S. Lee papers, Folio 9 (a)–9.37a, ISEAS Library.
11. Tan (2009).
12. Zheng et al. (2004); Lee (2007), pp. 152–55. See also unpublished essay by Hau-Shik's son Thomas Lee, made accessible to the author, titled "Tun Sir Henry Hau Shik Lee, SMN, KBE (1901–1988)". Family details were provided by Douglas Lee during the interview on 23 January 2013.
13. According to her son Thomas Lee, Choi Lin was not educated in English but taught herself enough functional English to accompany his father to public functions whenever she could, and when the couple entertained guests. Email correspondence with Thomas Lee, June 2019.
14. Zheng et al. (2004).
15. Tan (2009).
16. Lee (2007), pp. 154–55.
17. Hara Fujio, "An Alternative View of Tun Sir H.S. Lee: The Anti-Japanese Movement and His Dedication to China", *Journal of Asia-Pacific Studies* (Waseda University) 20 (February 2013): 53–63.

18. Zheng et al. (2004).
19. Lee (2007), pp. 154–55.
20. Yoji Akashi, *The Nanyang Chinese National Salvation Movement, 1937–1941*, International Studies, East Asian Series Research Publication, no. 5, Center for East Asian Studies, University of Kansas (New York: Paragon Book Gallery, 1970), p. 11.
21. Ibid., pp. 1–3.
22. Ibid., pp. 13–14.
23. Tan (2009).
24. Stephen Leong (1977), pp. 275–77.
25. A.H.C. Ward, Raymond W. Chu, and Janet Salaff, *The Memoirs of Tan Kah-Kee* (Singapore: Singapore University Press, 1994), pp. 2–4.
26. Emerson (1937), p. 505. (Reprinted by the University of Malaya Press in 1964).
27. Akashi (1970), pp. 13–32.
28. Sam King, *Tiger Balm King: The Life and Times of Aw Boon Haw* (Singapore and Kuala Lumpur: Times Books International, 1992), pp. 173–85.
29. Ward et al. (1994), pp. 260–61.
30. Ibid., pp. 123–30.
31. Akashi (1970), p. 79.
32. Masanobu Tsuji, *Singapore 1941–1942: The Japanese Version of the Malayan Campaign of World War II* (Singapore: Oxford University Press, 1988), p. 136.
33. H.S. Lee papers, folio 9 (a)–9.34.
34. Fujio (2013), p. 55. See also Tan Cheng Lock, "Memorandium on the 'Quisling' Resolution passed by the Malayan Association, Bombay, on 16th November 1942", in *Malayan Problems from a Chinese Point of View by Tan Cheng Lock*, by C.Q. Lee (Singapore: Tannsco, 1947), pp. 44–45.
35. H.S. Lee papers 121/005/001: 5.
36. H.S. Lee papers, folio 9 (a)–9.34.
37. Hara (2013), pp. 55–56. Hara's claim that the sea trip took 21 days seems slightly incorrect. Hau-Shik wrote elsewhere that he left Malaya

on 30 January and arrived in Calcutta on 14 February 1942, the day before Singapore fell. See H.S. Lee papers 121/001/001: 31.
38. Ward et al. (1994), p. 4.
39. Akashi (1970), pp. 82–84.
40. Emerson (1937), p. 505.
41. H.S. Lee papers 121/001/001: 31.

PART TWO
1942–45

Chapter 3

POLITICAL AWAKENING AMID GLOBAL WARS

> By December 1941, the Japanese government had come to the conclusion that diplomacy would not achieve its aims in Southeast Asia. It was essential to secure direct control over the region and also ensure that no power was in a position to threaten shipping links between Japan and Southeast Asia. The American navy posed the greatest threat, and on December 7, a surprise raid on Pearl Harbor in Hawai'i destroyed most of the American Pacific fleet.
>
> —Anne E. Booth[1]

IN ITS ATTEMPT to create the Greater East Asia Co-Prosperity Sphere, Japan deemed itself to be following the dictates of imperial economics. Tokyo's modernization was a defensive one, occurring in the wake of China's defeat in the Opium Wars. What it seemed to have learned from the process was how important a secure supply of resources was to industry. Its success in transforming its culture into one that could vie with Western powers was all the more extraordinary when compared to the failure experienced by other non-western polities of the time, especially the ailing Manchu dynasty that was ruling China.

The fall of the Qing in 1911 failed to place China onto any clear path of modernization, and the possibility of the empire being divided among properly modernized nations was all the stronger when the Versailles Treaty of 1919 saw German possessions in China being handed over by the victorious allies to Japan—which was then one of their numbers—instead of being returned to Chinese control. To be sure, no central government existed in China then. It was only after the Kuomintang under Generalissimo Chiang Kai-shek succeeded in defeating and co-opting the various warlords with his Northern Expedition in 1926–28 that such an authority came into being.

Chiang managed to complete this feat through violent campaigns that destroyed the urban presence of the Chinese Communist Party in 1927. This achievement did not stop the Japanese from invading Manchuria in 1931. In fact, it may have prompted them to act sooner rather than later. In retaliation for the bombing in Mukden (now known as Shenyang) of a railway line owned by the Japanese, an act many believed to be the work of an agent provocateur, the Japanese army began its invasion of the Northeast, the ancestral homeland of the now defeated and assimilated Manchurian conquerors of China.

All these incidents had great repercussions among Chinese communities throughout the world, leading them to contribute huge amounts in defence of the Middle Kingdom and to mitigate the sufferings of refugees.[2] The twentieth century did not look as if it would be any better for China and its peoples than the agonizing nineteenth century had been.

Modern times for China were choreographed around colonial intrusions and, most profoundly, Japanese invasions. In the propaganda of Japan's imperial occupations therefore, the liberation of colonized peoples [no doubt for incorporation into the Greater East Asian Co-Prosperity Sphere] seldom bothered to include the numerous and dispersed Chinese. By the 1930s, the Chinese—on the Mainland or overseas—had become the blood enemy hindering the creation of this Sphere. The war in Malaya would have at times been considered by the ground troops to be very much a southerly continuation of the conflict in China. Colonel Masanobu Tsuji, the strategist who planned the Malaya campaign hinted as much:

> On 11th January [1942] at 8 p.m. our troops entered Kuala Lumpur, capital of the Malay Federation, without serious enemy resistance. This metropolis presented a dignified and imposing modern appearance. There were Chinese merchants' shops on practically all the main streets, and from each of these hung the firm's name, written in *kanji*. We felt as though we had entered the crossroads of the central provinces of China.[3]

Hau-Shik and his family, along with thousands of others, had fled southward by then for the seemingly impregnable island of Singapore. As noted by Colonel Tsuji, it may have been true that Singapore could not be taken from the sea, but for some reason, the island was left without rear fortifications.

> In other words, to land in southern Thailand, brave the intense heat and the long distance of eleven hundred kilometres, and advance through dense jungle, was probably deemed an impossibility by [...] British common-sense judgment. A Japanese Army contemplating such operations in an emergency would, it appeared, in view of the long distance overland, have to labour for perhaps more than a year to reach Singapore from Thailand. In the meantime it was not difficult to imagine that the British would [have had time by then to] complete fortification of the landward front.[4]

As it turned out, the Japanese needed only 55 days after landing at Singora (Songkhla) in Southern Thailand to reach Singapore and to obtain an unconditional surrender from the British. The trudge northwards up the Tenasserim Coast saw them taking 20 days longer to capture the Burmese capital of Rangoon. But by May 1942, they had control over all of Burma except for a narrow northern strip.[5]

The Japanese would eventually retreat from Burma, and lose the war to the Allies. Their claim to be liberating Asia and Asians from Westerners, though historically impactful on some Southeast Asia nationalists more than others, was subsequently and rapidly "diminished, if not totally eradicated" by the returning colonialists.[6] Their perpetration of wartime atrocities and their links to the fascist powers in Europe, and the conquests that the creation of their Greater East Asian Co-Prosperity Sphere required, also damaged profoundly their image as Asian champions. As these colonial empires fought to replace each other, new imaginings of independence from external powers, paradoxically coupled with an imperative to ape political models developed in the west, began to appear in the colonies.

Japan's claim to be liberating Asia resonated most among the population in Indonesia, and to a lesser extent among Burmese. In Malaya, the lure of this narrative took concrete form in the creation of the Indian National Army (INA) on 17 February 1942, two days after the fall of Singapore. INA recruits were largely prisoners of war. By April, the All-Malayan Indian Independence League (IIL) had been formed by various Indian associations in Malaya and Singapore, with the INA subordinate to it. Formal recruitment began by May. Among the IIL's specific demands to the Japanese was the recognition of India as an independent nation and with the IIL as its representative. The Japanese did not give any proper response, and these organizations stayed irrelevant until their request to have the charismatic Subhas Chandra Bose, who was in Germany, brought to Southeast Asia was granted. Bose travelled back to the region on a German submarine and was transferred to a Japanese submarine which took him to Tokyo for talks with Japanese generals and the prime minister. He arrived in Singapore on 2 July 1943, and was made president of the IIL two days later. Under Bose, the INA, instead of relying on prisoners of war, succeeded in recruiting huge numbers from Indian communities in Malaya, arousing them with calls of "Chalo Dilli" (To Delhi) and descriptions of the INA as "Azad Hind Fauj" (India's Army of Liberation).[7]

The strong post-colonialist fervour whipped up by Bose and the INA can be seen, for example, in how it affected Johor-born James Joseph Puthucheary, who signed up as a 20-year-old and fought at the decisive Battle of Imphal in India. Of the 6,000 INA men who "marched to Delhi", only 2,600 returned. Puthucheary survived, and made his way back to Mandalay and then to Calcutta, where he hid for several months in the ancestral house of Bose. In 1948, after India's independence, he took a ship back to Singapore, joining up with the Malayan Democratic Union through his childhood friend William Kuok to continue the anti-colonial struggle. In his second stint as a political prisoner, Puthucheary finished the much-appraised *Ownership and Control in the Malayan Economy*. This was published in 1960.[8] Banished from Singapore in 1964, he would come to influence the comprehensive affirmative action plan that began to be implemented in Malaysia in 1970, thanks to his idea that only governmental intervention through public corporations could bring the Malay community into the mainstream economy.[9]

As has been noted by Wang Gungwu, the nationalistic fervour that was then engulfing East and Southeast Asia had many roots, and the gradual manner in which colonialism developed followed by its sudden decline in the wake of the Japanese invasion left deep impressions on the various peoples in the South Seas.

> As long as India was not independent, it was unthinkable for any of their [Britain's] other territories to ask for independence. And indeed, most unfortunately for Burma, it came to be administered as part of the Indian part of the empire, as were parts of the Malay Peninsula during the first half of the nineteenth century. But for the opening of China in the 1840s, the Malay states would also have been much more closely tied to imperial interests in India. As it happened, the invention of indirect rule reduced the urge to seek independence among the elite groups, who were given roles in the newly emerging modern administration. Thus, the question of providing a British model for a future nation-state to be formed out of what was called Malaya was simply not relevant before the Pacific War.[10]

For Peninsular Malays, political influence would come more cogently from Indonesia, where Japanese propaganda against Dutch colonialism took root on ground that was more fertile than in British Malaya. Being outside of British influence and its indirect means of colonialism, the arguments for full independence among the Indonesians were not tied to India's ability to throw off the colonial yoke, as was to a large extent the case in Malaya.

Sukarno and Muhammad Hatta declared independence for their country merely two days after Japan's surrender, although the Dutch would not accept it until late 1949. During that interim, the country went through a bloody social revolution that left a deep impression on the British and the Malay elite. During that time also, India gained independence, and this changed the British stance with regards to the future of Malaya.

After the First World War, the British had secured formal control over all the peninsular states, and following recognition of the fact that the Malays were involved in public administration only to a very limited extent, they implemented a "pro-Malay policy" of recruitment. Most positions were back then held by Europeans. In 1919, Malays made up only 10.5 per cent of the 1,001 clerks in the General Clerical Service of the Federated Malay States. They were even more weakly represented in the special services. Even in 1924, of the 5,500 subordinate officers in the railways, postal and medical departments, only 11 were Malays. In the late 1920s, long-domiciled Chinese began calling for equal rights with the Malays, and for a greater share in government. This threatened to upset the plural-societal balance that the British had come to rely on.[11]

For Malay activists of the time, such as those in the influential and impactful Kesatuan Melayu Muda (KMM, Union of Young Malays), such demands were a direct challenge to Malay rights. To KMM President Ibrahim Haji Yaacob, a Pahang-born teacher and journalist, the rights besieged by "foreign races" (*bangsa-bangsa asing*)—which did not include the British, who instead were named in the pre-war period at least as "our foster father" (*bapa angkat kita*)—were about positions in the government sector, creating a Malayan race (*bangsa Malayan*), having rice fields, abolishing the Jawi script and running primary schools in their mother tongue and funded by the government.[12] After the war, it became clear that Ibrahim, along with a large majority of Malayans, had lost their fascination with the British. He became more clearly an anti-colonialist agitator, condemning the British for their "open door" immigration policy and their capitalist exploitation of the region. He blamed the rulers for being feudalist and considered colonialism the root cause of the problems faced by the Malays.

A REGIONAL SINO-JAPANESE WAR

As has been mentioned above, the political stance of Malayan Chinese vis-à-vis Japanese military ambitions was configured by events in China which took place even before the fall of the Qing Dynasty, and for many of them, the coming of the Japanese to Southeast Asia in 1941 was simply the continuation of the war in East Asia.

This makes it necessary to consider the history of political consciousness among Malayan Chinese during the period just before the Japanese invasion. The origins of the political imaginings that came into play in Malaya after the Second World War were in fact regional, and even global.

Public outrage in China over the Treaty of Versailles of 1919 had led to an upsurge in Chinese nationalism, and the student-led May Fourth Movement begun that year pushed aside the obsession with elite concerns about cultural transformation in favour of political activism and populism.

Cultural transformation had also been a concern among the Nanyang Chinese as the fall of the Qing began to look more and more inevitable. Manchu attempts at reform tried to involve the elite in the Nanyang, with some impact.

> Overseas Chinese merchants and to a certain extent, the locally born Straits Chinese merchants and professional (who were British subjects) were in this way stimulated into a greater awareness of Chinese politics. Newspapers were started. Cultural and literary bodies were created to influence and to generate public opinion pertaining to the regeneration of overseas Chinese society. The Straits Chinese, in this respect, were also leading the China-born Chinese in social reforms such as the eradication of opium-smoking, the building of schools and the eradication of superstitious beliefs and practices. Overseas Chinese response as a whole was an emotive kind of nationalism

interpreted through what they could do to enhance their own image within a colonial society.¹³

However, it was revolutionaries such as Sun Yat-sen, who fervently worked to gain financial and other support for his cause who affected the region's Chinese most deeply. The Singapore branch of his Tokyo-based Tung Meng Hui was formed in 1906 to coordinate branches throughout the region. Its goal being a revolutionary one, it sought support from all Chinese from all backgrounds. With the success of the Wuchang Uprising of 1911 and the demise of the dynastic system in China, the path seemed clear. The Tung Meng Hui evolved through mergers with other political groupings to become the Kuomintang, and in Malaya its branches mushroomed along with the reading societies. This did not last though, and when China's revolution began to backtrack in the 1910s and British concerns over Chinese activism in their colonies grew, the patriotic enthusiasm of the Chinese in Malaya was channelled into the building of schools "to teach the young Chinese generation national pride and the glorious heritage of China".¹⁴

China's May Fourth Movement of 1919 fired the imagination of a whole generation of students and activists, and paved the way for the founding of the Chinese Communist Party on 1 July 1921. Political activism in the form of "militant nationalism, anarchism and communism" influenced the Chinese population in Malaya as well. Anarchism in Malaya was a worry until the enthusiasm of its supporters was absorbed by the Kuomintang's resurgence in 1924. Data from June 1924 numbered Kuomintang members in British Malaya at 5,998. While this made up an estimated measly 0.5 per cent of the relevant population on the peninsula, it worried the British.¹⁵

To the colonial government, the issue was tied up with the larger question of political stability in Malaya and the protection of

Malay sovereignty. It became even more serious when the issue of suppression of KMT branches was linked to the possibility of political repercussions on British interests in China.[16]

Between 1924 and 1927, during the period of collaboration between the Kuomintang and the Chinese Communist Party in China, Kuomintang branches in Malaya became increasingly associated with the dissemination of Bolshevik propaganda to such an extent that many wealthier members withdrew their support. This allowed for remaining members, many of whom were from the Hailam (Hainan) dialect group, to turn these branches in an even more anti-imperialist direction.[17] This had sociological and sentimental reasons. The Hailams had been the lowest in the Chinese social hierarchy, and often worked as servants and cooks in European homes or as water-carriers, hotel-boys and waiters.

In October 1925, the British ordered the dissolution of Kuomintang branches in Malaya.

In his excellent master's thesis on the Kuomintang and the Malayan Communist Party in the pre-war years, which is one of very few works on the subject, Leong Yee Foong notes:

> The Hailam community as such was largely a bachelor-migratory population, not family-centred and having the least economic and social stake in this country [British Malaya]. With their womenfolk in China, the Hailams maintained exceptionally strong emotional and social ties with their island home of Hainan. Such strong ties with China invariably induced them to be politically more aware than the other speech-groups of developments in South China.[18]

Back in its homeland, the Kuomintang under Chiang Kai-shek continued to gain ground, and finally reunited the country in 1928. After suppressing the northern warlords and massacring members of the then-city-based Chinese Communist Party, the Kuomintang formed a government in Nanjing, China's first central government since 1911. As the Kuomintang's right wing became dominant in China, a nascent communist movement began to take root in Singapore. It was not anti-colonial to begin with, but was instead a reflection of left-wing politics in China, and parochial in markedly having Hailams as its main supporters.

The 1925 ban on the Kuomintang in British Malaya was often ignored by the party's members, and it was with the arrival in early February 1930 of the former Governor of Hong Kong, Cecil Clementi, to become the Governor of the Straits Settlements and High Commissioner for the Federated Malay States that the situation had to be taken seriously. Clementi immediately set about "cutting Malayan Chinese political activism down to size through his attack on the KMT".[19]

He trained his efforts on Chinese vernacular education and exerted control over school curricula, the training of teachers, and funding. Restrictions on immigration, though couched in political terms, were significantly imposed at a time when the global recession was making workers redundant. By the end of 1930, he had two prominent Chinese banished. These were Teh Lay-seng, a British subject and prominent business and community leader, and P'ng Chi-cheng, a journalist. Teh was banned for two years, and P'ng for life. Six prominent Kuomintang leaders from the state of Selangor were also banned in February 1932.[20]

Considering the situation in Malaya to be such that Britain's wider interests were at risk when China was concerned put Clementi in immediate conflict with the Foreign Office's dictum for China "to achieve an independent Sovereign State while at the same time securing adequate guarantees for the lives, property and commerce of British nationals in China".[21]

[Clementi's] prime objective—protecting the Malay rulers according to the treaties—seemed to mean protecting the Straits-born Chinese from themselves and their errant countrymen indulging in disloyal political activities. By not recognizing any nationalist sentiment as legitimate, or any need to inform London of his measures, Clementi created chaos.[22]

The High Commissioner was steadfast in his conviction that the Rulers were not an anachronism and that they were valuable to the imperial system. His aim to raise the position of the rulers of the Federated Malay States through a looser federation incorporating all states was rejected in the end, not only by the Colonial Office but also by the rulers of the Unfederated Malay States, who "were fiercely independent and proved reluctant to accept any form of closer association with the other states".[23]

Clementi saw great value in the system of indirect rule that had been in place and that had over time been eroded. His experience serving in various imperial outposts convinced him that the Malay polities should be considered "a buffer between us [the British Empire] and political developments such as have taken place in Ceylon [and] between Government and the Chinese".[24] Throughout Clementi's four-year tenure in Malaya, tension mounted between the Colonial Office and its top official in Malaya. Clementi did not waver, and just before he was dismissed in early 1934, even expressed his intention to make Malay the basic language in Malaya.[25]

Outraged by what he and many other top colonial offices saw as Clementi's autocratic temperament and lack of understanding of how British Malaya had to be run, the Principal at the Colonial Office, J.A. Calder, poignantly altercated that "If their [Federated Malay States] rulers now aspire to be real rulers over States, it is because British officers have built up a Government machine for them."[26]

This profound conflict of views among British officials on the nature of indirect rule, the pluralistic nature of Malayan society and the status of the sultans and their states would resurface after the war to determine the unique federalist path and the development of a painful culture of consensus that sought to define the country after independence. The issue of education would remain a principal bone of contention.

A COLD WAR BEFORE THE COLD WAR

For the Malayan Kuomintang, the 1930s was a difficult period. Despite Clementi's efforts, the politicization of Malayan Chinese was not something that could be easily stopped, seeing how much of the process was fuelled by the growing conflict between Japan and China. In fact, by 1935, the British moved to exert more control over Chinese education in Malaya to counteract efforts being taken by Chinese consuls. Grants-in-aid were being provided to Chinese schools in which Mandarin was now officially recognized as the main medium of instruction.[27]

In mid-1936, Malayan Kuomintang members openly raised funds for the purchase of aeroplanes for China, and in December that year, sizeable demonstrations took place calling for the release of Chiang Kai-shek when he was kidnapped by Zhang Xueliang to force Chiang into cooperating with the Chinese Communist Party in resisting the Japanese invasion. By the time the Sino-Japanese war broke into the open in 1937, the colonial administration in British Malaya had grown concerned about the communist movement there, and when the European war began in 1939, the Kuomintang had gone from being seen as a threat, to being a nuisance, and finally to being a potential ally.[28]

The founding of China relief fund organizations throughout the region following the outbreak of war between China and Japan in 1937, like the one in Singapore by Tan Kah Kee and the one in Selangor by Lee Hau-Shik and Ang Cheng Chong, for example, was a deep expression of the concern for China's situation felt among overseas Chinese. Accordingly, the Malayan branches of Chinese political parties, namely the Kuomintang and the Malayan Communist Party, experienced an upsurge in support.

Although the non-partisan Tan Kah Kee would later break with the Kuomintang after his "Comfort Mission" to China in March 1940 left him disappointed with the Kuomintang government in Chongqing and highly impressed with the communist experiment at Yan'an, the Singapore China Relief Fund Association he founded in August 1937 was done with profuse support from Kuomintang leaders. This pattern was repeated when the Federation of China Relief Fund of the South Seas was formed in October 1938.

Administering Malaya at a time when its Chinese population was fixated with the political situation in China was a highly complicated matter. The British had also to consider their position and interests within the context of the Sino-Japanese war, as well as rising tensions in Europe. But even for the Kuomintang government in China, trying to control the Malayan Chinese was not a straightforward matter. Since the days of Sun Yat-sen, securing financial support through Chinese Chambers of Commerce had required good contact with these bodies. Already at its founding in 1928, Chiang Kai-shek promulgated the Chambers of Commerce Ordinance that required these bodies throughout the region to amend their regulations and register with the Kuomintang's Commission of Overseas Chinese Affairs. The Chambers in Batavia, Sandakan, Sibu and Siam complied. The Malayan Associated Chambers of Commerce would not.

The Kuomintang in its enthusiasm to project its jurisdictional influence over the overseas Chinese had failed to take into consideration the fact that overseas Chinese businessmen in the course of adapting and organizing themselves within a colonial economic environment had evolved their own unique patterns of leadership and authority in which socio-economic institutions such as Chambers of Commerce formed an integral part of the whole framework. The institutions formed the basis of their operative domain through which businessmen could project themselves into social and economic prominence and it was rather unlikely that they would readily subject themselves to outside control, however nationalistic they might be, when even the colonial government itself had theretofore allowed them plenty of room to operate freely.[29]

By 1936, the fear of Chinese communism had become palpable enough for the target of British anxiety to shift from the Malayan Kuomintang to the Malayan Communist Party.

Founded officially in 1930 through a change of name from the organization called Nanyang Provisional Commission of the Communist Party of China, which had emerged from the left-wing branches of the Malayan Kuomintang, the Malayan Communist Party sought to focus its efforts on British Malaya. Communist organizations such as those in Siam and Burma continued, however, to see that body as a regional operations centre. Be that as it may, this difference in view was probably not an important one in the larger scheme of things. Little or no evidence exists of direct communication between the Malayan Communist Party and the Far Eastern Bureau of the Comintern in Shanghai. Its own weakness was expressed at its Pan-Malayan Third Representatives Conference held in April 1930. The organization realized that its support was confined only to the Hailam section of the Chinese population, and that the labourer classes were not under party influence.[30]

But its influence did soon grow, and in seeking to develop beyond being a Chinese-based party, it implemented a multiracial policy to attract Malays and Indians into its anti-colonial struggle. Though not a failure, this strategy showed only limited success. Much of this had to do with the spatial aspects of the plural society in colonial Malaya. The Indians, for example, were mainly illiterate estate workers living in isolated enclaves. While the Malayan Communist Party may have hoped that the economic slump would have hit Malay peasants bad enough for them to oppose the British, this did not seem to have been the case, and in any event, the party lacked the ability to connect with and mobilize whatever disenchanted Malays there were.[31]

But Malayan society was changing along with the rest of the world as it came out of the recession. In the face of Indian and Chinese nationalism spreading ever more strongly into Malaya, the British colonial government implemented policies to favour Malays, in the process restricting non-Malays from taking government positions and enhancing Malay vernacular education. This mix of dynamics, local and global, alienated parts of the Chinese and Tamil population from the colonial masters and further encouraged communalism.[32]

THE DESCENDING RISING SUN

And in July 1937, Japan's invasion of China roused Chinese nationalism among Malayan Chinese to a degree never seen before. This hardly helped inter-ethnic ties or government policies in keeping social peace.

War was on the way for British Malaya, although hardly anyone there could have predicted a Japanese invasion on the scale that it came in. The ensuing occupation, though relatively short, changed everything. Colonialism was on its last legs and nationalism would be the sentiment and the rallying cry of the post-war period. In that sense, Japan acted both as disingenuous and as unwitting midwife for the nations—and the strong sense of nationalism—that would soon emerge throughout the region. The main actors had as yet to appear on the scene.

In any case, all this was understandably still not obvious to anyone, and certainly not to people like Lee Hau-Shik and his family, who were taking refuge in Calcutta. At the fringe of the great Pacific War, most of them were largely reduced to spectators as the whole of Southeast Asia became a buffer zone. It was in the Pacific islands, in Burma and within China that the battle lines were drawn. In Malaya, the war was largely fought by communist guerrillas against the Japanese invaders.

Malaya was now ruled centrally for the first time. The Japanese, in the form of the 25th Army, administered from Singapore and continued with the British practice of favouring Malays in the government service, and to much higher positions than had been the case.[33] In December 1942, a directive was sent out by Tokyo for the Military Administration in Malaya "to take a prudent attitude in treating Sultans" considering the importance of the policy for the rulers of princely States in India. This tactic was a reversed application of the indirect rule that the British learned from colonizing India which they then applied on the Malay Peninsula, but "remained merely a declarative statement and the real practice based on them was not thorough-going". Equally interesting was the establishment by the Japanese occupation forces of "reading clubs" (*Epposho*) in Malayan cities which were reminiscent of those started by young Kuomintang intellectuals before the war.[34]

The Japanese occupation helped to bring about certain changes in the structure of Chinese society in Malaya. Traditional Chinese leaders had either fled the country or were forced to cooperate with the Japanese if they remained. Consequently, the prewar elites were discredited and frequently despised. Their place tended to be filled by Chinese communists who were mostly of a younger generation. On the whole, the Japanese occupation and the war experience strengthened Chinese nationalism and their sense of ethnic identity.[35]

East Asia as it looked in 1942–45 was in dire and uncertain straits. Except for continental China, the whole of East Asia was under Japanese military occupation, and apart from guerrilla wars, the frontlines were in Burma, inland China and in the Pacific Ocean. For the Japanese, their impressive victories were difficult to sustain, and once these fronts stabilized, the limitations of their war machine and their world view became increasingly obvious. As claimed by K.G. Tregonning, overwhelming though their invasion had been, the ability of the Japanese to rule these lands and win the war was in serious doubt:

> [This] conquest should be seen as a brilliantly executed and skilfully planned campaign, not as a war, and the Japanese weakness in mistaking the former for the latter was soon apparent. After this campaign was over, its lack of plans, except a defensive determination to hold on to what it had secured, was clear. Japan had gone to war, but it had little appreciation of what that war would entail beyond this first campaign. For Japan to be successful, it had to defeat its enemies by achieving a total victory; but this it did not do, nor set out to accomplish. The Japanese had no strategic thought at all beyond the occupation of South-East Asia, and

while their tactics in the South-East Asian campaign were brilliant, their lack of thinking on a global basis led inevitably to their defeat.[36]

NOTES

1. Anne E. Booth, *Colonial Legacies: Economic and Social Development in East and Southeast Asia* (Honolulu: University of Hawai'i Press, 2007), p. 149.
2. See C.F. Yong, *Tan Kah-Kee: The Making of an Overseas Chinese Legend* (Singapore: Oxford University Press, 1987).
3. Masanobu Tsuji, *Singapore 1941–1942: The Japanese Version of the Malayan Campaign of World War II* (Singapore: Oxford University Press, 1988), p. 178.
4. Ibid., p. 218.
5. S.G. Chaphekar, *A Brief Study of the Burma Campaign 1943–45* (Poona: Maharashtra Militarisation Board, 1955).
6. Wang Gungwu, "Political Heritage and Nation Building", *Journal of the Malaysian Branch of the Royal Asiatic Society* 73, no. 2 (2000): 17.
7. Veena Sikri, *India and Malaysia: Intertwined Strands* (Singapore and India: Institute of Southeast Asian Studies and Manohar, 2013), pp. 288–95.
8. James Joseph Puthucheary, *Ownership and Control in the Malayan Economy* (Petaling Jayas: SIRD, 1960 (2004)).
9. Dominic Puthucheary and Jomo K.S., *No Cowardly Past. James Puthucheary: Writings, Poems, Commentaries* (Kuala Lumpur: Insan and SIRD, 2010 (1998)), pp. 21–28.
10. Wang (2000), p. 10.
11. Soda Naoki, "Indigenizing Colonial Knowledge: The Formation of Pan-Malay Identity in British Malaya", PhD thesis, Graduate School of Asian and African Area Studies, Kyoto University, 2008, pp. 140–41.
12. Ibid., pp. 142–51, 161–62.

13. Leong Yee Foong, "Chinese Politics and Political Parties in Colonial Malaya, 1920–1940: A Study of the Kuomintang and the Malayan Communist Party", Master's thesis, Universiti Sains Malaysia, Penang, 1977 [Microfilm at ISEAS Library], p. 13.
14. Ibid., p. 17.
15. Ibid., pp. 19–28.
16. Ibid., p. 29.
17. Ibid., pp. 30–33.
18. Ibid., pp. 32–33.
19. C.F. Yong and R.B. McKenna, *The Kuomintang Movement in British Malaya, 1912–1949* (Singapore: Singapore University Press, National University of Singapore, 1990), p. 138.
20. Ibid., pp. 141, 172.
21. FO 371/14728/1489, Enclosure, "Activities of the *Kuomintang* in Malaya", 17 March 1930; FO Memorandum by Sir John Pratt, 3 April 1930.
22. Yong and McKenna (1990), p. 143.
23. Simon C. Smith, *British Relations with the Malay Rulers from Decentralization to Malayan Independence 1930–1957* (Kuala Lumpur: Oxford University Press, 1995), p. 29.
24. Note of Conference at the Colonial Office, 15 May 1931, CO 717/76, no. 72483/1931, cited in ibid., p. 23.
25. Straits Settlements Legislative Council Proceedings, 1934, B. 18, cited in Leong (1977), p. 71.
26. Minute by Calder, 13 April 1931, CO 717/81, no. 82395/1931, cited in Smith (1995), p. 24.
27. Leong (1977), p. 72.
28. Yong and McKenna (1990), pp. 184–88.
29. Leong (1977), pp. 77–79.
30. *Monthly Review of Chinese Affairs* 5 (January 1931), p. 13, CO273/571, cited in Leong (1977), pp. 79–82.
31. Leong (1977), pp. 82–103.
32. Ibid., p. 105.

33. Cheah Boon Kheng, "The Social Impact of the Japanese Occupation of Malaya (1942–1945)", in *Southeast Asia under Japanese Occupation*, edited by Alfred W. McCoy (New Haven: Yale University Southeast Asia Studies, 1980), pp. 116–17.
34. Yoichi Itagaki, "Some Aspects of the Japanese Policy for Malaya under the Occupation, with Special Reference to Nationalism", in *Papers on Malayan History*, edited by K.G. Tregonning (Singapore: Journal South-East Asian History, 1962), pp. 257, 261.
35. Cheah (1980), p. 117.
36. K.G. Tregonning, *A History of Modern Malaysia and Singapore* (Singapore: Eastern Universities Press, 1964), pp. 217–18.

Chapter 4

FINDING REFUGE IN INDIA

In the months immediately following the collapse of British administration in Malaya, widespread American criticism of Britain's alleged "bungling imperialism" induced the Colonial Office to press for the formulation of an official post-war reconstruction policy, in order to forestall probable demands from Washington and Chungking for the dismantling of British colonial rule in Southeast Asia.

—C.M. Turnbull[1]

IN THE CHAOS of the times, the future of East Asia was apparently being fought over between its two political giants, China and Japan. To what extent the colonialists could return in triumph to regain their stature and power was a grave matter for consideration, especially for the peoples they had ruled. For most, nationalism was as yet just an interesting but impractical thought rather than an ideological conviction.

For Malayan Chinese, two stances were prominent and possible at this time. Does the post-war future for them lie with China, or with the European colonialists, damaged though their reputation and their right to rule had been by the Japanese?

Japan's Greater East Asia Co-Prosperity Sphere was not acceptable to them, and the idea of small nation states growing out of the disparate colonies was for most as yet a fantastical myth.

Surviving this period of global conflict and planning loosely for the time of fragile peace that must surely follow occupied the minds of displaced persons such as Hau-Shik. The active and influential person that he was, Hau-Shik's sentiments at this time was more clearly China-oriented, and it was towards Chungking that his thoughts initially went. There was no clear reason why the Japanese would not continue their expansion into India, and therefore inland China seemed at this point a safe place to be.

Generalissimo Chiang Kai-shek happened to be in Calcutta on the final leg of his visit to India when the Malayan evacuees arrived. Serendipitously, the two men met for the first time.

A short note hastily typed on 27 April 1942 by Hau-Shik to a friend he called Martin, apparently someone he played golf with in Kuala Lumpur, provides some scant details on the crossing from Singapore to Calcutta. "Martin" was Major J.M. Bell, whom he learned had successfully escaped via the Riau Islands and Sumatra to Bombay, and who was now based in Colombo.

> I had the greatest difficulty in getting to India as my ship was originary [sic] intended for Rangoon. Fleming of the Passport Office, Singapore, refused to give a Vise [sic] to India and so it seems wanted us to be killed in Rangoon. Our ship however altered course for Madras after a few days' sailing, not without danger of bombing etc. My brother was with me while our wives and children left two days earlier for Bombay which was reached after two weeks' troublous voyage; their ship being continuously bombed for several days. Eventually we all met at Calcutta safe and intact though all the personal effects were lost. We came here [to Mussoorie] in March, and are staying in this place to wait for developments. There is great uncertainty

in this country and our family of 16 members requires a lot of looking after. [...] What do you think of the India situation? Things and ways Indian being so different from what we are used to simply drive[s] one crazy sometimes.[2]

Hau-Shik's meticulously kept private papers also include a "To whom it may concern" note written for him on 12 February 1942 by O.H. Farrar, the Master of the S.S. *Haiching* that was ferrying them away from Singapore. It was written at Hau-Shik's request, troubled as he must have been when their destination had to be changed.

> The bearer is Mr. H.S. Lee who is Chairman of the Evacuees Committee of this vessel, acting on behalf of a party of 108 Straits-born Chinese (mostly women and children) who were evacuated from Singapore by arrangement with the S.S. Government and the Chinese Consul General. The ship was originally scheduled to call at Rangoon and visas were obtained for Burma, but ship was later diverted to Madras and it was not possible to obtain visas for India in time owing to Air Raids, before ship sailed. ... Any assistance regarding landing and exchange facilities and shore accommodation would be greatly appreciated by these unfortunate people, many of whom have been bombed out of their homes.[3]

Singapore had not fallen into Japanese hands yet, as the *Haiching*, whose regular route was actually between Hong Kong and the Chinese ports of Swatow and Amoy (Xiamen), sailed 3,000 miles on its maiden voyage across the Indian Ocean. The Evacuees Committee was something that was quickly formed by the 108 passengers on board on learning that they would not be going to Rangoon after all. Hurriedly made chairman of this ad hoc and anxious group, Hau-Shik took charge. He wrote a short note on their stop in Madras on the way to Calcutta, meant for some authority in Singapore, which most probably was never posted, commending Captain Farrar and his crew for "careful and brilliant navigation". From the note, we learn that the *Haiching* was sent to Singapore "at the request of the Chinese Consul General Kuo Ling Pak to the Governor of the Straits Settlements for the evacuation of the Chinese to Rangoon". About 75 per cent of the evacuees were women and children. When writing the short note, Hau-Shik was clearly oblivious of how bad the war in Singapore was going. He wished to inform the immigration officer to change his visa procedures—and in this, we may assume that he and the other Chinese civilians, in the chaos of the war, had encountered much trouble in getting visas when leaving Singapore. The surrender of Singapore seemed unthinkable as yet. Significantly, the *Haiching*, ferrying this group of Chinese to safety, was a vessel sent by the Chinese government. Evacuation procedures were otherwise meant for Europeans before anyone else.

> Our impression when leaving Singapore is that though we suffer a setback at the commencement of the War in the Far East, we are confident that with increasing reinforcement the final victory will be ours. In the meantime, we hope that the Immigration and Passport Officer in Singapore will now be able to see his way to give easier facilities for Visas so that more Chinese civilians whose presence in the Colony can only contribute to the consumption of water and food will be evacuated.[4]

Particulars Hau-Shik inked on the registration form for "Overseas Chinese evacuated from Malaya, Netherlands East Indies and other countries to India", filled in sometime later to prepare for his family's foreword journey to Chungking, provide further details of interest. He stated that his native place in China was

Shun Yu district in Kwangtung; he was a tin miner and lawyer now living at Devonshire House, The Mall, Mussoorie, India; his sister-in-law was accompanying him and his wife; they had eight children with them, aged two to 18; they were evacuated from Kuala Lumpur, F.M.S, from 16 Golf View Road; they left Malaya on 30 January 1942 and arrived in Calcutta on 14 February; he had means of subsistence "up to certain period"; he desired to return to Chungking "to serve China"; and he had not joined any political organization.[5]

Hau-Shik received news in April 1942 that an acquaintance from Kuala Lumpur, K.L. Yuen, had been appointed Special Commissioner by China's Ministry of Overseas Affairs "to deal in all matters relating to Overseas Chinese evacuated from Malaya, Dutch East Indies and other countries, who are now in India".[6] Yuen had immediately written to inform Hau-Shik of this good news.

On arrival in India, Hau-Shik had immediately settled his family in two flats at Mullingar, a military settlement in the mountainous province of Uttarakhand. But as families of troops from Burma began being evacuated into the town, his family was told to leave. Protests did not help, and it was only after much trouble and time that they found and rented Devonshire House in Mussoorie, a hill station situated in the Himalayan foothills 290 km north of New Delhi. S.H. Sih, the Consul for China in Calcutta, who had been China's Consul in Kuala Lumpur, wrote to inform Hau-Shik on 16 April that "The situation in India seems to be very precarious."

Those evacuees who were Rotary Club members were apparently quickly contacted by fellow Rotarians in India. This would have brought some comfort to them in these dire times. In Hau-Shik's case, the Rotary Club of Dehra Dun wrote to him already on 29 April to invite him to attend their lunch meetings.[7]

Hau-Shik's plans remained unchanged. He told Yuen that he had informed General Wu Te-chen, the secretary-general of the Central Executive Committee of the Kuomintang that "I intend to take the whole family back to China, if the question of remittance and transport could be satisfactorily arranged." He added that "I may be able to play my part as a son of China to some degree in our Fatherland, though meagre it may be", and agreed with Yuen that "there is no place safer than Free China".[8] He was also planning to bring along a shipment of medicine.[9]

The inflation rate in Chungking was extremely high at this time, and Hau-Shik was advised by Sih to remain in Mussoorie instead at least till after August, and even then to fly to Chungking by himself, and not with his family.[10] Throughout this period, Hau-Shik received much help from Sih, while dealings with Yuen, though important, were less gratifying.

Hau-Shik's plans to move to Chungking were not going well. As one can see in the record of correspondences at times, letters were crossing each other quite badly. The Chinese government had refused to make an exception for Hau-Shik where remittance limits to China were concerned. In confidence, Yuen offered a black market contact to Hau-Shik if he should wish to get better rates. Flights from Calcutta to Chungking, which had to land in Lashio in Burma were in danger of being suspended. In fact, the outpost soon fell to the Japanese on April 29 and would not be regained by the Allies until March 1945. Flights to Chungking did continue however, via other routes, but at prices about 50 per cent higher due to shortage of high octane fuel and other reasons.[11]

Hau-Shik declined the offer to buy Chinese dollars on the black market, and politely rebuked Yuen that, "As my decision will very likely be followed by other Overseas Chinese evacuees, it devolved on me that I should give this matter very considerable thought." He also decided not to meet Yuen in Calcutta, and instead asked the latter to come to Delhi instead, which the latter did. Flights from Calcutta to Chungking had for the moment been suspended in any case.[12]

A transfer of a sufficient and substantial sum of money to Chungking by Hau-Shik was finally facilitated by Sih to the Chungking branch of the Kwangtung Provincial Bank.[13]

Hau-Shik was now intending to charter a plane for his party of four adults and seven children to get to Chungking, but learned from Yuen that the Monsoon and the shortage of planes made that impossible. He was to rest assured that "special attention is given to Overseas Chinese evacuees". This upset Hau-Shik deeply. He replied in a letter written on 13 June 1942, more agitatedly than was normal for his communication with Yuen thus far. His frustration with the Special Commissioner had in fact, fairly or not, been growing over time.

> I am greatly disappointed at Chungking's refusal to allow the chartering of planes. What has the Monsoon got to do with chartering when the charterer has enough passengers for a plane is a mystery to me. Our Government firstly cannot and will not do anything to compensate the Overseas Chinese who in the past have both morally and materially done their best to help China, for the loss they incur in the question of remittance though it is well-known that what they have is only an infinitesimal part of their fortunes and is much less than the contributions they have given to the China Relief Fund during the last five years. Secondly there is no chartering of planes even if the Overseas Chinese evacuees can arrange amongst their relatives and friends sufficient number of passengers to fill up the quota. It appears to me that the "Special Attention" to Overseas Chinese evacuees are given only in words and not in deeds.
>
> The refusal to allow the chartering of a plane has completely upset my plans, and I do not see how I could take my family

back with only a luggage allowance of 30 lbs. each, in view of the large number of children and of the exorbitant prices of clothing in Chungking. Surely I do not want to let the members of my family become beggars in China, though the attitude of our Government seems to aim at that way.[14]

He ended his letter with a request for Yuen to send him "two kerosene tins of Chinese sauce from Chinatown".

In the meantime, news reaching Hau-Shik from Chungking were causing him to rethink his plans. Living conditions there had become "appalling and impossible", he told Yuen, and "India is heaven compared with Chungking for the present at any rate." Indeed, life was pleasant enough in Mussoorie, and Hau-Shik got to play tennis as many as three times a week. On the war front, the Japanese seemed by now to have shifted their efforts from the Burmese border to inland China, so he thought it best that he travelled to Chungking alone, and after the Monsoons.[15]

A letter written to General Wu that same day—13 June 1942—revealed the sense of desperation settling on Hau-Shik by this time.

> Much as I desire to return to China, I am extremely sorry that I am unable to do so owing to the low rate of exchange and the lack of accommodation in air-transport. At such a rate of exchange, what I have in Rupees will, when converted to Chinese dollars, not last me very long because of my large family and the high cost of living in Chungking. [...] Under such circumstances I have no alternative but to remain in India until the Japs drive me out again. If they do come, I presume that I would have to leave everything behind once again as I did in Singapore. This is, I am afraid, the plight of the Overseas Chinese.[16]

It was also during these weeks that Hau-Shik was embroiled in an argument with the medical doctor which his family consulted on arrival in Mussoorie, a Dr Edmund R. Ronald. Hau-Shik resented having a huge bill sent to him without details of the costs, the two could not agree on the sum due to the doctor, and the matter went to the lawyers. How the matter ended is not clear but it did seem from the correspondence left behind that Hau-Shik got his way.[17]

On 17 June, a letter from Sih brought some welcome news about the unfolding war and the threat to India.

> From General Loo [of the 6th Army Corps that fought in Burma], the invasion of India cannot come from Assam. The enemy may attempt a landing near Calcutta. My point is that if a landing is attempted, it must be accompanied by large naval and air forces. After Midway action, it is doubtful whether the enemy dares to launch out what is left of his aircraft-carriers. My conclusion is that for the coming two months or so, India or at least North India will not be in serious danger unless the Germans can drive down from the Caucasus.[18]

Sih later shared with Hau-Shik that in his opinion, it was the fighting in Egypt that would decide whether India would remain safe or not, and advised him to leave his family in India for now.[19]

As things were developing, however, the direct and indirect pressure Hau-Shik had started putting on his high-level contacts in Chungking began paying off, and he soon received notice that he would be allowed to charter a plane to evacuate his party to Chungking.

At this point, fate stepped in. Mussoorie was quite an isolated place, located about 1,000 feet above the bus terminus at Kineraig, and was not approachable by car. On 14 July, Hau-Shik and his brother Hau Mo rode on horses down to the terminus to see Yuen off. About 100 yards from the station, Hau-Shik's mount suddenly fell, throwing Hau-Shik headfirst onto the road. Bleeding from badly lacerated lips, he fainted. The fall was an especially bad one that took him 40 days in bed to recover. Apart from superficial injuries to his cheek, lower jaw and the back of his left hand, his upper lip just below the nose had to be stitched together, six teeth were chipped and loosened by the fall, and his right wrist fractured. To add to the misfortune, Yuen, who came running to help on hearing of the accident, was bitten on the leg by a dog, while his bus drove off with his baggage. All in all, a very bad day for everyone.[20]

On receiving news about the accident, Sih wrote to Hau-Shik: "I hope you are now recovering and will find yourself in perfect health pretty soon. Since Mr. Yuen brought you ill-luck, your plan of going back with him may be very well postponed for the time being." Lau Pak Khuan, a Kuomintang member and prominent Ipoh personality, who had also fled ahead of the Japanese advancement with British help, had through Sih been trying to raise financial interest among the Malayan refugees to establish a bank in Chungking, to be called the Overseas Chinese Industrial Bank. Hau-Shik replied that he was "very interested in his banking project and wish to take an active part in it. [...] Kindly tell him also that I have myself worked in a big bank before and have run through every department in the course of eight months."[21] Hau-Shik was of course referring to his experiences working at the P&O Bank in Hong Kong in 1924–25.

And so, just at the point of succeeding after four frustrating months overcoming hurdles getting his family to Chungking, Hau-Shik's trip, to his exasperation, had to be postponed again.

A letter from Sih dated 9 September brought news that a Japanese invasion of India was now most unlikely: "American aircraft going to China is increasing. The number ferried over last month was quite considerable. A few hundred more are now in Karachi. So I think the tide is definitely turning, and it will do you no harm if I keep you waiting in Mussoorie for a couple weeks more."[22]

IN WARTIME CHINA

So it was only in late September that plans could be actualized for him to finally get to Chungking. By now, news of rising prices in Chungking and tight luggage restrictions placed by Indian customs on Chinese travellers had greatly dampened his enthusiasm to move his family. "Allies indeed", he grumbled of the Indian government.[23]

Hau-Shik's trip was further inconvenienced when he finally did make it. This was despite the fact that he had with him a certificate dated 21 October 1942 issued by the Consulate General of the Republic of China in Calcutta, introducing him as "chairman of Chinese General Chamber of Commerce and China Relief Fund, Selangor, Federated Malay States" who was travelling to Chungking "in accordance with the instruction of the Chinese Government".[24]

According to a message from the travel agent, he travelled from Calcutta to Chungking on 23 October, a Friday. On his arrival in Chungking, Yuen was too sick to meet him (and would remain so for five weeks), and this seemed to have led to "extreme inconvenience" for Hau-Shik, as Yuen put it when apologizing to him several months later in a letter dated 19 February 1943, also thanking Hau-Shik for having visiting him in his sick bed. Apparently, the visit had not gone smoothly and despite having prearranged as much as he could, Yuen "could not but feel equally sad and disappointed with the manner you had been treated". No details were mentioned.

> I know how you felt. But one good thing you had done was that you had told them in the face of your disappointment and dissatisfaction which nobody else ever dared to say about.[25]

In reply, Hau-Shik wrote that "Except the first night on my arrival at Chungking my stay there was quite comfortable because I myself succeeded in securing accommodation at the Victory House on the next morning." This short letter provides what may be the only record that still exists, apart from a slight mention in a concurrent letter to Martin Bell, his golfing buddy from Kuala Lumpur, of what he did in Chungking.

> The subject of reconstruction in Malaya mentioned in your letter formed the second part of my Memorandum handed by me personally to the Generalissimo during my interview with him, and it would be rather out of place to state its contents in this letter. The essential factors seem to me to be complete unity amongst the Overseas Chinese, the energetic backing of our Government for such [an] Overseas Chinese organization, and the skilful handling of the problem by our delegates at the Peace Conference. If these were done there might be some share of Government for our countrymen. I advised Mr Lau Pak Kwun, Mr Lin Ying Show and Mr Ho Poh Jin to form an association in our Wartime capital for the Malayan Chinese in China so that a nucleus might exist for future development, but they did not seem to appreciate my point of view. If I should get instructions from our Government, I would not mind going round India to approach the rest of our Malayan Chinese to start something of the sort here. There is already a Malayan Association here started by Europeans, and I think the Chinese will be worse off without a corresponding organization. [...]

The trouble with the Overseas Chinese before the War was, as you must be aware, no unity of purpose, no unity of thought and no unity of objectives.[26]

To Martin Bell, Hau-Shik said that he "paid a flying visit to Chungking where I stayed for a week, and came back to India in the early part of Nov". He told Bell that "In the Chinese Wartime capital I met many high officials including the Generalissimo, and found that everybody was full of confidence of final victory."[27]

On his return from Chungking, Hau-Shik also wrote a letter to Shang Chen, the Director of the Foreign Affairs Bureau of the National Military Council. Shang seemed to have gotten on well with Hau-Shik, and said of their new-found camaraderie: "I am very much pleased to know that you have carried away with you the indominable spirit of our Leader, which is the only infallible motive power in continuing and prosecuting the present armed resistance against Japanese aggression until victory is ours."[28]

New Year came, and with it a letter from a G.S. Rawlings from the Far Eastern Bureau of the British Ministry of Information based in New Delhi. The Bureau was looking to recruit "any people from Malaya, now in India, whose talent, enthusiasm and experience in matters connected to Malaya could suitably be utilised for broadcasts" and was wishing "to examine any proposals for broadcasts of propaganda value".

Apparently, Tan Siew Sin and his father Tan Cheng Lock, the Malaccan tycoon, were both presently settled at Dehra Dun, near New Delhi. Siew Sin had suggested Hau-Shik as someone who could broadcast to occupied Malaya in Hokkien and English. This was of course mistaken. Hau-Shik knew very little Hokkien. Nevertheless, this offer interested him, and although he was not willing to be "a regular announcer in Hokkien", he wished to discuss "the subject of broadcasts to Malaya" with Rawlings "because it appears to me that suitable propaganda will undoubtedly help in our War effort and may even quicken the time of final victory".[29]

Hau-Shik would later provide at least one name as possible announcer to Rawlings. This was Robert M.K. Lim, a Cantonese-speaking architect from Singapore. Hau-Shik also informed Rawlings that he was Chief Air Raid Warden in Kuala Lumpur, something he certainly seemed very proud to have been, and in that capacity had made broadcasts "with reasonable results, to recruit members for the Civil Defence Services". In a rare boast, Hau-Shik went on to present his credentials:

> The Officer in charge of information and propaganda in Malaya was Dr Victor Purcell, M.C.S., who is a personal friend of mine and we were at Cambridge at the same time. He and I very often discussed problems under his care and my advice, mostly in connection with the Chinese community, was usually sought.[30]

It can be gathered from Hau-Shik's various correspondences, especially with a much younger friend, Chan Kwong Hon, also a miner from Kuala Lumpur and who worked as translator and broadcaster at the Chinese Unit of All India Radio (A.I.R.), a government-run radio station in Delhi, that he did do some work for the Ministry of Information, at least by contributing articles.[31]

As winter approached, Hau-Shik moved his family to Dehra Dun, and away from harsh winter conditions in Mussoorie. Chinese New Year in 1943 was on 5 and 6 February, but celebrations were extended a day by the Kuomintang in exultation over an agreement reached with the British and the Americans that they would relinquish their treaty rights in Chinese ports acquired since the Opium Wars a century earlier.[32] In truth, the Japanese occupation had already made these rights obsolete.

On 8 March 1943, the family relocated back to Mussoorie, but to a new address: Savitri Villa, on Camel's Back Road. This was to allow for good schooling for the children. A letter that Hau-Shik wrote to General Wu on 5 March provides some insight into his state of mind at this time. He seemed to have given up altogether on the idea of moving his family to China. Instead, he was thinking of touring India to reconnect with Malayan Chinese, many of whom were now settled in Bombay and Bangalore, and to discuss matters of reconstruction in Malaya "when the final victory is won, with particular reference to the political, economic and social problems of the Overseas Chinese". The fact that a Malayan Association had already been formed in India by Europeans bothered him greatly, "and unless we Chinese from Malaya will also organize ourselves beforehand, we may lag behind in looking after our interests".[33]

Although Hau-Shik was technically a British colonel, he feared that a Chinese citizen travelling in India as a British officer would prove awkward. To ease his travels therefore, he asked both General Wu and General Shang for assistance, seeking "an appointment from our own Government, carrying only a title simply for facilitating my travelling in this country".[34]

These being difficult times, for correspondence and otherwise, Hau-Shik received a reply from General Shang only at the end of May, in which he offered the position of "advisership of the Foreign Affairs Bureau attached to its Ramgarh Office which has been newly opened with Brigadier General Yeh Nan as its Officer-in-Charge". Hau-Shik very gladly accepted the offer, which meant that he would now be a uniformed colonel in the Chinese Army. This entitled him "to travel throughout India without hindrance", and put him in the strange position of being a colonel in two different armies at the same time.[35]

Yuen's reply to his letter sent in March came only three months later. He was being sent as Deputy Consul to New York and would leave within a few months. Written on 16 June 1943, the letter contained interesting facts concerning their common ambition to organize the Overseas Chinese for the war effort and in preparation for post-war difficulties.

Apparently, an organization already existed in Chungking called South Seas Chinese Association, established at the end of 1942 under General Wu. This was intended as "the parent association serving as a nucleus for future developments, and all kindred associations, formed subsequently, shall be linked to it and shall be centralized, thus ensuring unity of purpose, unity of thought and unity of objectives even of actions amongst such associations". The general had been told of Hau-Shik's concurrent wish to start a Malayan Chinese association in India and was therefore supportive of it. The appropriate name for such an organization, given related developments, was quite naturally, South Seas Chinese Association Malayan Branch.[36]

As winter neared, Hau-Shik brought his family to stay in Bombay, "as the climate here is more like that of Malaya and we need not go to any other place for the summer".[37] He told General Shang in a letter written on 27 December 1943 that Bombay was where they would stay "for the duration of the war". All he seemed to be doing was "just idling away the time unprofitably", and so wished to be of use to the Bureau, doing "liaison work with the British and American forces at Bombay". As it turned out, the Bureau could not afford to take on any new personnel.[38]

In a note written on 17 November 1943 seeking ration cards from the authorities in Bombay for members of his family, Hau-Shik listed 14 people apart from himself, and four servants (the cook, two bearers and a chokala[39]). These were his wife and her sister, five sons and two daughters, his brother and his wife and their three sons—quite a party to take care of under their trying circumstances.[40]

It was also around this time that Hau-Shik had to contact the Dehra Dun police to have his eldest son Douglas taken off its registry for foreigners. Douglas was by birth a British citizen and carried no other passport. Somehow, Douglas' name had been processed together with his uncle Hau Mun, who was a Chinese citizen. Hau-Shik argued his case proficiently and the matter was cleared up by the end of the year.[41]

With the advent of the New Year, the weather got warmer, and Hau-Shik played less and less tennis and began to spend time on golf, "the golf course being only 1 mile away".[42] In fact, he would go on to win a golf trophy there.

Throughout 1944, Hau-Shik's correspondences with the Chinese government seemed to slow down. General Shang Chen was posted in May that year to lead the Chinese Military Mission to America.[43] The letters that have survived from this time were about plans for a trip to Kashmir with Sih and others, difficulty in getting maid-servants, and optimistic views about the war. The "War in Europe" was often expected to be coming to an end earlier than the Pacific War.

On 3 December 1944, Sih wrote worriedly about a rumour he had heard:

> It is learned that the Malays evacuated from Malaya have formed an association and have sent a petition to the Colonial Office requesting, among other things, the ban of entry into Malaya after the war of Chinese nationals unless they will become Malay citizens. The Colonial Office have sent an official with the name of Paddy to India with a view to making an investigation along that line.[44]

Hau-Shik replied that he was now "a Committee member of the Malayan Association (consisting of all nationals) for the year 1944–45, and this Association is in touch with all Malayan matters". Despite that, he heard of no such development as suggested by the rumour, so the claim was probably nothing more than that. Incidentally, Tan Chin Tuan, a renowned banker from Singapore was elected president for the association for that year.

A DIVISIVE COMING TOGETHER

The forming of associations among refugees in India in 1942–45 was an interesting phenomenon whose significance for the postwar period has not been fully explored. Although there was fear that a Japanese invasion was impending, India remained a safe haven from which the World War could be observed and the future planned by the individuals for themselves or in anticipation of what the political condition of their homes would be after the Japanese had been defeated.

Refugees from Malaya did form or involve themselves in several associations with which to maintain contacts among themselves and to provide advice and voice worries to the British authorities regarding their own lot and the future of Malaya.

As has been mentioned, among those spending the war years in India and based in New Delhi, was the Malaccan Tan Cheng Lock and his family. The distinction between the orientation taken by Tan, a highly respected community leader by this time, and by Hau-Shik, whose view of the world included the Republic of China to a much greater extent than Tan's did, reflected clearly not only the uncertainties felt by these refugees personally but also the few big powers that would be of consequence in the region even after the War. As yet, there was no talk of the rise of nation states to replace the colonized territories.

On 24 September 1943, a body called the Overseas Chinese Association (OCA) held its inaugural meeting. As its founder and president, Tan Cheng Lock gave the opening speech in which he stated that the association's goals were "to protect and further the important interests of ourselves as Oversea-Chinese and to consider the many problems of post-war settlement affecting the Oversea-Chinese in the Eastern Asia Territories now in enemy occupation". Although the OCA claimed to have members from "Burma, China and the other territories", most of them were in fact Malayan Chinese.[45] Tan Siew Sin, Cheng Lock's son, was the OCA secretary and treasurer.[46]

In a letter sent to the Secretary of State for the Colonies in London later that year introducing the OCA, Tan Cheng Lock stated more clearly what the OCA's "principal objectives" were:

a) To deal with the problems of Chinese evacuees.
b) To consider problems relating to war damage and losses sustained by the Chinese in the Japanese-occupied eastern territories and all other post-occupational and post-war problems affecting the Chinese therein.
c) To study means of assisting the efforts of the United Nations in regaining these occupied territories and of co-operating in the war efforts of China.[47]

What the OCA was aiming for were basically two things: to be entrusted by the British with the responsibility of caring for "needy Chinese evacuees of British nationality in India, whose conditions and circumstances [the OCA] should have a better knowledge [of] than any other body and with whom we are in direct and constant contact", and to gain British agreement to include in their colonial register "particulars of war damage and loss sustained in Malaya and the other Eastern

Territories", collected by the OCA, "so that records may be compiled now relating to possible claims". These appeared to be their immediate worries. It would seem that the retrieval of Malaya by the British was either not in doubt in their minds, or that they were simply preparing for the eventuality that the Japanese would fail in their venture, at which time the regaining of ownership of lost properties would a major concern.[48] The need to limit the great damage done to them by the war was an understandable one, their worrying over which should be properly considered in any analysis on the lot of the Malayan refugees in India and elsewhere.

While the impact of a short-lived organization like the OCA on the post-war situation was small, what is of longer-term historical and political interest are the tactical notions embedded in its transcripts, such as the following:

> My Committee wish to co-operate in every way with all those concerned with the task of restoring normal conditions, economic, domestic and otherwise, in Malaya on its reoccupation, and we trust that His Majesty's Government will see their way to recognise the Association as representing the Chinese community of Malaya... On our return to Malaya those of our members who are Malayans will constitute themselves into a Malayan Chinese Association devoted to the interests of the country.[49]

Hau-Shik was in Mussoorie when Cheng Lock, who was then based in Bangalore wrote to him on 27 June 1943 informing him of his plans for the OCA. According to Cheng Lock, the OCA has "already the support of practically all the important Malayans and other Oversea-Chinese in Bombay, Calcutta, Madras, Bangalore and Delhi". His son Siew Sin was to liaise with Hau-Shik on OCA matters and had in fact also already written to the latter at the same time. In trying to gain Hau-Shik's support, the 60-year-old Cheng Lock wrote as follows:

> You are a man of great ability and considerable experience of public life in Malaya, where you are well-known and where you have had a good deal of influence. So your support of the Association and active participation in running it will do much to make it a success and also a strong body. [...] I understand you are also well-known amongst the Chinese officials both here and in Chungking, so that if you should associate yourself with this movement for the good of our people, you would be extremely useful to the Association and helpful to its members.[50]

To Siew Sin, Hau-Shik replied that the Malayan Chinese community-in-exile should "aim at practical usefulness rather than at ostentation and the enlargement of its precincts that would lead to internal complications". They should instead form "a solid body, which, though small and less pretentious, will nevertheless serve us now and have unlimited scope to work for the benefit of the Chinese in Malaya later".[51] This initial contact between Hau-Shik and the Tans appears to have been rather tense.

Hau-Shik's reply to Cheng Lock, a very established figure in Malayan life who was 17 years his senior, provides some insight into how he was thinking about the situation of the overseas Chinese at this point, seven months after visiting Chungking. He was more interested in forming a purely Malayan body but one that was linked to Chungking's own South Seas Chinese Association than one "covering such wide territories and grouping so many people with divergent interests". The OCA, he thought, "would be unwieldy and impractical".

> If, however, you and your sponsors condescend to form a body as suggested by Chungking, the object of which is to unite

all the Malaya Chinese now in India with a view to looking after our evacuees and the postwar problems of the Chinese welfare in Malaya, with the Chungking association as its parent body, it will not only be practical but extremely useful. It would, I venture to say, receive more than the goodwill of our Government, if the man at the helm has in the past represented Chinese interests in Malaya and has also some standing in the eyes of our officials. After all what could an oversea-Chinese organization hope to achieve for its members if it were not supported by their own Government?[52]

Hau-Shik was more opposed to Cheng Lock's idea than might appear in these first letters between the two Malayan Chinese who would become the top players in Malaya's post-war struggle for independence. He stated his case more intensely in a letter to Cheng Lock written on 19 August 1943, two days after Siew Sin had visited him in Mussoorie. Considering all overseas Chinese as the represented constituency was not a practical approach, he thought, and any organization built on them would disintegrate once the war was over. The only thing these people now had in common was the fact that they were temporary evacuees in India. Hau-Shik believed it best to focus on "reconstruction problems after the war", and therefore welcomed "affiliation so as to maintain connection", but was at the same time convinced that "amalgamation will not only be useless but lead to prolonged meetings due to divergent views and natural ignorance of subjects of two different places [Burma and Malaya]". In any case, he continued, long-term success for any such organization would depend on backing from Chungking.

> You say there is no harm in embracing all classes of Oversea-Chinese. I beg to differ, because your proposed association will in fact not embrace them. You may have some China-born

Chinese in India, some Burma Chinese, some Malayan Chinese and a few others, but that is far from saying that your association represents the Oversea-Chinese as the name implies. It would be a misnomer, and tantamount to misrepresentation of facts. It would be like naming a shop general provision store, when only selling fish and chips.

I wonder whether you remember Mr. Tan Kah Kee of Singapore. Supported mostly by his ex-employees, and armed with a very large amount of funds, he got himself called the Chairman of the Federation of the China Relief Committees in the South Seas, and announced that he alone represented 6 millions of Oversea-Chinese. To the ignorant he appeared most powerful, but really his influence could not even command the unanimous support of his own town Singapore, because of the presence of Mr. Aw Boon Haw. By the well-informed he was simply regarded as an over-ambitious old man who had been led astray by his own vanity and self-glorification. His speeches after his return from China caused the Chinese in Malaya not a little embarrassment and Chungking contemptuous amusement. But nothing good came out of it though lots of Chinese money were wasted.[53]

Hau-Shik was not pulling his punches. To the older man, he further wrote that "If we had really our common interests at heart and no personal or ulterior motives, [...] I would certainly try to avoid any suspicion that may be cast upon us as an emulation of Mr. Tan Kah Kee's performance" and added that "Too big a tail is a hindrance to wagging".[54]

What may have escaped Hau-Shik's notice was that the connections between Burmese Chinese and the Straits Settlements were more intimate than he, living in the Federated Malay States, might have realized. Tan Cheng Lock, being a Straits Chinese, would have felt that to be the case much more than Hau-Shik, a

Kuala Lumpur Cantonese could have done. The cultural niceties of the Chinese overseas were—and are—multi-layered, and clashes among the many communities that comprised them, especially when they were living under uprooted conditions, were to be expected. Below is a summary that explains in short but profound detail the social and strategical considerations the Rangoon Chinese tended to have in relating to Malayan Chinese culture in the Straits Settlements.

> Baba-Nyonya culture was emulated by the Chinese in Rangoon not only because it provided a way to maintain their shared Hokkien heritage but also because it represented modernity in British Burma. Migrants from southeastern China were more established in Penang, Melaka, and Singapore because of their earlier arrival and larger numbers. Unlike in Rangoon, the local Chinese were the dominant foreign population and enjoyed direct access to colonial trade. In addition, the Straits Settlements, as a British Crown colony, were directly administered by the Colonial Office in London instead of the Indian government in Calcutta. This meant that Straits Chinese dealt more directly with the British government and quickly learned to champion their causes by adopting British conduct. The Peranakan led the way in learning English, courting British officials, buying European luxury goods, and building eclectic villas...[55]

As predicted by Hau-Shik, the OCA did fail—for lack of support as much from Chungking as from its diverse constituency. His own aspiration for a Malayan Branch, based in India, of Chungking's organization, fared even worse, however. It never materialized at all. Instead, he joined the multiracial Malayan Association of India that had been formed by Europeans, Jews, Malay royalty and Chinese who were sitting out the war in India.[56]

Be that as it may, such gatherings provided a platform for Malayan evacuees to acquaint themselves with each other, and this would have allowed their members to discuss and prepare for the radically changed post-war world to come. Having been relatively side-lined for almost three years, most of them were ready to dig their heels in on their return to a Malaya they may no longer know, in order to safeguard their own welfare, the interests of their communities and the future of Peninsular Malaya as a whole. There was bound to be much tension—within each major community as much as without.

In Malaysian historiography, for example, one stubborn and infected controversy has been over who the real founder/s of the Malayan Chinese Association (MCA) were, which held its inaugural meeting on the early morning of 27 February 1949 at the Selangor Chinese Assembly Hall in Kuala Lumpur, and which would play such a pivotal role in Malayan history.[57] If the complex processes and the chaotic conditions which key figures of the Malayan Chinese community were trapped in during and after the war are given the importance due to them, the question becomes rather moot. A conflation of factors were definitely involved, including British uncertainties over how to regain their colonies, fight the Cold War, and maintain their authority long enough to secure a pacific and beneficial retreat; not to mention the unavoidable speculation about what global politics would be like after the Axis powers were defeated.

Most of them being effectively exiled in India, it would seem that the time had not yet come for the Malayan Chinese—diverse in origin, interests and even culture—to collaborate effectively.

Hau-Shik's disapproval of Cheng Lock's project, apart from the reasons he listed in his letters, may also have had to do with the larger conflict going on between the Chinese Communist Party and the Malayan Communist Party (MCP) on the one hand, and the Kuomintang on the other. For the MCP, this gained expression at exactly that time in the significant difference it made between "Malayan Chinese" (*mahua*) and "Overseas Chinese" (*huaqiao*). It considered the former group to be politically passive and lacking in anti-colonial sentiments; and thus partly due to its "mixed parentage" of having drawn inspiration from Indonesian, Chinese, Comintern and Vietnamese sources and to its membership being excessively Chinese and therefore not representative of the Malayan populace, the MCP sought as international a character as it could. "Overseas Chinese", in this context, was thus its favoured term for Chinese living in the region outside of China.[58] This MCP preference for "Overseas Chinese" may well have influenced Hau-Shik's dislike of the OCA initiative.

The Chungking government did not approve of the OCA and Chinese in India were advised to withdraw from it. Refugees of Chinese origin from other parts of Southeast Asia also felt uncomfortable over the dominance that the Malayans had in the organization. This lack of support doomed it to irrelevance. In a letter to Sih dated 7 January 1944, Hau-Shik stated: "With regard to Tan Cheng Lock's association, I am afraid that [some people] have been very misled by him, and it would not be too easy to stop his activities unless our Government take more drastic actions than gentle persuasion by our Consuls."[59]

The serious consideration that Hau-Shik requested of the Tans for Chungking's approval of their organization could very well have had to do with the fact that 2,000 Chinese seamen who were in India when war broke out were being organized around this time into the "Work Force of the Stranded Chinese Seamen in India" by the Kuomintang government's Overseas Department, working together with Britain's Special Operations Executive (SOE). The SOE was the body responsible for building Force 136 to assist resistance groups in Burma, Thailand, Indochina and Malaya, and was basing it on the Work Force.

Among the British officers who founded the Malaya section of Force 136 in July 1942 were J.L.H. Davis and R.N. Broome. These two had between 21 December 1941 and 30 January 1942 been training 165 recruits supplied by the MCP for guerrilla warfare around Kuala Lumpur and further south against the advancing Japanese. Training of Kuomintang supporters by the British was also carried out in Kuala Lumpur, but almost as an afterthought and very late in the day, starting only on 21 January.

Among the refugees in Calcutta was Lim Bo Seng, a Singapore businessman who was a prominent Kuomintang official and who had dramatically made his escape in a small sampan to India via Sumatra and Ceylon. Davis and Broom decided that Bo Seng was the right person to use as a recruiter for the Malayan section.

> After being contacted by Force 136, Lim Bo Seng flew to Chungking for consultations. He obtained the consent of Generalissimo Chiang Kai-shek for the Force 136 assignment through General Wu Te-chen. Lim was explicitly instructed to ensure that all the Chinese trainees for Force 136 missions were KMT men. [...] To demonstrate he had official backing, Lim was appointed the Chinese Government's representative in Force 136.[60]

The new position conferred on Lim Bo Seng the rank of Major. Force 136 made its first landing in Malaya only in June 1943, in the state of Perak. Until then, the MCP guerrillas in Malaya, the main resistance fighters on the peninsula, had had to rely entirely on their own devices.[61] Proper contact between Force 136 and the MCP took place only on New Year's Eve 1943, with Bo Seng acting as interpreter. Bo Seng had returned to Malaya in

November 1942 in a submarine, and in the guise of a trader in Ipoh managed to organize an intelligence network in the area.[62] He was finally betrayed by the notorious Lai Tek, the MCP's secretary-general who was later revealed to have been a Japanese spy. With Bo Seng's arrest, the KMT-based intelligence network collapsed, leaving the British to rely fully on the MCP-controlled Malayan Peoples' Anti-Japanese Army (MPAJA).[63]

LIVING IN BOMBAY

A letter written on 19 December 1944 by Hau-Shik, in reply to his friend Kwong Hon who was planning to visit Bombay, provides some interesting details about how the family had been living for the past year, at Flat No. 8, 69 Marine Drive, Bombay.

> My flat is rather small, consisting of 2 bedrooms, one sitting-room and one dining room. We have turned the dining room into a bedroom, but all the rooms are very small, much smaller than those in Savitri Villa. My wife and I and the two youngest children have one room, Douglas and three other boys the second one, and KS and the two girls the third one. The rooms are so small that at present they are all jammed up with beds leaving very little empty space in the middle. If you can bring the necessary folding camp-beds to put out at the centre of the room at night and have them folded up in the daytime, you are welcome to stay at my place, coming either in one party or two batches.[64]

By the end of February 1945, the optimism felt by the Malayan refugees had grown greatly. Consul-General Sih seemed sure that the Americans would land in China by the end of the year or even in Japan itself, which would end the Pacific War before Hitler could be defeated. As it turned out, the Third Reich surrendered first, and unconditionally on 7 May.

On 1 August, Sih wrote to Hau-Shik that "the reconquest of Malaya will be a reality within the year, but the return of civilians to that land will be allowed at a much later date".[65]

The end to the World War was indeed nigh. Events were moving fast. By the time Hau-Shik received Sih's letter, the first atomic bomb had been dropped on Japan. This was on 6 August. The Soviet Union invaded Manchukuo on 9 August, and later that same day, the second atomic bomb was detonated over Nagasaki. It took another week, but Japan finally surrendered, on 15 August.

The slow but steady retreat of the Japanese in the Pacific in the face of American naval strength had raised worries about how, rather than if, the war would end, and if the Japanese home territories would surrender at all or be defended to the last man, woman and child.

In the territories it had occupied where nationalist movements had grown strong, the Japanese moved step by step to grant token independence. And so, Burma nominally gained independence in August 1943 and the Philippines in October 1943. The groundwork for a declaration of independence by Indonesians was already laid when Emperor Hirohito surrendered on 15 August 1945, and so, Sukarno and Hatta defiantly claimed independence two days after that, in the face of the return of the Dutch colonialists.

The case of Malaya was quite different. There, the issue of independence was kept off the agenda, at least until the very end, when it became undeniable that Indonesian independence may have unpredictable repercussions on the peninsula. Discontent with the Japanese had been growing among the Malays, and inflation had been high. Furthermore, the cession of the four northern states to Thailand in October 1943 had reduced the Malay population radically, most significantly in relation to the other ethnic communities. The Japanese Military Administration initiated the KRIS (*Kekuatan Rakyat Istimewa*) movement in mid-1945 to project the idea of Malaya being part of Greater Indonesia and to stimulate political consciousness among the Malays. With the sudden fall of the Japanese, elements from KMM and KRIS gathered to found the Partai Kebangsaan Melayu Malaya (PKMM; Malay Nationalist Party, MNP) in Ipoh in October 1945.[66]

The Malayans who had found uneasy refuge in India for almost four years could now seriously plan to go home, pick up the pieces, and negotiate their way into the future.

Consul Sih's last letter to Hau-Shik, written from New Delhi on 15 September 1945 informed him that Sih would soon be returning to Shanghai by sea via Singapore: "It seems to me that you as President of the Chinese Chamber of Commerce in Kuala Lumpur and Mr Lau Pak Kwun as President of the Chinese Chamber of Commerce in Ipoh should also return to help in the task of reconstruction and rehabilitation." Should the timing be right, Sih hoped to pay Hau-Shik a visit to "enjoy a little swim on the beaches of Port Dickson provided your bungalow is still intact".[67]

A circular from the Malayan Association in India, issued on 23 November 1945, titled "Preparations for Return to Malaya— No. 4", provided its members with details about what was allowed in their baggage for their trip home. It was not much. Each person was allowed only 5 lbs in weight "excluding tea", and could not bring along any unsown textile. Items such as cars and large electrical appliances needed special permits, unlike sewing machine, typewriter, camera, fountain pen, binoculars, watch and "home cine equipment".

NOTES

1. C.M. Turnbull, "British Planning for Post-war Malaya", *Journal of Southeast Asia Studies* 5, no. 2, The Centenary of British Intervention in Malaya (September 1974): 242.

2. H.S. Lee papers 121/8/30.
3. H.S. Lee papers 14 (a)/1/4.
4. Ibid.
5. H.S. Lee papers 121/1/31.
6. H.S. Lee papers 121/1/1.
7. H.S. Lee papers 121/8/33.
8. H.S. Lee papers 121/1/3.
9. H.S. Lee papers 121/1/65.
10. H.S. Lee papers 121/1/46.
11. H.S. Lee papers 121/1/10.
12. H.S. Lee papers 121/1/11–12.
13. H.S. Lee papers 121/1/50, 55.
14. H.S. Lee papers 121/001/15
15. H.S. Lee papers 121/001/18.
16. H.S. Lee papers 121/001/107.
17. H.S. Lee papers 121/001/109–118.
18. H.S. Lee papers 121/001/001: 58. The Battle of Midway took place on 4–7 June 1942, just six months after the Pearl Harbor bombardment, and ended with a clear victory for American forces. The Japanese navy suffered heavy maritime casualties, see http://www.history.com/topics/world-war-ii/battle-of-midway.
19. H.S. Lee papers 121/001/001: 64.
20. H.S. Lee papers 121/1/22–25, 84.
21. H.S. Lee papers 121/1/68, 70.
22. H.S. Lee papers 121/1/82.
23. H.S. Lee papers 121/1/30.
24. H.S. Lee papers 14 (a)1.
25. H.S. Lee papers 121/8/1.
26. H.S. Lee papers 121/8/3. "Lau Pak Kwun" is more recognizably known as "Lau Pak Khuan". His life story had strong parallels to that of Hau-Shik except that Lau was a Hakka who came from the underclass. Born in China in 1894, he was 19 when he boarded a junk to Malaya. Settling in Perak, he went from being a tin-mine pushcart boy to having multiple mines of his own, and an Officer

of the Order of the British Empire. He was a member of the KMT, spent the war years in India as well, and later, alongside Hau-Shik, was a founding member of the Malayan Chinese Association (MCA). In 1956, he left the MCA due to intra-party differences over how Chinese Malayan rights were to be defended. He was later conferred the honorific of Datuk Seri by the Sultan of Perak, and had a street named after him in Ipoh. A highly influential man and philanthropist, he was president for an extended period of the Chinese Chamber of Commerce, the Perak Chinese Assembly Hall, the Perak Kwantung Association and the Perak Chinese Mining Association.

27. H.S. Lee papers 121/8/38.
28. H.S. Lee papers 121/5/1.
29. H.S. Lee papers 121/8/51, 52.
30. H.S. Lee papers 121/8/52. Victor Purcell (1896–1965) was a writer who, besides being a colonial civil servant, was a prolific historian and respected Sinologist. Many of his books were on the Chinese in Malaya and Singapore. Hau-Shik's connections from his Cambridge University days apparently played a substantial role in gaining him relevance and prominence in the eyes of the Malayan British administration. Apart from Prince Albert (later King George VI) and the influential Purcell, Hau-Shik was in Cambridge at the same time as Tunku Abdul Rahman, who would later become the first Prime Minister of Malaya, and "father" of the country. Although it is doubtful that Hau-Shik had any intention while in England to have a career in British Malaya, the lives of several of his Cambridge mates would nevertheless overlap with his later in life, in Malaysia and India; the British Empire still stretching as it did across the globe.
31. H.S. Lee papers 121/7/8.
32. H.S. Lee papers 121/5/4.
33. H.S. Lee papers 121/5/7.
34. H.S. Lee papers 121/5/8.
35. H.S. Lee papers 121/5/16, 30, 35.
36. H.S. Lee papers 121/8/6.

37. H.S. Lee papers 121/5/51.
38. H.S. Lee papers 121/5/50, 53.
39. "Chokla" is noted to mean "mixed up" in J.L. Dillard's *Perspectives on Black English* (The Hague: Mouton & Co., 1973), p. 253. It would appear to be a colloquial term, therefore, denoting someone of mix parentage, rather than a function or role.
40. H.S. Lee papers 121/8/10.
41. H.S. Lee papers 121/8/71–73.
42. H.S. Lee papers 121/5/69.
43. H.S. Lee papers 121/7/18.
44. H.S. Lee papers 121/5/76.
45. Tan Cheng Lock, "The Oversea-Chinese Association, India. President's Speech at Inaugural Meeting, Bombay, 24th September 1943", in *Malayan Problems from a Chinese Point of View by Tan Cheng Lock*, by C.Q. Lee (Singapore: Tannsco, 1947), pp. 1–3.
46. Tan Miau Ing, "The Formation of the Malayan Chinese Association (MCA) Revisited", *Journal of the Malaysian Branch of the Royal Asiatic Society* 88, part 2, no. 309 (December 2015a): 111.
47. Tan Cheng Lock, "Letter from the President of the Association to the Secretary of State for the Colonies, London", in *Malayan Problems from a Chinese Point of View by Tan Cheng Lock*, by C.Q. Lee (Singapore: Tannsco, 1947), pp. 4–7.
48. Ibid., pp. 6–7.
49. Ibid., p. 7.
50. H.S. Lee papers 121/3/1.
51. H.S. Lee papers 121/3/5.
52. H.S. Lee papers 121/3/6.
53. H.S. Lee papers 121/3/45–47.
54. H.S. Lee papers 121/3/47.
55. Jayde Lin Roberts, *Mapping Chinese Rangoon: Place and Nation among the Sino-Burmese* (Seattle and London: University of Washington Press, 2016), pp. 41–42.
56. Tan (2015a), pp. 110–11.
57. Ibid., pp. 108, 119.

58. Cheah Boon Kheng, *From PKI to the Comintern, 1924–1941: The Apprenticeship of the Malayan Communist Party. Selected Documents and Discussion Compiled and Edited with Introductions by Cheah Boon Kheng* (New York: Southeast Asia Program, Cornell University, 1992), pp. 38–40.
59. H.S. Lee papers 121/5/67.
60. Cheah Boon Kheng, "Some Aspects of the Interregnum in Malaya (14 August–3 September 1945)", *Journal of Southeast Asian Studies* 8, no. 1 (March 1977): 54.
61. Paul H. Kratoska, *The Japanese Occupation of Malaya: A Social and Economic History* (London: Allen & Unwin, 1998), p. 293.
62. Cheah (1977), pp. 53–56. The imprisoned and tortured Lim Bo Seng died of dysentery in Batu Gajah, Perak, in 1944. A plaque at his graveside at MacRitchie Reservoir in Singapore states the following:

Lim Bo Seng was born in China, the 11th child and first son of wealthy businessman Lim Loh. He arrived in Singapore in 1917. He studied at Raffles Institution and later at the University of Hong Kong. In 1930, he married Gan Choo Neo and they had 8 children, one of whom died in infancy.

During the Second Sino-Japanese War, Lim was active in the Nanyang Federation's resistance activities. On 1 February 1942, Lim and other Chinese community leaders left Singapore for India where they recruited and trained hundreds of secret agents, mainly Malayan Chinese, for the Sino-British guerrilla group, Force 136.

The first Force 136 agents were deployed in May 1943 in Operation Gustavus to establish an espionage network in Malaya and Singapore. Lim returned to Malaya in November 1943. Unfortunately Operation Gustavus failed. Lim was captured on 25 March 1944 and taken to the Kempeitai headquarters for interrogation. He was subsequently imprisoned at the Batu Gajah Gaol in Perak.

Despite severe torture, Lim refused to divulge any information. Incarcerated under appalling conditions, he fell ill with dysentery towards the end of May 1944 and died in the early hours of 29 June 1944. He was buried behind the Batu Gajah Gaol compound in an unmarked spot.

In December 1945, after the war ended, Lim's widow travelled with her eldest son Lim Leong Geok to bring her husband's remains back to Singapore. A funeral service was held on 13 January 1946 at City Hall and Lim's remains were brought to MacRitchie Reservoir where he was buried with full military honours. He was posthumously conferred the rank of Major-General by the Chinese Nationalist Government.

63. Cheah Boon Kheng, *Red Star over Malaya: Resistance and Social Conflict During and After the Japanese Occupation of Malaya, 1941–46*, 4th ed. (Singapore: NUS Press, 2012 (1983)), pp. 95–96.
64. H.S. Lee papers 121/7/38, 40.
65. H.S. Lee papers 121/5/79–80.
66. Yoichi Itagaki, "Some Aspects of the Japanese Policy for Malaya under the Occupation with Special Reference to Nationalism", in *Papers on Malayan History*, edited by K.G. Tregonning (Singapore: Journal South-East Asian History, 1962), pp. 264–66.
67. H.S. Lee papers 121/5/81.

PART THREE
1945–59

Chapter 5

POLITICS IN A MESSY NEW WORLD

> The average person in Southeast Asia has little knowledge of, or interest in, foreign policy. Attitudes towards foreigners are often based on personal contacts. [...] Nevertheless, events are moving rapidly in Southeast Asia, and generalizations that may be true at present may not be valid in the not too distant future. Attitude-forming groups—religious, educational, military, labor, and others—as well as political parties are active in varying degrees of intensity.
>
> —Russell H. Fifield, 1958[1]

THESE WERE tumultuous times, and the World War that was now ended ushered into being a world that none could recognize. Not only did individuals have to adapt to new situations, the political map of eastern Asia was about to change dramatically, and new security alliances were emerging that would include actors whose birth, one could say, was fanned by the fires of war. Conditions in Malaya changed as much with events happening in the region and the world as they were by domestic dynamics. The age of nation states had arrived in Asia.

As Josef Silverstein noted, the Japanese invasion of Southeast Asia had a profound impact on all affected by it. No doubt, conditions were very different in different countries, but despite that, with some "modification and reformulation" here and there, some general propositions can be made on the matter:

(1) The swift victories of the Japanese over the colonial defenders destroyed the myth of Western superiority and the need for alien guardians in these countries, (2) the goodwill of local populations toward the Japanese at the outset of the occupation gradually turned to hostility in the face of the invaders' cruelty and neo-colonial policies, (3) nationalism, which had first appeared before the war, accelerated under Japanese rule and emerged at war's end as the most powerful force in Southeast Asian politics, (4) evolutionary social change metamorphosed into revolutionary upheaval, producing new attitudes, awareness, organizations, and occupations, and (5) the local population gained experience in administration, political organization, and military affairs, with a resultant confidence in their ability to govern and defend themselves.[2]

European colonialism in the region had in fact been dealt a death blow by the Japanese invasion. But what would take its place was far from certain. Amid the chaos of surrender, the badly weakened European powers tried their utmost to regain their former territories in Southeast Asia. None had an easy time of it, and only the British succeeded in Malaya, but even that was only for a few years.

On 26 November 1943, American President Franklin Roosevelt, British Prime Minister Winston Churchill and Chinese President Generalissimo Chiang Kai-shek met in Cairo and issued a press release that day announcing their resolve "to restrain and punish the aggression of Japan". For China's part, the three leaders agreed that "all the territories Japan has stolen from the Chinese, such as Manchuria, Formosa, and the Pescadores, shall be restored to the Republic of China".[3] Plans for Japan's "unconditional surrender" were laid out in somewhat greater detail in the so-called Potsdam Declaration, issued by the allies on 26 July 1945, in Potsdam, Germany following the fall of the Third Reich on 8 May.[4]

FROM HOT WAR TO COLD WAR

Japan's capitulation on 2 September saw Taiwan shaking off 50 years of colonial control. Korea's liberation from Japan came in the form of the Soviet Union expanding down to the 38th parallel, and by the United States holding ground south of that. The peninsula quickly became the first major battlefield for the Cold War in Asia. The Korean War was fought out between June 1950 and July 1953, with North Korea, supported by the Soviet Union and Maoist China, going into open conflict with South Korea, backed by United Nations forces made up mainly of American personnel.

It is as much a twist of fate as it is a revelation of political expedience that China, from having been an ally of the Americans during the Second World War, quickly became their key enemy— just as Japan became their key ally after its adoption of a liberal democratic constitution in 1947. In fact, Japan's industrial recovery at this crucial time in her history was heavily aided by the substantial "special procurements" ordered by the United Nations during the Korean War, and by the United States thereafter for the maintenance of its military forces in Japan.[5]

With the end of the war with Japan, China regained all the territories of the Qing except for Mongolia, which had declared independence under a communist regime supported by the Soviet Union in July 1921. The British had relinquished through a treaty signed on 11 January 1943 the privileges gained through the unequal port treaties of the nineteenth century. To be sure, they had already lost those ports when the Japanese invaded in 1937.

Civil war in China now saw the Communist Party successfully purging the mainland of Kuomintang forces, and Mao Zedong could already declare on 21 September 1949 the founding of the People's Republic of China.[6] Chiang Kai-shek's forces found uneasy refuge on Taiwan, and with these developments, the geopolitical map of East Asia was radically redrawn. For Beijing, the exclusion of Taiwan was not only an unsettled historical embarrassment but also symbolic of the continuation of its inability to exert maritime influence in its own domains. China was an original signatory of the United Nations Charter, and despite the expulsion of the Kuomintang from the Mainland, her seat continued to be kept by Taipei. Beijing—the People's Republic of China—had to wait until 25 October 1971 to take it over.

These were globally uncertain times indeed, and new political entities were taking shape throughout Asia—and the world—within the larger trends of decolonization and the struggle for supremacy between the communist realm and the capitalist world.

In Southeast Asia, only Siam had remained nominally uncolonized and unoccupied. During the Japanese expansion into its neighbourhood, Siam had in fact, albeit as a puppet state, regained territories bordering Cambodia and Laos from the French, as well as the Malay states in the south from the British. All these were lost again with the surrender of the Japanese, and the British, on their return to the region, sought to style the country over which it had once had predominance, into a protectorate. Thailand's alliance with the Japanese in fact saw the country officially declaring war on the Allies.

Opposition from Siam's leaders, the Chinese government and, more covertly, the Americans, forced the British to relent in their ambition to exert stronger control over Thailand after the War. What emerged instead was agreement by Bangkok to allow British air rights over its territories, to relinquish the Malay states, and to guarantee that no canal at the Isthmus of Kra would be built without British consent. In return, London sponsored Siam's entry into the United Nations, which took place on 16 December 1946.[7] The United Soviet Socialist Republic agreed to support Siam as well, on condition that it revoked the anti-Communist law it had passed in the 1930s. Siam reassumed the name of Thailand in 1949, and the United States became the single important factor in Thailand's development in the post-war era, with the Thai military dominating the government for a quarter of a century.[8] This legacy of military dominance continued in fits and starts until today.

The Philippines, ceded by the Spanish to the Americans in 1898, was granted independence on 4 July 1946. It was nevertheless already able to have the honour one week earlier, on 26 June, of being one of the original signatories of the United Nations Charter. Philippine independence had certain limitations, however, and was qualified by legislation favouring American access to Philippine natural resources, and import quotas on Philippine goods whenever these should come into substantial competition with American products. Dozens of American military bases were retained as well, including several major ones.

Collaboration between the French Vichy government and the Axis powers starting in August 1940 saw Japan's control over Indo-China grow to the point where it could launch attacks on the British and Dutch colonies when the time came in late 1941. In Vietnam, as the end drew near for the Japanese, they ended their alliance with the French and gave support on 9 March 1945 to the Emperor of Annam, Bao Dai. The moment Tokyo surrendered, however, the Vietnam Independent League led by Ho Chi Minh took over and Bao Dai abdicated on 25 August. The nationalists then declared Vietnam independent a week later, on 2 September. The French were of course not about to depart without a fight.

> The possibility of control was, however, initially reduced by the transfer of Japan of authority to Indo-Chinese governments. It was still further lessened on account of the fact that sufficient time elapsed between the Japanese surrender and the arrival of Allied forces to take over from the Japanese forces to enable the proclaimed Viet Nam Republic to establish itself in Tongking, Annam and Cochin China.[9]

The Japanese surrender in Vietnam was received in the north by Kuomintang troops and in the south by the British. In Saigon, imprisoned French troops were released and armed before control over the territory was handed over to them. This led to the expulsion of the Vietnamese regime, and a guerrilla war ensued with British, French and Japanese troops fighting the Viet Minh. By the end of 1945, the French had regained control over the south, which they knew as Cochin China. With the Japanese already disarmed, the British then left, their mission accomplished.

Mao's victory in China in 1949 changed the equation in Vietnam as much as it did in Korea. Northern Vietnam now had a friendly neighbour up north ready to supply material and men in the slow war to rid the country of foreign powers.

The Associated States of Indochina was formed in 1950, consisting of Cambodia, Laos, Vietnam and France. This was an economic union aimed at prolonging French influence in Indo-China. In the fight against the Viet Minh, the costs for maintaining such a disparate army were exorbitant for France, and America's Truman administration soon felt compelled to provide supplies and weapons free of charge. The first delivery arrived several weeks after the Korean War began. Containing the spread of communism out of China, which was how the Americans read the situation, led Washington to increase its military and economic support to such an extent that by 1954, they were footing 80 per cent of France's war costs.

After the Viet Minh decisively defeated the French at Dien Bien Phu in May 1954, the Associated States began to unravel. Both Laos and Cambodia became members of the United Nations on 14 December 1955, and on New Year's Day 1955, new currencies were issued by them and by South Vietnam. There were now two effective Vietnamese currencies in circulation, and two Vietnams at each other's throat.[10]

Support for the Republic of Vietnam saw the United States taking over from France in the battle against the Viet Minh, and its marines landing on Vietnamese soil for the first time in 1965. Their numbers reached half a million by 1967. America's Vietnam War ended in April 1975 with victory for the North, by which time the country had been left devastated and military casualties amounted to over a million on the Vietnamese side, and 58,200 on the American side. Civilian deaths climbed beyond half a million.[11] Both Laos and Cambodia had been drawn into the war in the process, with equally devastating results.

In 1976, the North and the South merged to become the Socialist Republic of Vietnam, and joined the United Nations the following year. Vietnam's long war of unification cast a long shadow over international dynamics and strategic thinking in the rest of the region until the end of the Cold War in 1991.

The journey towards independence and national stability was an equally bloody one for the peoples of Indonesia. Unlike British Malaya, anti-colonial sentiments were already strong in the Dutch Indies before the Japanese invasion. The Japanese "liberation" of the colony began on 28 February 1942, two weeks after the fall of Singapore, with troops mobilized from Indo-China and from the Philippines. Dutch defeat came rapidly, and already on 12 March, the commanders of the Allied forces had been gathered at Bandung to formalize their surrender.

> However, disillusionment with the Japanese as liberators was quite rapid in Indonesia. As elsewhere in Southeast Asia, the Japanese conquerors moved to Japan, without exchange, as much of everything already produced as possible, and proved unsuccessful in re-establishing production, in the exports' fields, on a reoriented (to Japan) exchange basis. Thus the years of Japanese rule were years of increasing economic deterioration and impoverishment.[12]

As Japan's far-flung and short-lived empire rushed towards a close, Indonesian leaders led by Sukarno, Muhammad Hatta and Radjiman Wedyodiningrat flew to Dalat, Vietnam, in early August 1945 for hurried discussions on independence with Field Marshal Terauchi Hisaichi, the commander of Japan's Southern Expedition Army Group. All ideas for a formation of a new nation spanning all of maritime Southeast Asia were shelved with the surrender of the Japanese on 15 August in 1945. Sukarno and his group went ahead nevertheless to declare independence for Indonesia alone on 17 August, with him as president and Muhammad Hatta as vice president.[13] This republic, centred in Java, was equipped with a constitution and "supported by forces equipped with Japanese arms seized and turned over to it after the surrender".[14]

The region that now constituted Indonesia was diverse not only in ethnic terms but also in administrative experience, both under the Dutch as well as the Japanese, and most importantly, in political consciousness. Furthermore, the complicated process for regaining the islands added to the confusion.

By the time, in late September, that British forces of the Southeast Asia Command, of which war theatre Indonesia had become a part, arrived to receive the Japanese surrender, [the republican government] had been able to establish and consolidate its authority in Java, Madura, and Sumatra.

HANDLING THE SURRENDER

The British seemed concerned largely with handling the Japanese surrender and freeing prisoners. Dutch colonial matters were not their concern and expediting them were in any case not in their interest. This led to the Dutch putting some of the blame for the expectedly strong opposition to their return on the British.

> For, although Netherlands sovereignty over Indonesia was recognized by both the United States and Britain, authority over these areas was placed in the hands of the Commander-in-Chief of the British troops sent to disarm the Japanese. The British Commander did not side with either the Dutch or the Indonesians... It is only natural that the Republicans construed this British policy as a recognition of their authority. In any case, the British decision not to intervene gave the Republicans a strong weapon with which to consolidate their position and to convince the masses that Great Britain recognized the Republic.[15]

From this point until Indonesia finally became a member of the United Nations on 28 September 1950, difficult negotiations between the Dutch and the Republican government, with occasional and effective appeals to the international community and to the United Nations, took place alongside armed conflicts. The Netherlands transferred sovereignty to what was called the United States of Indonesia on 27 December 1949, but this federal union soon fell apart and was replaced on 15 August 1950 by the unitary Republic of Indonesia.[16] The territory this republic now controlled included all of what had been the Dutch East Indies except West Irian (later West New Guinea). For some Indonesian nationalists, this fell short of the dream of an Indonesia Jaya, which would have included British Malaya and its possessions on the island of Borneo.

Also of special relevance to British Malaya were the developments surrounding the Japanese surrender in Sumatra. This island forms the western littoral of the Straits of Malacca, and has, especially the central and southern parts of it, strong cultural links with the Malay Peninsula itself. These links were radically diminished on 17 March 1824 through the Treaty of London, which by drawing a line down the middle of the straits sought to defuse any potential for conflict between the British and the Dutch over their respective areas of influence in the region following the Napoleonic Wars. The founding of Singapore five years earlier had led to great tension between the two powers, with the Dutch claiming that the British agreement made with the Sultan of Johor was invalid and a clear intrusion into the Dutch sphere of influence. This treaty created the expedient colonial divide between what would become Indonesia and what would become Malaysia and Singapore over a century later. It also assured the British of unhampered and vital access to the Chinese market, which they properly secured through their victory in the Opium War 16 years later.

When Sumatra fell to the Japanese in 1942, one of the first things the invaders did was "to insulate Sumatra, as far as possible, from the relatively advanced political climate of Java". In fact, Japan's initial plans for the occupation of the Southeast Asian archipelago was to administer Java, run by its 16th Army, separately from all other parts of the Dutch East Indies. Political activities were allowed, and even encouraged, in Java, leading to the appearance of nationalist leaders such as Sukarno. The navy controlled Borneo, Celebes and the Lesser Sundas, retaining them "in future for the benefit of the Empire", while Malaya and Sumatra, ruled by the 25th Army, were considered "the nuclear zone of the Empire's plans for the Southeast Area". Tellingly, the urban population of Penang Island was described as "the new Japanese people", in apparent reference to it being a core for the colonial future of the region. This joint administration of Malaya and Sumatra lasted only until April 1943, and Japan's plans for the archipelago had to be adjusted as the fortunes of war quickly turned against it. It was only in April and July 1945, that higher authorities overruled the 25th Army's insistence that Sumatra not be included with Java in plans for an independent Indonesia. Sumatra under Japanese rule had in fact been tightly controlled and any form of organization was kept at a very local level.[17]

Sumatra is in truth a culturally chequered place. For about a month in December 1945 and January 1946, a successful revolutionary movement led by religious leaders in Acheh, the northernmost end of the island, ousted the 102 aristocratic rulers that the Dutch had put in place in 1904 to replace the Sultan of Acheh, and assassinated half of them.[18] As noted by Anthony Reid, "The final consequence of the Dutch occupation of Acch was a bitterly divided society."[19]

A so-called social revolution also broke out in the East Coast Residency of Sumatra, a region that under the Dutch had been Indonesia's most important plantation-based exports. It was run by local aristocrats, who over the years had become extremely unpopular.

> Not only did few of the aristocratic rulers govern in the interests of the local population, but also most of them took pains to emphasize their Malay peninsula ancestry and cultural

orientation, rather than identifying themselves with the local population. Moreover, they served the Japanese as well as they had the Dutch. [...] Thus, when after the launching of the Republican revolution most of these rulers held back from joining the movement, the long-smoldering popular hatred of them markedly increased. When in late February reports circulated that these rulers were contacting the Dutch in the hope of reinstating themselves in their old positions, a spontaneous movement to oust them quickly developed.[20]

This uprising was "wantonly brutal", and the killing of aristocratic families were accompanied by many fatal and indiscriminate acts against those who were too visibly wealthy and westernized. This contrasted sharply from events in Malaya occurring more or less at the same time, and the crucial lessons that were there to be learned in the half decade following the fall of Japan by the British colonial and traditional Malay leaders watching from across the Straits of Malacca were many, and these should not be disregarded by historians seeking to understand the difference in political developments on the two sides of the straits. The Malayan sultanates were definitely less authoritarian under British supervision than their counterparts in Sumatra had been under Dutch rule, and the level of colonial disruption of Malayan village life was much less as well.

> Our Sumatran societies all broke more sharply with their past than did Malaya. Traditional restraint and enforced respect gave way before the astonishing new confidence of youth. Ancient, privileged dynasties were torn down, regional particularities glossed over, old loyalties swept away. The way to the future was sought through heroic myths of unity and struggle rather than through the channelling of traditional group loyalties. Many of the new forces unleashed by the revolution were difficult for a

large new multi-ethnic state to absorb. Sumatra became harder to govern than Malaya, with more frequent resort to force at the local level, until direction passed altogether to the military whose specialization it was.[21]

As noted above, the British spearheaded the return of Allied forces to Southeast Asia. But after administering the surrender of Japanese forces, they were quite happy leaving the colonies of other European nations to their own devices. Being a major colonialist themselves, they had already too much on their hands trying to regain power and status in the colonies and territories of influence they lost to the Japanese challenge—the Federated States of Malaya, the Unfederated States of Malaya, the Straits Settlements, Brunei, Labuan Island, British North Borneo, Sarawak, and Burma. On the Chinese Mainland, Hong Kong was all that remained under their control following the termination in 1943 of the unequal treaties placed on China since the Opium wars.

And India, the Jewel in the Crown, though saved from Japanese invasion, was about to fall away. The Indian movement towards self-government and independence had been going on for decades, if not since the very beginning of British power in India; and from 1919 onwards, this had come to be intimately associated with Mahatma Gandhi and his idea of *satyagraha*—non-violent civil disobedience. For all its weaknesses, Gandhi's charisma and his teaching seemed to have "turned the [Congress] party away from the paths of Communism and armed revolution". In fact, in 1942, the Indian Communism party had only a membership of 5,000.[22]

Local and provincial elections held in December 1946 and March 1946, however, returned results that showed the division between Hindus and Muslims to be too deep to be bridged by checks and balances, and by political negotiations. And so when independence came on 15 August 1947, it was in the form of the partition of the British Raj into Hindu India and Muslim Pakistan. This was accompanied by massive bloodletting that overshadowed earlier inter-ethnic massacres in northern India, and left, at a modest estimate, over half a million people dead.[23]

Pakistan became a member of the United Nations on 30 September that year, and India followed a month later, on 30 October. The island nation of Ceylon off southern India gained independence on 4 February 1948 and joined the United Nations on December 1955.

In Burma, where "British rule was disliked by many sections of Burmese society", the Japanese invasion in 1942 saw the Burmese being "inclined towards their conquerors while the inland hill tribes, the Karens and the Kachins, supported Britain, which had protected them from their lowland neighbours". The Japanese declared Burma independent in August 1943, under the Burma National Army headed by Thakin Aung San. In March 1945, however, Aung San and his followers switched sides and went over to the British "when it was clear that they would expel the Japanese".

A partially boycotted election in April 1946 saw Aung San's Anti-Fascist People's Freedom League gaining an overwhelming majority. Three months later, however, political rivals gunned down Aung San and six ministers in the cabinet room. Independence was nevertheless granted by the British on 4 January 1948, and rebellions by communists and Karen separatists ensued.[24] On 19 April 1948, the Union of Burma, nevertheless, joined the United Nations.

The post-war years were busy ones indeed for the British colonial office. After overseeing the surrender of Japanese forces in the region, the British had to prepare for the imminent loss of the Indian subcontinent, and Burma. Where withdrawal from their Malayan possessions was concerned, it has to be said that they fared relatively well.

The resource-rich island of Borneo—made up of the British possessions of Brunei, Labuan Island, British North Borneo and Sarawak, plus Dutch Borneo—was a prioritized target for the Japanese invaders in 1942, but that was not the case for the Allied forces led by American forces under General MacArthur when they began reoccupying the war theatre named the South-West Pacific Area (SWPA), which included Borneo. The thankless task of retaking the giant island fell to Australian forces instead, whose commanders, though filled with doubt about the necessity of the difficult campaign at a time when the Japanese were obviously losing, failed to take a stand against the American general. On 1 May 1945, Australian forces began landing on Borneo, and after two months, on 9 July, defeated Japanese forces based there. This was two weeks before the atomic bombs ended the war with fateful finality on 14 August.[25] Allied bombing had, however, devastated most of the towns in these territories.

The commanding officer, Lieutenant-General L.J. Morhead, had declared martial law in the British territories in northern Borneo on 10 June 1945.[26] The surrender of Japanese forces took a while, however, and it was only on 9 September that this took place in a ceremony at a beachside village in Labuan. Trials for war crimes were held against the Japanese invaders in the following months, based on evidence on the so-called "death marches" involving prisoners of war in the British areas, and on the mass beheadings of civilians in the occupied Dutch territories in southern Borneo which were described as "the worst Japanese war crimes on Indonesian territory". The three-week interregnum between Tokyo's surrender and the arrival of Australian military authorities allowed for mob rule exacting acts of retribution on the Japanese, which sometimes took the form of lynchings.[27]

Brunei followed its own political course, and stayed under British protection until 1 January 1984, after its withdrawal from the plan to join the Federation of Malaysia in 1963. The administration of North Borneo was taken off the hands of the North Borneo Chartered Company, and the territory—together with Labuan—became a crown colony on 15 July 1946 and was granted self-government on 31 August 1963 in time for it to join the Federation of Malaysia as the state of Sabah. Sarawak was made a crown colony on 1 July 1946, and gained self-government on 22 July 1963. Together with Singapore and Sabah, it joined the Federation on 16 September 1963.

BRITISH MILITARY RULE

Already on 15 August 1945, as soon as the Japanese Emperor had announced his country's full surrender, Louis Mountbatten, the Supreme Allied Commander for South East Asia, had proclaimed the Malay Peninsula to be under military administration "by reason of military necessity and for the prevention and suppression of disorder and the maintenance of public safety".[28] However, it took three weeks before the first British Royal Marines landed on the peninsula, at Penang on 3 September, and at Singapore two days later. This period was sadly marked by violent acts of retribution often between different ethnic groups. Inter-ethnic relations had been tense even before the war, but the Japanese occupation and the viciousness of the immediate post-war period worsened matters and poisoned politics in Malaya for decades to come.

What remains a curiosity to historians is the fact that although the communist-controlled Malayan People's Anti-Japanese Army (MPAJA) had a chance during these weeks to take over Malaya and Singapore, it did not.

On the other hand, its counterpart in Vietnam under Ho Chi Minh, in similar circumstances, acted quickly to seize the country's key centres of power in order to present the returning French forces with a *fait accompli*. In Malaya, the MPAJA took over only the regional government in scattered areas, but made no moves to seize the key administrative centres such as Kuala Lumpur and Singapore which were in Japanese hands. The British were allowed to return without any opposition.[29]

The Malayan Communist Party (MCP) may not have been the united and powerful force at this time that it was often assumed to be. For one thing, it had serious leadership issues in the wake of huge Japanese successes in eradicating top communists in Singapore in August 1942 and the imperial army ambushing and eliminating almost the MCP's entire central executive committee on 1 September 1942 at Batu Caves in Kuala Lumpur.[30] In fact, the man accused of providing information to make these hits possible was no other than Wong Kim Gjuck, alias Lai Tek, the party's secretary-general who had been suspected of being a spy for the Japanese as well as for the British, and even for the Russians (via the Comintern) and the French.[31] Lai Tek's multiple roles could have determined the adoption of a policy of "abandonment of revolution and cooperation with the British" at a crucial time for the MCP.

Also, not only was the MPAJA relying on Force 136 for funding, arms and other supplies, it lacked correct knowledge of the situation outside their limited domains. Most seriously, there were rumours circulating in the MPAJA, which seemed strong enough not to be ignored, that Chiang Kai-shek's army would be handling the Japanese surrender in Malaya. In fact, this was only true for Vietnam, and only above the 16th parallel.[32] Thus, when British troops reoccupied Malaya, "and received an enthusiastic welcome from the Resistance movement", they noticed "as in Burma, that the flags displayed were rarely British; honour was accorded mostly to the Chinese flag".

> A sprinkling of British, American, and Russian flags did not really conceal the facts that the Chinese had expected the reoccupation to be performed by Chinese troops and that they were inclined to believe that it was the Chinese guerrillas who had defeated the Japanese.[33]

More concretely, violent clashes involving Chinese secret societies and Kuomintang guerrillas at the end of the war also showed how divided and diverse the Malayan Chinese community really was at this time. Their interests and loyalties seemed as complex as they had been before the war, if not more so.

Tan Chong Tee, whose remembrances of the struggle suggest a much stronger contribution by the Kuomintang through Force 136, helps answer the question why the MCP did not—or did not think it could—grab power before the British could return. Tan joined the Force immediately after meeting fellow Singaporean Lim Bo Seng in Chungking while the latter was there to discuss Kuomintang participation in Force 136 with Chiang Kai-shek.

Allied forces were in fact planning a final assault on Malaya for 9 September 1945 and for that purpose had been parachuting personnel and supplies to over 30 spots on the peninsula.

> Once the communications network was completed, more military personnel, including the Gurkha force, were sent to major strategic spots. The jungles of Malaya were practically controlled by the Allied forces now. The Japanese [would] not stand a chance.[34]

Although the sudden surrender by Tokyo made the invasion unnecessary, the British decided to keep to their plan. But instead of landing at Port Swettenham and Port Dickson, and heading for Kuala Lumpur and then Singapore, the last expected to be regained within three months; it was decided that Penang and Singapore be reoccupied first ahead of the execution of the original proposal.[35]

Whether biased or not, Tan's comment at the end of the war, as he collected information from his fellows emerging from the jungles, remains fascinating:

> What interested me most was the role of the Kuomintang government in the counter-offensive operation. For more than two years, they worked very hard to recruit the best youths from China and overseas for the resistance movement. [...] The Allied Forces set up a strong frontline force in Malaya through a series of operations via air and sea routes. This was critical in their eventual takeover of Malaya.[36]

The immediate problems faced by the British Military Administration (BMA) in Malaya concerned re-equipping the police and boosting morale. Apparently, by the time the Malayan Union took over, "the police forces were approaching pre-war strength, though there was still a severe shortage of European officers and inspectors".[37]

Public health was another key issue to manage. Shortage of most things, including drugs and equipment, as well as the lack of proper training and knowledge among the existing staff, had to be overcome. What the BMA found was that "malaria, pulmonary tuberculosis, and venereal disease, had greatly increased during the Japanese occupation [and] malnutrition was marked and general". Fortunately, during the BMA period, there were no serious epidemic outbreaks in Malaya. Given the dire conditions then, the consequences of these could have been horrendous.[38]

Despite the disruption caused by the Japanese occupation, however, there was continuity where British anxieties over how Malaya was to be governed were concerned. In the early 1930s, the Governor of the Straits Settlements and High Commissioner of the Federated Malay States, Cecil Clementi, had been at loggerheads with the Colonial Office over the nature of Malaya's plural society. He had tried to champion the benefits of indirect rule and the status of the sultans in conflict with the centralization that many colonial officers saw as a necessary development in the administration of the peninsula.

The break in British rule offered a chance for its simplification once the Japanese were defeated. A War Cabinet on Malaya and Borneo was set up on 6 January 1944 to study a proposal for constitutional changes put up by the Secretary of State of the Colonies. The changes were accepted as policy by July that year. What drove this process was the conviction that "decisions could not be postponed as planning for military government could not proceed until these [changes] had been taken".

> At this stage [in July 1944,] planning was to proceed on the basis that a Malayan Union would be constituted in the Peninsula (excluding Singapore but including the settlements of Penang and Malacca) with a strong central authority under a Governor, and with local authorities which should be in some degree representative of the principal communities and interests. Concurrently there was to be created a new Malayan Union Citizenship for persons born, or ordinarily resident, in the Malaya Peninsula, or who, in future, became ordinarily resident. This new citizenship was intended, in the words of the White Paper, to enable "all those who have made the country

their homeland to have the opportunity of a due share in the country's political and cultural institutions", and to include "without discrimination of race or creed all who can establish a claim, by reason of birth or a suitable period of residence, to belong to the country".[39]

The BMA thus understood that its task from Day One was to pave the way for the Malayan Union that was to replace it. The main hurdle standing in the way of these ambitions was the official status of the sultans, whose power would need to be curtailed through fresh treaties. The modifying of treaties with the Rajah of Sarawak and the Sultan of Brunei was also on the cards. The North Borneo Company had already opened negotiations in 1944 with the British government to transfer power to the latter, with Labuan being incorporated into the future Sabah.[40]

The man chosen to explain to all the sultans—and to elicit from them—the required surrender of sovereignty was Sir Harold MacMichael. He arrived in Malaya on 11 October 1945, and already by 22 January 1946, a White Paper was released proposing the formation of the Malayan Union comprising the nine Malay states and the settlements of Penang and Malacca, and the separate crown colony of Singapore.

Without doubt, the Japanese occupation of the Far East helped change the whole region forever. Colonialism's time was now ending in haste. And unlike the "hot war" that was the Second World War and that lasted six years in the West and nine years in East Asia, the "cold war" that followed it, within which new post-colonial nations were being painfully born, would last 45 years.

Learning to live in—or to construct—this new era was not going to be easy, not for exhausted individuals and not for emergent nations.

NOTES

1. H. Russell Fifield, *The Diplomacy of Southeast Asia: 1945–1958* (New York: Harper & Brothers, 1958), p. 58.
2. Josef Silverstein, "The Importance of the Japanese Occupation of Southeast Asia to the Political Scientist", in *Southeast Asia in World War II: Four Essays*, edited by Josef Silverstein (New Haven: Yale University Southeast Asia Studies, 1966), p. 3.
3. The Cairo Declaration states:

    The several military missions have agreed upon future military operations against Japan. The three great Allies expressed their resolve to bring unrelenting pressure against their brutal enemies by sea, land and air. This pressure is already rising.

    The three great Allies are fighting this war to restrain and punish the aggression of Japan. They covet no gain for themselves and have no thought of territorial expansion. It is their purpose that Japan, shall be stripped of all the islands in the Pacific which she has seized or occupied since the beginning of the first World War in 1914, and that all the territories Japan has stolen from the Chinese, such as Manchuria, Formosa, and the Pescadores, shall be restored to the Republic of China. Japan will also be expelled from all other territories which she has taken by violence and greed. The aforesaid three great powers, mindful of the enslavement of the people of Korea, are determined that in due course Korea shall become free and independent.

    With these objects in view the three Allies, in harmony with those of the United Nations at war with Japan, will continue to persevere in the serious and prolonged operations necessary to procure the unconditional surrender of Japan.

    See USA Department of State document 740.0011 European War 1939/32623, http://www.documentcloud.org/documents/1341677-cairo-declaration-1943.html.

4. See Proclamation Defining Terms of Japanese Surrender issued, at Potsdam, 26 July 1945, https://www.documentcloud.org/documents/1341676-potsdam-declaration-1945.html#search/p1/Potsdam.
5. Harold M. Vinacke, *A History of the Far East in Modern Times*, 6th ed. (New York: Appleton-Century-Crofts, 1959), p. 745.
6. Ibid., p. 679.
7. United Nations, United Nations Member States, 3 July 2006, http://www.un.org/press/en/2006/org1469.doc.htm.
8. M.C. Ricklefs, Bruce Lockhart, Albert Lau, Portia Reyes, and Maitrii Aung-Thwin, *A New History of Southeast Asia* (New York: Palgrave Macmillan, 2010), pp. 360–62; also Vinacke (1959), p. 777.
9. Vinacke (1959), pp. 763–64.
10. Hugues Tertrais, "France and the Associated States of Indochina, 1945–1955", in *The Transformation of Southeast Asia: International Perspectives on Decolonization*, edited by Marc Frey, Ronald W. Pruessen and Tan Tai Yong (New York and London: M.E. Sharpe, 2003), pp. 72–82.
11. Ricklefs et al. (2010), pp. 346–55. See also National Archives, "Statistical Information about Casualties of the Vietnam War", undated, https://www.archives.gov/research/military/vietnam-war/casualty-statistics.html.`
12. Vinacke (1959), p. 820.
13. Soda Naoki, "Indigenizing Colonial Knowledge: The Formation of Pan-Malay Identity in British Malaya", PhD thesis, Graduate School of Asian and African Area Studies, Kyoto University, 2008, pp. 156–58.
14. Vinacke (1959), pp. 821–22.
15. Netherlands Information Bureau, *The Political Events in the Republic of Indonesia: A Review of the Developments in the Indonesian Republic (Java and Sumatra) since the Japanese Surrender*, 1947(?), pp. 8–9.
16. Vinacke (1959), pp. 827–29.
17. Anthony Reid, "The Birth of the Republic of Sumatra", *Indonesia* 12 (October 1971): 22–25.
18. George McTurnan Kahin, *Nationalism and Revolution in Indonesia* (New York: SEAP Publications, 2003), p. 179.

19. Anthony Reid, *The Blood of the People: Revolution and the End of Traditional Rule in Northern Sumatra* (Kuala Lumpur: Oxford University Press, 1979), p. 31.
20. Kahin (2003), pp. 179–80.
21. Reid (1979), p. 263.
22. Lawrence James, *The Rise and Fall of the British Empire* (London: Abacus, 1998 (1994)), p. 421.
23. Ibid., pp. 552–54.
24. Ibid., pp. 546–47.
25. Ooi Keat Gin, *Post-War Borneo, 1945–1950: Nationalism, Empire and State-Building* (London and New York: Routledge, 2013), pp. 32–48.
26. F.S.V. Donnison, *British Military Administration in the Far East 1943–46*, History of the Second World War, United Kingdom Military Series, edited by J.R.M. Butler (London: Her Majesty's Stationery Office, 1956), pp. 452–53.
27. Ooi (2013), pp. 32–48.
28. Donnison (1956), pp. 450–51.
29. Cheah Boon Kheng, "Some Aspects of the Interregnum in Malaya (14 August–3 September 1945)", *Journal of Southeast Asian Studies* 8, no. 1 (March 1977): 49.
30. Ibid., p. 53.
31. Chin Peng, *My Side of History (as told to Ian Ward and Norma Miraflor)* (Singapore: Media Masters, 2003), p. 82; ibid., pp. 70–74.
32. Cheah (1977), p. 74.
33. Donnison (1956), pp. 384–85.
34. Tan Chong Tee, *Force 136: Story of a WWII Resistance Fighter*, translated by Lee Watt Sim and Clara Show (Original title: *Wo yu 136 budiu*) (Singapore: Asiapac Publication, 1995), p. 300.
35. Donnison (1956), p. 154.
36. Tan (1995), p. 300.
37. Donnison (1956), p. 158.
38. Ibid., pp. 158–59.
39. Ibid., p. 137.
40. Ibid., pp. 137–39.

Chapter 6

MOVING TOWARDS MERDEKA

> As Britain brought the peninsula under control, tin and rubber would eventually make it a jewel of British possession in Southeast Asia. With that knowledge, Britain knew what it needed to do and why it should stay when at the end of the Second World War it was challenged by an anti-colonial movement of some force and legitimacy.
>
> —Yao Souchou[1]

HAU-SHIK had returned to Malaya without his family, and was living at 12–14 Sultan Street in Kuala Lumpur when he wrote to his wife on 26 November 1945:

> As soon as I finish inspecting the tin mines and have made my report to General Hone, I shall come back to Bombay. I hope you will look after everything in the flat. The cost of living here is very very high indeed, and it will be better for our family to remain in India until things become more normal.[2]

Incidentally, Hau-Shik's departure from India was saddened by a breakdown of relations between his family and that of his brother Hau Mo. The two families had by then been staying together in India for three years.³ On 13 December, he wrote to his children, telling them that he had moved back to 16 Golf View Road at the beginning of the month, and had employed two maid servants to prepare the house for their return even though he did not know when that would be. He was also arranging for their schooling: "I have got all the beds for you but there is no mosquito net, no mattress, no bed sheets and no pillows so you had better bring these things back yourselves."⁴

It was indeed a new Malaya they were all returning to. In fact, they were entering a new world into which much adaptation was needed. Hau-Shik was positioned to play an essential part in this new world, not least in the founding of a new troubled but optimistic country. Tan Cheng Lock, whose reputation after a lifetime spent in business and public administration was already an extremely impressive one, would soon take on an even more prominent role in history. Cheng Lock returned to Malaya only in June 1946.

Thus, while Hau-Shik had come back to a land run by the interim British Military Administration (BMA) which was trying to manage the chaos of re-occupation and the inter-ethnic strife that followed the Japanese surrender, what greeted Cheng Lock on his return was the Malayan Union, a Malaya that was restructured in a way that he and others in pre-war years had been fighting for—a Malaya run as one country (or one colony). In fact, while in India, Cheng Lock, on learning that the Colonial Office was considering how post-war Malaya was to be governed, had written a very long memorandum on 1 November 1943 to Edward Gent, the man in charge of the project, to provide him with background knowledge about Malaya and the inter-ethnic situation there. It was then published, and according to the historian K.G. Tregonning, "It had some influence in London."⁵

Cheng Lock wrote in the memorandum, as advice to the British, that

> The best way of treating the Chinese is to trust them and to give an opportunity to those of them who have resided in Malaya, especially if they have done so with their families, for a sufficiently long period and have become domiciled in the country, to acquire the right of Malayan citizenship by naturalisation, so as to enable them to identify themselves completely with the interests of the land of their adoption.[6]

The transformation from the BMA to the Malayan Union was completed by 1 April 1946, and Edward Gent was sworn in as Governor and Commander-in-Chief. The new polity was however an ill-starred creation. A month before it was officially established, more than 40 Malay organizations had already come together to oppose it. This had deep repercussions, and was in fact the beginning of a process that led to the founding of the United Malays National Organisation (UMNO), the party that would dominate Malaysian politics until 2018.

> Most unusual was the violent political agitation of the Malays. This was a factor Tan Cheng Lock and others found difficult to accept for some time. The upward surge of the Malays, however, so quiescent before, was not merely to disturb but to dominate political developments from here on. Indeed Malay political power was to be the mainstream of the movement for *merdeka* which now gathered way. Important though the work of Tan Cheng Lock was to be, it was only when it joined this mainstream that it became successful, and his long-held visions were realized.[7]

It was also this latter mainstream that Hau-Shik and many Malayan Chinese like him who still had strong emotional ties to

China would find themselves drawn into. But already then, this China-orientation was moving in two violently opposed directions, reflecting the ongoing struggle in China between the Kuomintang (KMT) and the Chinese Communist Party (CCP). For many other Malayan Chinese though, especially Straits Chinese such as Tan Cheng Lock and his family, British Malaya was the only home they had known, and with the ability of the returning British to control the peninsula in doubt, their future was equally uncertain.

Thus, while political consciousness among the Malays following the war centred on the ultimatum of ethnic unity amidst external threats, confusion reigned among the Malayan Chinese as a community. Within the Chinese population had already existed intrinsic and inherited tensions based on "occupational divisions, education background, locally born or China-born and speech group-prejudices".[8] More significantly, these tended to be expressed differently and divisively in political leaning and affiliation.

Hau-Shik, on his return to Malaya, very quickly became an important figure involved in the rebuilding of the regained colony. In a list made by Hau-Shik in 1979, over 30 years after returning to Malaya in late 1945, can be noted the positions that he had held since leaving Hong Kong in the 1920s. This displays some continuity in a time of commotion and chaos. For example, while he saw himself as returning with a break between 1941 and 1945 to continue as President of Kuan Cheng Girls School and Member of the Kuala Lumpur Sanitary Board, he considered his time as President of the Miners' Association of Negeri Sembilan, Selangor and Pahang, and the Selangor Chinese Chamber of Commerce and as Member of the Council of the Federated Malay States Chamber of Mines, to be unbroken during the war.[9] He would leave all the above mentioned and important positions only in 1955.

From that list alone, one can see how Hau-Shik's prominence increased after the war, and how his influence rocketed under the returning and uncertain British regime. Positions that he took on in the late 1940s included the directorship of the Operations Committee (1948–55); the presidency of the All Malaya Chinese Mining Association (1946–55) and of the Associated Chinese Chambers of Commerce, Malaya and Singapore (1947–55); and Member of the Malayan Union Advisory Council (1946–47), of the Chinese Tin Mines Rehabilitation Loans Board (1946–59), the Malayan Tin Delegation to all International Tin Meetings (1946–60), the Tin Advisory Committee (1946–55), the War Damage Commission (1946–56), the Federal Finance Committee (1946–56), the Federal Executive Council (1948–57) and the Federal Legislative Council (1948–57).[10]

The political situation was no doubt a volatile one after the war, but much of the concern in the government and among the elite was social and economic in nature as well. This can be clearly seen in the type of organizations and institutions into which Hau-Shik went. The War Damage Commission was founded to assess claims for compensation made by companies and by individuals, while the Chinese Tin Mines Rehabilitation Loans Fund was established to revive Chinese mines, with Hau-Shik requesting $20 million for this purpose from the government. Kick-starting the local economy also required that the Selangor Chinese Chamber of Commerce and the Associated Chinese Chambers of Commerce for the peninsula be reactivated. When the government finally did provide loans to the tin mines, however, three-quarters of the $78 million allocated for this purpose went to European companies. The industry was slow in reviving itself, and even in 1949, tin production was still a third lower than it had been before the war.[11]

Recognition by the British colonial authorities of Hau-Shik's contributions in the immediate post-war years was rewarded with the award to him of the CBE (Commander of the Most Excellent Order of the British Empire), by King George VI on 1 January 1948.

The Japanese surrender had come very suddenly, and the return of the British, their reputation for invincibility now thrashed beyond redemption, heralded desperate attempts to kick-start a colonial economy that had been badly damaged, and to bond a population deeply divided by violence and distrust. As succinctly stated by Leong Yee Foong:

> The colonial government saw in the KMT an attempt to establish an *imperium in imperio* and the MCP as politically subversive. Both parties were inimical to the interests of law and order in Malaya and had to be suppressed. Colonial policy which hinged on the preservation of Malay interests looked upon the development of Chinese political enthusiasm as particularly undesirable and various measures were introduced to curb this tendency.[12]

The *Report on the 1947 Census of Population for Malaya*, showed Malaya having a population of 5,848,910. All major communities had grown in number despite the war, except the Indians, who shrank by 20 per cent from 744,202 to 599,616 (making up 10.25 per cent of the population). There were 2,614,667 Chinese (Singapore's 730,133 included), who made up 44.7 per cent of the population, compared to the 2,543,569 Malays who made up 43.5 per cent of the population. If Singapore is excluded from the calculus—which perhaps it should be since the British omitted the island from the Malayan Union—then the Malayan Chinese share was down at 32 per cent and the Malays' was up at 61.8 per cent.[13]

It is estimated that as many as 50,000 Indian immigrant labourers lost their lives during the Japanese occupation of Malaya, many in forced labour schemes. With the end of the war, however, the traditional "docility" of the Indian labouring community was replaced by new confidence and pride. This was partly due to the returning Indian National Army soldiers leading them to question their harsh conditions. Indeed, for several months after the Japanese surrender, the South East Asia Command administered the region as one, with Indian troops as the mainstay in the reoccupation of Burma, Malaya and Singapore, as well as in the initial retrieving of Vietnam for the French, and Indonesia for the Dutch. In fact, 37,000 Indian soldiers were dispatched to Japan. This excessive deployment of Indians troops after the travails of the war led to mutinies and desertions, such as for example the strike by 4,000 men at Seletar Airbase in Singapore.[14]

Where the Chinese community was concerned, the major political force to emerge from the war was the Malayan Communist Party (MCP). When Singapore fell in 1942, the Japanese had carried out mopping up operations that "lasted for days during which several thousand Chinese suspected of being Communists were seized and shot".[15] Those who managed to flee went into the jungles on the peninsula to become members of the MCP-based Malayan People's Anti-Japanese Army (MPAJA). After the war, this guerrilla army and its support network became the biggest sustained security threat to the British and to successive governments of independent Malaysia.

> [The MPAJA] drew on a civilian body called the Malayan People's Anti-Japanese Union for food and financial support. ... [It] was divided into eight regiments, based in Selangor, Negri Sembilan, North Johore, South Johore, Perak, West Pahang,

East Pahang and Kedah, although coordination was difficult and these groups generally operated autonomously. By July 1945 the MPAJA was reported to have grown to around 10,000 members, mostly working-class Chinese with a smattering of intellectuals and non-Chinese.[16]

Between 20 October and 21 December 1945, Harold MacMichael managed to obtain the signatures of all the Malay sultans through which their power would be transferred to the British Crown. The Malayan Union proposal released in January 1946 replaced the British tried-and-tested system of indirect rule with a centralized system, meaning the loss of sovereignty for the Malay rulers; and proposed the creation of a common citizenry, a "Malayan public" to prepare for self-government. This quickly led to heated debates, with much of the initial groundswell going against the British and against the Malay rulers for signing away their powers. Onn Ja'afar, who was district officer in Batu Pahat, Johor, when the British returned, on learning about the British plan, started a movement called *Pergerakan Melayu Semenanjung (Johor)* (Peninsular Malay Movement, Johor Chapter) on 3 January 1946.

His aim was to establish an organization that could unite the Malays throughout the peninsula. This was achieved at amazing speed. The Pan-Malaya Malay Congress was held on 1–4 March that year, with Onn as chairman. The Congress's first item of business was to endorse the formation of an umbrella party that would act on behalf of the many state-based organizations that had come into existence.[17]

When the Malayan Union came formally into being on 1 April 1946, it was amid a hugely successful boycott fiercely incited by Onn, by the Malay sultans and by other leaders, of the installation of its first governor, Edward Gent. Gent, who had been Assistant Permanent Under-Secretary for the Colonies, was the man behind the working out of the details of the Union.[18] The boycott succeeded very well and effectively and immediately restored the status of the sultans in the eyes of their traditional subjects.[19]

This turn of events was not welcomed by all Malay nationalists. Overwhelmed by the conservative bent that the Malay unity movement had now taken, the Parti Kebangsaan Melayu Malaya (PKMM) and other left-leaning groups left in April to go their own way.[20]

Riding nevertheless on a wave of widespread exuberance, Onn founded UMNO on 11 May, and became its first president. UMNO would go on to become Malaysia's major political force.

Within a month of the party's founding, the Colonial Office had begun looking for a replacement plan for the Malayan Union which the exultant Malays could accept.[21] This was the Federation of Malaya Agreement. Already in July 1946, the Political Working Committee was formed, consisting of six British officials, four royal delegates and two UMNO representatives, expressly to work out a new constitutional framework acceptable to UMNO. Whether or not the exclusion of all other ethnic groups reflected a reassertion of the traditional paternalistic concerns that certain British officials harboured for the Malays, anxiety over rising leftist activism in Malaya and in the region, fear of contamination from the social revolts in neighbouring Sumatra, or more likely a combination of these; an agreement was quickly reached between the colonialists, the sultans and UMNO on a new polity to replace the stillborn Union.

The Federation of Malaya Agreement was made public in December that year. This hasty backtracking by the British on the Malayan Union—a strategy that had been on the colonial agenda for decades—was astounding, to say the least.

Apart from the crucial founding of UMNO, the Malayan Union controversy pushed the Malay rulers into a new role. They became "symbols of the nation, both constructing and helping Malays to picture their future" as well as "icons of traditional Malay culture, or rather a new rendering of tradition which facilitated aristocratic ascendancy in postwar politics".

> Icons, being invented symbols, have no intrinsic value beyond that ascribed to them. The rulers were, in a sense, invented by colonialism, and then reinvented by Onn and the furious public debate over their behaviour. In 1946 their continued existence, role and meaning were no longer self-evident, even though their representation of tradition was accepted. The ambivalence shown towards them was the ambivalence of the Malays towards their invented tradition, with all its disadvantages in a changing world.[22]

With the Federation Agreement, UMNO and the aristocratic class that led it in effect saved the sultans' reputation and provided them with a new status around which the idea of a Malay nation state could be conceived. But in achieving that through the Agreement with the British, it "adopted a course that closely resembled collaboration".[23]

The proposals made by the Working Committee left no doubt that the intention was now to re-establish Malaya as a Malay country. It was still possible for non-Malays to become citizens, but the regulations governing their eligibility were undoubtedly stringent; the Sultans were to be given more authority, and the Malays were to receive "special treatment" in certain vital fields.

Resentment against being excluded from discussions was strong among the non-Malays, and this was clearly reflected in memoranda submitted to the Consultative Committee that was formed after the Agreement was achieved. This Committee, although meant to reflect public opinion, was made up of five Europeans, two Chinese and two Indians. The two Chinese were Hau-Shik and Leong Yew Koh. The memorandum submitted by the Selangor Chinese Chamber of Commerce, of which Hau-Shik was president, stated that

> we and those before us have lived and toiled in this country and have contributed in a very large measure towards the development and progress of Malaya. [...] The Chinese should have the same representation as the Malays for they have contributed the most in the development of this country and have to pay the greatest share of the taxes and rates.

Apparently, the Chinese paid as much as 70 per cent of total taxes collected at this time.[24]

Spontaneous opposition to the Agreement's curtailing of citizenship rights and the expansion of royal power led to the formation by a string of Malayan and Singapore organizations, including trade unions and political parties across the left-right spectrum, of the Pan-Malayan Council for Joint Action (PMCJA). Tan Cheng Lock was its chairman, with John Eber of the Singapore-based Malayan Democratic Union (MDU) as its secretary. In February 1947, Malay organizations opposed to the Agreement came together in the form of Pusat Tenaga Rakyat (PUTERA). The following month, these two new groupings decided to come together to form an alliance.[25]

The PMCJA-PUTERA managed a general strike—a *hartal*—on 20 October 1947. As noted by Mohamed Noordin Sopiee, the hartal (termed "the hurt-all" by those opposed to it) "was a tremendous success in its execution... [but] a complete failure in its effect". It could not accomplish what its organizers were so optimistically hoping for, i.e. a second *volte face* by the British in deciding on a plan to govern post-war Malaya. Not only did PMCJA-PUTERA lack singularity of purpose, they also lacked tactically skilled leaders. Apparently, the only leader they had whom the British respected was Tan Cheng Lock, and even he began losing their respect through his association with the leftists.[26]

While opponents of the Federation may have been failing, they did show that a host of political issues still needed to be overcome before the Agreement could effectively function as the vehicle for national independence. This was most succinctly expressed by UMNO's founder, Onn Ja'afar, in his ultimatum to his followers that the party open its doors to non-Malays, in effect turning it into the United *Malayans* National Organisation. On having his proposal rejected, Onn resigned in August 1951 to form the Independence of Malaya Party (IMP), constituted in the form that he had failed to turn UMNO into. Few Malays joined. The most prominent Chinese who did was Tan Cheng Lock who, although he was present at the launch of the party, assumed a rather inhibited role.

If one considers the period between 1937 and 1945 as a Sino-Japanese war fought across all of East Asia, then the occupation of most of that region by Japanese forces was a tremendous victory over the Chinese government of the day, the KMT. In Malaya, it decimated the KMT networks and dispersed its leaders throughout the region. Regrouping after the war had to be done in the face of organized Malay nationalism, inconsistent British colonial policies, and rising aggression from the MCP. It was most successful in the crown colony of Singapore. In December 1946, its Overseas Department Office was founded there, marking a shift in control from Nanking to local leaders. Competent party organizers were at the same time sent from Nanking to help operate Malayan party branches. A study of Malayan KMT leaders in the post-war years shows the following: some of them were now Malaya-born and bilingual; many were tin and rubber magnates who were prominent community leaders involved in the chambers of commerce and the vernacular schools and charitable organizations. Often charismatic, they were articulate anti-communist activists with close ties to Chiang Kai-Shek. Perhaps most interestingly in this context, many of them were founders of the Malayan Chinese Association when this impactful party was established in February 1949.[27] Significantly, KMT influence over the Chinese chambers of commerce in the states of Kedah, Malacca and Negri Sembilan was weak.[28]

Although Hau-Shik was not elected a KMT executive committee member in Selangor in 1948, the general profile of Chinese community leaders presented above describes him rather well. KMT influence was also very strong in Chinese vernacular schools and social clubs. Reflective of the underlying ideological and class war taking place between the KMT and the CCP in China, the union movement in Malaya was to a very large extent controlled by the communist faction. The Chinese triads, on the other hand, became brothers-in-arms against the MCP, whose activities had encroached into their areas of business.

Another area where the KMT had the edge over their communist opponents was in journalism. The largest of the KMT newspapers at this time was the *Nanyang Siang Pau*, followed by the *Sin Chew Jit Poh* and the *Kwong Wah Yit Poh*. The first two were based in Singapore and the last in Penang. *China Press* was the one with the largest circulation based in Kuala Lumpur at that time.[29] It was officially founded by Hau-Shik already on 1 February 1946, which would mean that it was probably one of his first major projects on returning to Malaya from India.[30]

As the Cold War dawned, the essential disunion between the MCP and the Malayan KMT cut all the deeper. British gratitude towards their wartime allies, the MCP-run MPAJA, could not last long, and the basic anti-colonial stance of the communists soon led to open conflict. MCP activities included a 24-hour general strike called on 29 January 1946, and as many as 300 strikes organized in 1947 alone. In June 1948, with chaos threatening and the killing of estate owners by communist guerrillas accelerating, a state of emergency was declared by the British authorities; and a full-scale guerrilla war began which would last until 1960. This was an opportune signal for the KMT organizations in Malaya to seek closer ties with the British colonial authorities. However, overt cooperation with the colonialists brought swift retribution from the MCP. In July 1948, 27 KMT members were killed by the communists. The following month, 40 more lost their lives. A teacher at Penang's Chung Ling School was killed in 1949, followed by another in 1951, and this spate was topped by the assassination of the school's highly-respected and long-time principal and prominent KMT man, David Chen, in February 1952.[31] The times were turbulent indeed. Just a few months earlier, on 6 October 1951, High Commissioner Henry Gurney was killed in an ambush up Fraser's Hill by communist guerrillas.

Despite the collaboration between the government and KMT supporters, the movement towards self-rule based on the Federation of Malaya Agreement nevertheless necessitated the re-banning of the KMT. The last meeting of the Malayan KMT took place in Penang on 28 August 1949, where a resolution was passed to close all branches by 11 September that year. Thus, the nationalist Chinese movement in Malaya which began in 1912 after the fall of the Qing Dynasty, officially ended in 1949. For KMT supporters in Malaya and elsewhere, the loss of China to the CCP by October 1949 required them to rethink their local strategies—and their lives. There were few who did what Tan Kah Kee, the prominent leader of the Malayan Chinese before the war, did. Though a naturalized British citizen, Kah Kee became an official of the Communist government in Beijing at its inauguration in October 1949, as a member of the People's Political Consultative Conference and of the Overseas Chinese Affairs Commission. This caused the British in Malaya some diplomatic difficulty. Kah Kee's decision to leave Singapore for good to settle in China on 21 May 1950 came therefore as a relief to the local colonial authorities.[32]

Mao Zedong's victory changed not only the strategical map of the world, it also altered the list of possibilities for all Chinese outside of China. Not willing to return to China, they had to recalibrate their options—and their loyalties. Things looked all the more dire for the Chinese in Malaya since the Federation of Malaya Agreement announced in early 1948 had excluded them from all rights to citizenship.

The need for a non-communist organization among the Malayan Chinese—and not necessarily in the guise of a political party—had become irrefutable. Beating the communists in Malaya was now the common goal and the highest priority for the British, the Malay leaders and a large segment of the Malayan Chinese population, especially those who had been strongly affiliated with the KMT. In the end, the communists in Malaya were beaten, and in the very process of that victory, the pillars of Malayan politics were put in place—contingent at first but fated to last, for better or worse.

> When the Emergency began in June 1948, after an initial setback, British resolve never wavered. The marriage of imperial prestige and the colony's earning power, we might say, provided the men in Whitehall with commitment and clarity of purpose in regard to Malaya. When Britain left in 1957, it march out in triumph: imperial prestige was restored, its economic assets were secured by the country's pro-British market-friendly government. [...] Yet, if the colony did not increase the heartbeat of imperial enthusiasts, it was Empire's rustic possession in Southeast Asia that kept Mother Britain from the poor house.[33]

THE FOUNDING OF THE MCA

Discussions about the origins of the Malayan Chinese Association (MCA) tend to get mired in heated controversies, and agreement on them are rare. No doubt, Tan Cheng Lock did establish the Overseas Chinese Association in India, but as we have seen, the official constituency for that body was not confined to Chinese in Malaya and Singapore, and was an expedience of a different period. Despite his undisputed reputation as a spokesman for many Malayan Chinese, especially vis-à-vis the British, Cheng Lock, being a Straits Chinese, lacked the intimate and broad support that China-born Malayan Chinese could command. Henry Gurney, the British High Commissioner of Malaya, is also often credited for pushing the Chinese guilds, associations and chambers of commerce to form a party to counteract the influence of the CCP. By and large, the need for an organization uniting non-communist Malayan Chinese had come to be keenly felt within the community as a whole.

Three groups of conservative-minded Chinese leaders cooperated in setting up the MCA: English-educated professionals, many of whom were Straits-born; leaders of Chinese guilds and associations; and Chinese educationists. The first group was important not only because of their wealth and education but also because of their links to the British and to the English-educated Malay leadership. The leaders of guilds and associations, for their part, connected the MCA to the broader Chinese community. The third group, the Chinese educationists, were key players in shaping Chinese political opinion.[34]

Hau-Shik provided his version of the establishment of MCA in a speech made on 19 January 1969, over a decade after he had left politics. He titled it "The History of the Formation of the Malayan Chinese Association in 1949". The party was celebrating its 20th anniversary, and Hau-Shik, "being one of the founders of the Association", wanted to "recapitulate from memory the events of 1949", and present the opportune conditions surrounding its founding and the strategical reasons for it. His speech is offered here at length to avoid loss of significant nuance.

> The Emergency was declared in June 1948 because the Communist terrorists began to murder planters and miners in various parts of the country. Shortly afterwards the High Commissioner for the Federation of Malaya, the late Sir Edward Gent, on his way to report to the British Government, was killed in an air crash in England. The late Sir Henry Gurney was appointed to succeed Sir Edward Gent and he arrived in Malaya in December 1949.
>
> As most of the Communist terrorists in the jungle were persons of the Chinese race, certain persons in the country cast unjust suspicions on the Chinese people that they were sympathisers of the terrorists, specially the Chinese squatters living near the jungle. Although there were numerous Chinese organisations in the country representing districts, Provinces, clans, mining, planting and other industries, there was no public body which represented the Chinese community as a whole. Consequently there was no unified Chinese institution to represent the Chinese either to co-operate with the Government in its efforts to combat the terrorists or to organise the Chinese community to resist the communist threats or to [refute] unfounded allegations.
>
> After attending an International Tin Conference in Europe I came back to Penang by ship in December 1948 and met Sir Henry Gurney for the first time in the island. I then returned to my home town, Kuala Lumpur, and met my Chinese colleagues in the Federal Legislative Council during a meeting of the Council in December 1948. We discussed the problems in connection with the Emergency particularly as it affected

the Chinese community and came to the conclusion that it would be essential to establish an organisation to represent all the Chinese in the country. At the same time it was felt that the establishment of such an organisation was a very delicate matter and the motive might be misunderstood by either the Federal Government or by the UMNO which represented the Malay community and was a very strong political organisation.

Sixteen Chinese Legislative Councillors decided that the best approach was to have a frank talk with the High Commissioner of the Federation of Malaya. It was then arranged to invite the late Sir Henry Gurney to a dinner to meet the Chinese Federal Legislative Councillors at the late Mr Yong Shook Lin's residence on the 15th of December, 1948.[35] Being a member of the Federal Legislative Council I was given a seat next to the High Commissioner and during dinner I tried tactfully to find out Sir Henry Gurney's reaction to the suggestion of the formation of a unified Chinese organisation embracing all the Chinese interests. To my very pleasant surprise he agreed with our views readily and urged the Chinese Legislative Councillors to initiate ways and means to form the organisation without any delay, because he wanted all the help from the Chinese to combat the Emergency.

The late Mr Yong Shook Lin, the late Mr Khoo Teck Ee[36] and I were asked to draft the Rules of the new set-up to be called the Malayan Chinese Association and to prepare a circular to be sent to the leading Chinese public bodies in the country. The circular was sent out in January 1949 in the name of the sixteen Chinese Legislative Councillors, and addressed to the Chinese Chambers of Commerce and other leading Chinese organisations in the various States, requesting them to call meetings of the representatives of the Chinese public bodies in the particular State in order to elect delegates to represent the State at the Conference to be held at the Selangor Chinese Assembly Hall, Kuala Lumpur on the 27th February 1949 to discuss the formation of the Malayan Chinese Association. The drafting of the Rules was no easy task because there was no other organisation of a similar nature, the rules of which could be used for guidance. The Rules were duly prepared by the three of us and published in the China Press on the 4th February 1949. The reaction from the Press and the public was very favourable.

On the 19th February, the Selangor Chinese Chamber of Commerce called a meeting of the representatives of registered Chinese guilds and associations in Selangor at which an Organising Committee was established and the Selangor delegates to the Conference to be held on the 27th February 1949 were elected. At this meeting it was reported that over 3,000 persons had agreed to become members of the organisation about to be formed.

On the 27th February 1949 more than 300 delegates from all over the country attended the Conference which was presided over by Mr Ee Yew Kim, a Chinese Federal Legislative Councillor. Twelve of the sixteen Chinese Federal Councillors were present. The speakers included the late Tun Tan Cheng Lock, Dato Lau Pak Khuan and myself and the speeches all stressed the necessity of forming an organisation to represent all the Chinese interests so that the Chinese as a community could maintain friendly relationship with Malays and the other races in order to assist in every way the Federal Government to fight the Communist terrorists whose victims were mostly Chinese.[37] The main object of the Malayan Chinese Association, namely to promote and maintain inter-racial goodwill and harmony in Malaya so as to ensure the peaceful progress of the nation and to foster, safeguard, advance and secure the political, social, educational, cultural, economic and other interests of the Chinese by legitimate and constitutional means were accepted with loud applause.

After deliberation for 5 hours, the Conference, while accepting the draft rules in principle decided to form a temporary Organising Committee of 100 persons with a time limit of 3 months to make preparations for the official formation of the Malayan Chinese Association after further examination of the draft rules. The late Tun Tan Cheng Lock was elected Chairman of this temporary Organising Committee with 11 Vice Chairmen from each State or Settlement, the late Mr Khoo Teck Ee was elected Hon. Treasurer and the late Mr Leong Cheung Ling and Mr Yong Shook Lin were elected joint Hon. Secretaries. The Organising Committee was to meet in Ipoh at the end of a period of 3 months.

The Conference on the 27th February 1949 was the first Chinese meeting attended by the delegates from all walks of life, at a time when the Chinese community was suspected of being un-cooperative, slurred for being cowardly, and disparaged for being neutral in a grave situation in the country. [...][38]

Despite Hau-Shik's obvious importance in the forming of the MCA, he did not begin by holding any central position, and stayed officially prominent in the organization only at the Selangor state level. To be sure, the support he enjoyed even at that level was not strong, as would be borne out by later developments.

British support for the MCA was due largely to the objective of fighting the communists. For the Chinese community, the party provided a platform for communal unity and for opposition against the Federation Agreement. It fought to limit deportation orders of Chinese by the British, and functioning as a welfare organization in many ways, it offered material aid to the sizeable squatter population and to the needy.

In his speech on the inaugural day, Tan Cheng Lock stated: "It is a matter of supreme significance and indisputable necessity that a basic purpose of this organization must be the attainment of inter-communal understanding and friendship, particularly between the Malays and Chinese."[39]

His path to that fateful meeting was quite unlike that of many others among the founders of the MCA. It saw him joining the motley PMCJA-PUTERA protests and participating in the 1949–50 Community Liaison Committee (CLC) discussions initiated by Malcolm Macdonald, the British Commissioner General, which functioned as damage control following the inter-ethnic distrust that stemmed from the exclusion of non-Malays from the Federation of Malaya Agreement, which obliged him later to lend support to Onn Ja'afar's IMP.

COMMUNITY LIAISON COMMITTEE

The CLC had begun with a meeting of 22 attendees at the home of Onn Ja'afar in Johor Bahru on 29 December 1948 to discuss ways of reversing the downward trend in inter-ethnic relations. Self-rule seemed impossible without some drastic change taking place.

> [The CLC] considered a number of ways in which a united country could be created. Tan Cheng Lock took an active part in this. New members were added from time to time, always of the highest calibre. It was an unofficial body, but by reason of the support given it by these men, and by the Government's concern, which made its offices available for meetings and its civil servants for questioning, its recommendations were treated with respect. It did much good work. Perhaps coincidentally, race relations began to improve again from the moment these men gathered at Dato Onn's to discuss the problems that faced them.[40]

One of the suggestions aired at the very first meeting was for the Malayan Chinese to follow the example of the Malays and Indians and create a national organization to represent their interests. Crucially, the CLC may have played a part in convincing Onn to adopt the tactic of opening up UMNO to non-Malay membership as a quick fix.

Things were certainly moving beyond the stalemate caused by the exclusively achieved Federation Agreement. The CLC gave to Tan Cheng Lock, after the dismal failure of the PMCJA-PUTERA, new reason to hope for a change for the better. The Straits Chinese British Association (SCBA) of which he was a key member, was no longer relevant, especially with the dismantling of the Straits Settlements through the advent of the Malayan Union. But outside the CLC, other new initiatives were brewing.

Hau-Shik had been travelling a lot throughout 1948, being "sent abroad five times in 1948 to represent Malaya in various International Tin meetings". He had, however, advocated at a public dinner held on 13 January 1948 in his honour on receiving the CBE, "the establishment of ... one organisation which could represent the whole Chinese community ... in view of the difference of conditions prevailing in the country after the war, especially as other communities had formed such organizations". As mentioned earlier, Hau-Shik had on 15 December 1948 "pleaded with Sir Henry the necessity of forming the Malayan Chinese Association". Sir Henry agreed and, under the names of the 16 Chinese Federal Legislative Councillors, a circular was sent out to the various Chinese Chambers of Commerce in the States and Settlements, urging them to establish the Malayan Chinese Association (MCA) and recruit members.[41] It seems therefore that the need for proper Chinese representation was strongly felt among different parties at the time. But organizing such a body was not possible for the aged Cheng Lock, and yet there was no one else who could really head it.

Leong Yew Koh, a Chinese community leader from Perak, and Yong Shook Lin from Kuala Lumpur agreed with Hau-Shik that it was vital that Cheng Lock be persuaded to be the first party president. Interestingly, support also came from the Chinese government, who saw the creation of an anti-communist body to replace the Malayan KMT to be very much in its interest.[42]

> Symbolic he may have been, but it would be a mistake to imagine Tan Cheng Lock as figure-head. It is customary in Chinese and Japanese organizations to conceal the chief executive, and many mistakes are made by people unaware that the man on top is not necessarily the top man. The MCA was the concern of H.S. Lee, Yong Shook Lin, Leong Yew Koh, and others constantly involved in the affairs of the capital. But particularly until 1952, Tan Cheng Lock was an active President, and one of those who were responsible for saving it from collapse a few years after its birth.[43]

As with UMNO, whose original strength lay in the defence of Malay establishments, the MCA, whose original goal was to stem communist strength, was soon in need of a larger mission. Both parties would find this in the coming of local elections, and in the promise these represented of independence for the whole country and unity for its diverse population.

> Although Tan [Cheng Lock] was elected the first president of the MCA, the Selangor MCA branch remained very much in control, something that became evident when H.S. Lee, without the concurrence of Tan and the other MCA Central Committee members, worked with UMNO to form an UMNO-MCA Alliance that contested the 1952 Kuala Lumpur Municipal Council election. Tan did not support the coalition between the MCA and UMNO, but instead threw his support behind Onn Jaafar's cross-communal Independence of Malaya Party.[44]

Fatefully, what turned the MCA into an important political force in Malayan history was exactly its political collaboration with UMNO. This began in 1952, and Hau-Shik played a major role in this, as he would in subsequent negotiations with the Malays and the British made possible by that collaboration, for a national independence that would not disfavour the Chinese.

The dominant dynamic behind these events was the Cold War. In the local context, this took the form of the Emergency. In early 1948, the MCP had begun a campaign of violence and terror, fuelled by the Federation Agreement announced in February that year. The Pan-Malayan Federation of Trade Unions that it controlled also initiated a serious of labour conflicts. But after some brutal murders carried out by the MCP on 16 June, the British authorities declared a state of emergency. This covered only Perak and Johor at first, and a concerted operation was launched to capture members of the MCP. Almost 1,000 were arrested while many others managed to slip away into the jungle. These moves appeared to wrest the initiative away from the communists, and on 18 June, the Emergency was expanded to cover the whole federation. But it remained a Malayan matter.[45]

> The Malayan Emergency might be called the Quiet War. Except for the occasional bad incident, such as the ambushing and murder in 1951 of the High Commissioner, Sir Henry Gurney, the Emergency seldom made headlines in the world press. From the world's public, there was therefore little reaction other than predictable, verbal support [for] the MCP and attacks on the British by Communist countries and left-wing groups. [...] The Emergency was a localized war fought by British and Malayans, assisted by Commonwealth countries and territories, and the predominantly Chinese MCP. There is no evidence to show active or material assistance to the MCP from outside the country, and neither was there sufficient moral or other

pressure on Britain to cause her to deflect from or moderate her intention to defeat the Communists.[46]

Some profound and lasting measures taken by the government at this time included the Emergency Regulations Ordinance of 1948 that allowed for detention without trial for up to a year.[47] Another was the creation of the Special Branch, which was—and is—the intelligence department of the police force and was the sole instrument of the government for the collection, collation, assessment and dissemination of all internal intelligence affecting the security of the country. But perhaps the most dramatic of the tactics used to fight the communist rebels was one that affected hundreds of thousands of Malayan Chinese. This was the efficacious Briggs Plan, named after the first director of operations, Lieutenant General Sir Harold Briggs. It aimed at cutting communist access to the rural Chinese community.[48] Fenced off from the jungle, these people were isolated from the communist guerillas.

> The New Villages were similar in appearance. Many of them were little more than closely packed shanty-towns, with small houses and large *kongsis* (communal dwellings) made of wood, with roofs of *atap* thatch, *lalang* or zinc, and with bare laterite roads and unfinished drains, all fenced in with barbed wire.[49]

Figures from 1954 show that 604,208 squatters had been resettled into 480 so-called "new villages", 94 "regroupment areas" and 50 "Malay regroupment areas". The overall number resettled under the Briggs Plan may have been as high as 1.2 million, placed in over 600 such settlements.[50] And it was here that the MCA came to play a deeply influential role in the "quiet war", and in the process establish for itself a base of support that would carry it through many elections in the coming decades. Many of these Chinese squatters, as mentioned earlier in this book, had over decades and desperate times settled in rural areas to become agriculturalists during periods of unemployment in the rubber, tin, and other industries. MCA aid given to these populations went on for 2½ years and amounted to 4 million Malayan dollars, with funds being derived from a lottery that it sponsored. Once it became a political party, however, this lottery was banned. But with the establishment of party branches throughout the new villages, the MCA could finally come into direct contact with the villagers, and no longer functioned merely as an external charity and welfare organization.[51] In fact, already by October 1950, the MCA had grown impressively and was claiming a membership of 150,000.[52]

> It was essential, however, that those who for so long had been exposed to the subversive influence of Communism should be given an opportunity to begin a new life where they could make a satisfactory living from the land or in a salaried job. It was also necessary for them—particularly the squatters—to develop a sense of identity with the rest of the community. The resettlement program therefore became a vast social and economic undertaking in which there was close cooperation between the civil administration, voluntary welfare organisations, and other public bodies. Health and welfare services were provided by the government and private organizations. The villagers were identified with their own defense by enrolment in a Home Guard organization. Gradually, the New Villages became economically viable communities and were given a say in the conduct of their own administrative affairs through Village councils.[53]

As local elections were being planned throughout Malaya as part of the preparation for self-rule for the colony, the communist insurgents managed their biggest success: on 6 October 1951, they ambushed and killed High Commissioner Henry Gurney. The fact that participation in the first local election, which was held in Malacca the following month, was disappointingly poor added further to the sense of despondency. The candidates were all returned unopposed. The Chinese community was not responding as positively as had been hoped to the series of measures being taken to fight the communists.[54]

It is a quirk in Malaysia's history that the two parties that would represent the two largest ethnic groups, began as social organizations and pressure groups more than as political parties. UMNO is designated an organization while the MCA is but an association. But having huge followings, with the coming of elections, it was natural that they would comfortably and conveniently transform into political parties. Signficantly, other parties formed just as elections were being introduced were indeed promoted as political parties in their names. These include the UMNO splinter parties Pan-Malaysian Islamic Party (Parti Islam Se-Malaysia, PAS) founded on 24 November 1951, and the Independence of Malaya Party (IMP), established on 16 September 1951.

COMMUNISTS AND ELECTIONS

On 31 December that year, municipal elections in Penang, a state whose population was 73 per cent Chinese, saw the Radical Party, a non-racial but pro-Chinese party, taking the most seats. The next such election was to be held in Kuala Lumpur on 16 February 1952. In a turn of events that proved a game-changer, the Kuala Lumpur Division of UMNO and the Selangor Branch of the MCA, which was very much under Hau-Shik's control, announced on 8 January 1952 that they would be contesting as a coalition. This was aimed at challenging the favourite at that time, Onn Ja'afar's new party, the nominally multiracial IMP. Ironically, the chairman of that party's founding committee was Tan Cheng Lock, the MCA's president.

In the meantime, the fight against the communists gained further momentum with the swearing in of Sir Gerald Templer on 8 February 1952, not only as High Commissioner but also as Director of Operations "to assume complete operational command over all armed forces in Malaya to bring about the defeat of the communist insurgents".[55]

The Kuala Lumpur election gave nine of 12 seats to the new coalition—the Alliance. To many in UMNO and the MCA, this now seemed the obvious path to take. The short report on the genesis of the impactful Alliance provided in *Monthly Review of Chinese Affairs*, the internal periodical brief circulated by the Secretary of Chinese Affairs in Kuala Lumpur, is illustrative of the conflicted conditions surrounding the initiative. It seemed to show that Hau-Shik himself, in coming up with the coalition, was reacting to the immediate situation, and was not strategizing for the future. The full impact of what he pulled off may have surprised even him.

> The K.L. Municipal Elections were causing little comment, in fact it began to look as if Kuala Lumpur might follow the example of Malacca and return candidates unopposed. The Parties, however, began to crystallise out and by nomination day there were 34 Candidates for 21 seats. The biggest surprise was the UMNO/MCA Merger. IMP, the Labour Party, PMU and Selangor Ratepayers Party had put forward their candidates and IMP had raised 12 Candidates for the 12 seats and was considered to be a certain winner in that no one dreamt of the possibility of UMNO and MCA joining and producing 12 Candidates.

There is no doubt that the merger was a complete surprise and that it seriously shook the IMP who immediately attacked the alliance as "Shameful", "Marriage of Convenience", etc. Such remarks were not allowed to go unchallenged by H.S. Lee, President of the Selangor MCA, and the real architect of the merger. H.S. Lee forestalled a lot of IMP criticism by saying that both parties had united on purely local Municipal Affairs and at the moment the larger issues of National Elections were not under consideration. As H.S. Lee put it.... "The Municipal Councillors will only be responsible for the running of Municipal Affairs. They are not concerned with issues such as self-government for Malaya, nationalisation of industry or mobilisation of manpower. If an improvement in the collection of night refuse and night soil is desirable the Councillors should devise ways and means to improve it and not debate whether such an improvement conforms with the political theory of Liberalism, Conservatism or Socialism."

Dato Thuraisingham, the Member of Education stood staunchly by Dato Onn and gave a very impassioned speech. He accused the two parties of wanting "the country to remain under a foreign power", "causing a split in two dignified organisations" and "that certain Chinese gentlemen because of their opposition to IMP did not want to see a free Malaya." Dato Thuraisingham was very ably answered by Mr Ong Yoke Lin, who refuted all Dato Thuraisingham's charges by such remarks as: "The UMNO and MCA not only wanted a free Malaya but wanted to free themselves from IMP domination. If there was a split in either UMNO or MCA, would not that be to the advantage of IMP?" In actual fact the merger was likely to cause a split in the IMP.

If one is to judge progress in democracy by the spirit of the give and take at the Meetings then K.L. is making good progress. This merger has, if nothing else, produced a lively interest in the elections, and lots of good "slanging matches" even vulgar ones.

> The Chinese generally favour the merger. It has heightened the antagonism between H.S. Lee and certain other Chinese Leaders, and H.S. Lee and IMP. IMP supporters refer to H.S. Lee as the "Lilliputian" and "Accuse him of sabotaging a possible MCA-IMP Alliance. H.S. Lee's Chinese critics (in particular the Hokkiens) consider him to be arrogant, and refer to MCA candidates as [...] Rice Bucket Candidates, or the Miners' Club's clique. The Central MCA with Tan Siew Sin as spokesman have frowned on the merger and considered it a breach of discipline but have apparently not thought it advisable to try and call H.S. Lee to heel. The Candidates of UMNO-MCA will get good support from the Chinese. The Selangor MCA and the Selangor Chamber of Commerce have conducted a very thorough campaign and there is little doubt that the non-English speaking Chinese will vote for the MCA candidates.[56]

Tan Cheng Lock wrote to congratulate Hau-Shik on the success of the Alliance, a success that bulldozed to the ground many of the uncertainties that post-war political developments had aroused in the major players. The electoral triumph in Kuala Lumpur for the Alliance provided a viable path towards independence from the British. It triggered the end of Cheng Lock's dealings with the IMP and with Onn Ja'afar, and led to Onn Ja'afar giving up on his new party in 1953 to form Party Negara, which like UMNO was an all-Malay organization. The Tunku cabled to say: "Alliance great achievement profiting Malaya. May it be everlasting and may it spread". Hau-Shik replied to humbly say that he was not in a position to spread the Alliance beyond Selangor, and that Cheng Lock and the Tunku "might profitably have a discussion on this matter [and] if UMNO-MCA alliance could be established in the other parts of the country, it would go a long way to achieve a united Malaya".[57]

The two party presidents did quickly meet, already on 18 March in Kuala Lumpur. It resulted in a letter to UMNO branch leaders suggesting that they contacted MCA branches to arrange cooperation in coming elections.[58] The next municipal election was in Johor Bahru, where both the local committees of UMNO and MCA quickly adopted the new formula. It proved the right thing to do. Lead by Dr Ismail Abdul Rahman, the Alliance in Johor Bahru managed to better the result in Kuala Lumpur, winning all the seats to the Johor Bahru Town Council.[59]

The MCA reorganized itself at this time to work out the practicalities of electoral cooperation with UMNO. The central committee was now reduced from 17 to six members, apart from the Chairman. Hau-Shik was, needless to say, one of them. In the round of local elections carried out in 1952–53, the MCA won 94 of the 124 seats it contested in.[60] The peninsula-wide Alliance was thus born out of the string of municipal elections.

The Alliance successes prompted Templer to offer it two positions in the Federal Executive Council. The Tunku appointed Ismail and Hau-Shik for that honour, while calling for federal elections to be held by the end of 1954. While Ismail was made Member for Lands, Mines and Communications, Hau-Shik became Member for Railways and Ports. Ismail was the only one of the "founding fathers" of Malaya who was not trained in the United Kingdom. Instead, he gained his medical degree in Queen's College at Melbourne University and was in fact marooned in Australia for the length of the Japanese Occupation of Malaya. Hau-Shik, who spent the war years in India, was of course well-versed in English culture and mannerisms, having spent years at Cambridge University studying economics. This background equipped him well in communicating and dealing with the British colonialists, and in representing British Malaya at congresses such as the International Tin Agreement.

A federal elections committee was formed by Templer in mid-1953 to which the Alliance, despite its electoral triumphs, was given only a minority role. The Alliance pushed for a more focused and fast path towards independence than the majority in the Legislature did. Instead of the suggested 92-member Council of which 44 would be elected and the rest nominated, the Tunku called for a 100-member Council that had 60 elected members.[61] He also suggested that elections be held at an unspecified date in the future. The Conference of Rulers sought a compromise with a 98-member Council with 52 elected members.

The Alliance stuck to its guns and sent a delegation to London in April 1954, led by the Tunku. The elderly Cheng Lock was advised to stay behind. But who would go instead? The negotiations were going to be tough, especially since Oliver Lyttelton, the Secretary of State for the Colonies, was not predisposed to even meet the group.

> H.S. Lee, leader or delegate to many a International Tin Conference, a member of the Legislative, familiar with the procedures and precedents of Parliament, younger and stronger, also with the complete trust of the Tengku—here was the man, and Tan stayed in Malacca.[62]

Back in Malaya, Gerald Templer took matters into his own hands and declared his adoption of a 98-member Council with 52 elected members; with elections to be held in early 1955. Lyttelton now agreed to meet the group, and conceded that "if majority rule [were] obstructed he would as High Commissioner [have] to consider appropriate steps". The victory was a small one. Also of interest was the fact that Abdul Razak Hussein, who would become Malaya's first deputy prime minister, decided during this stay in London "to leave the Government service and swim with us in the flood of political work", as the Tunku said in a letter written home to Ismail Abdul Rahman at this time.[63]

On their return, the Tunku and Hau-Shik, accompanied by Leong Yew Koh, handed over a memorandum to Templer warning him of an Alliance boycott if his declaration on the Council should become law. UMNO and the MCA then followed it up with a press statement threatening to withdraw from the Legislative Council. The threat "to take strong action such as resigning from all positions from top to bottom levels" was first raised by Hau-Shik at the UMNO-MCA Roundtable held at his home at No. 16 Golf View Road on 17 March 1954.[64] This threat was carried out by the Alliance on 18 June.

Fearing that the communists would make use of the impasse to manipulate the elections, the British quickly called for a meeting with the Tunku, Ismail and Hau-Shik on board the *HMS Alert*, anchored off Singapore's Seletar Naval Base. The three thought that they might be exiled, and began making plans for how their struggle would continue should that turn out to be the case. As Ismail remembered it, they arrived at the ship at 11 p.m. on 2 July.

> Sir Donald [MacGillivray, the new High Commissioner] was there, waiting for us in the captain's cabin. He told us that he was going on a cruise for a fortnight up the east coast of Malaya and that he wanted to see us before we left. He said he was not at all happy at the turn of events and that the Alliance by its boycott of the Government was playing into the hands of the Communists who were already taking political advantage of it. He assured us that the six nominated seats reserved at the discretion of the High Commissioner would not be used to frustrate any political party which secured majority seats at the elections. We had to think fast and although the three of us had no time to meet to discuss matters we knew that if we did not offer some sort of compromise we might be taken away

and exiled. If that were to happen, we knew the movement for independence would pass from the hands of the moderates to the hands of the extremists who because of the methods which they might employ would never achieve their goals. I therefore suggested that we were willing to show that we were responsible leaders by proposing that in exercising his discretion in nominating the six, the High Commissioner should do so only after consulting with the leader of the majority party. Sir Donald at first rejected this compromise because he said that this would fetter the discretion reserved for the High Commissioner. We said that was as far as we were prepared to concede and that we were prepared for the worst. Finally seeing that we could not be moved from our stand he agreed to think over our proposal during his voyage and would let us know his reply when he returned. It later turned out that the object of his voyage was to gauge the feelings of the East Coast Malays and if possible win them over to his side. When he found that the Malay support for Umno was absolute and that he had failed to persuade them in spite of everything, he agreed to our compromise on his return to Kuala Lumpur.[65]

The Alliance ended its boycott on 7 July, and Ismail and Hau-Shik were reinstated in the Legislative Council on 1 August. The wind appeared now to be in the Alliance's sails, and with the approaching state- and federal-level elections, other parties began showing interest in collaborating with UMNO-MCA. The Malayan Indian Congress (MIC), after failing to be accepted by the IMP, had already decided in April 1954 that it would join the Alliance. At the Alliance Roundtable held on 13 November 1954, again at Hau-Shik's house, the Tunku and Ismail shared with their comrades that at an UMNO meeting held on 15–17 October in Penang, leading members of the Pan-Malayan Labour Party had queried about the possibility of their party joining the coalition.

The Tunku had denied them that possibility because "the Alliance wanted communal parties to get together and form a united national movement". The point of this united front was to gain independence, after which "it was possible that the various parties in this national movement would break into groups according to their political philosophies". Ismail added that his objection to the Labour Party was over the issue of nationalization of resources; and when he raised it with them, they said they were prepared to forego nationalization, which he thought strange since that would involved them giving up on their principles.

Discussions were indeed ongoing at this time at subnational levels between UMNO-MCA and the MIC and the Labour Party, and the Roundtable decided that it would be best for discussions to take place at the local level first, and for the state-level Alliance to then decide on the inclusion of these subnational parties. The Secretary, T.H. Tan, informed the Roundtable that the Radical Party in Penang under Dr Lim Chong Eu, for example, had in fact on being rejected spots on the Alliance National Council that was soon to be formed, responded in the correct manner by joining the Penang Alliance.[66]

With federal election on the way, the Alliance now moved towards securing the support needed for independence to be possible within four years. Months of discussions at various levels led by early 1955 to the MIC becoming an official member of the Alliance.[67] In March that year, the colonial government announced that elections would take place on 27 July.

The manifesto that the Alliance put together for the occasion was a very thorough one. While considering the interests of the various communities—and these included most crucially the issues of citizenship and education where the Chinese were concerned—, it highlighted the longing for Malayan independence to take the heat off the other issues.[68]

To afford a sense of the pathos and ethos of the Alliance in 1955, a shortened transcript of the Radio Malaya broadcast that Hau-Shik delivered on 13 July "on behalf of the UMNO-MCA-MIC Alliance", is provided below. Interestingly, the gaining of independence by all neighbouring countries is used to highlight the anomaly of British Malaya still remaining under colonial rule. Equally interesting is the sad fact that Hau-Shik's criticism of the types of rhetoric used by opposition parties appears so relevant in describing Malaysian politics at this point of writing, in 2019, after the fall of UMNO from power. It would appear that there is a constant in political polarization in the country, which six decades of nation building has failed to dismantle.

> [...] Ever since the formation of the Alliance in Kuala Lumpur in 1952 the electors have supported the Alliance in every election which has enabled the Alliance in the past to win all the elections. In some of the elections, notably the last State Elections in Johore and Trengganu and the last Settlement Election in Penang, every Alliance candidate was returned with large majorities, and not a single candidate from other Parties was returned. In the elections held so far the Alliance published manifestoes appertaining to the affairs which are the concern of the various Towns, Municipalities, Settlement and States. This time the Alliance took very great care in producing our manifesto and Book of Guidance outlining our policies in all the principal matters which any responsible government must face. I would like just to touch upon a few of the main features of our policies.
>
> Our Book of Guidance is called "The Road of Independence" because we place independence uppermost in our minds. Looking round our neighbouring countries we find that those countries which have no greater importance than Malaya in the world have emerged after the second world war as free and independent nations. Malaya must therefore gain her

independence since the peoples of Malaya have not only the right but also the will, ability and integrity to govern themselves. The Alliance therefore has pledged to achieve independence by constitutional means within the next four years. We are convinced that only independence will give the peoples of Malaya the sense of responsibility, so that by our joint efforts Malaya will be developed rapidly to take the place with the other nations in the world for the benefit of not only the Malayan people but for the benefit of the world at large. Independence for Malaya does not mean that Malaya will stand aloof in isolation. Indeed it is the policy of the Alliance that an independent Malaya will remain a member of the British Commonwealth so that Malaya, treated as an equal partner in the great Commonwealth, will strengthen the ties amongst the constituent members, thus contributing to the welfare of mankind.

The Alliance has stated emphatically to uphold the positions of Their Highnesses the Rules as Constitutional Rulers in their respective States and Heads of the Muslim religion. As Constitutional Ruler, occupying the highest position of respect and dignity, His Highness will be the symbol of loyalty from his subjects, and as Head of the Muslim religion, His Highness will be in a position to maintain the very great importance attached to it by a very great many people in this country.

The Alliance has also declared that the present emergency must be terminated at the earliest moment so that peace can be restored to the country. When peace is restored the country will then be able to spend the very large sums of money, previously required to fight the emergency, towards the expansion of our education, health and social services. Moreover, when the emergency is terminated the people can devote their time and energy towards the economic development of the vast areas in the Federation in order to increase our national wealth. Fully realising that in the economic progress of the country there must be the closest co-operation and happy relationship between capital and labour, the Alliance has pledged that the welfare of the workers must be regarded as of paramount importance. Each worker must be rewarded with a reasonable wage for his work. There must be schemes to guard against unemployment. It is axiomatic that [a] happy and contented labour force is a prerequisite to the productive capacity of any industry. [...]

The other Parties have not devoted their time to criticising our programme. One Party has been preaching racial differences. How can any responsible politician say things which are aimed at creating a cleavage between the two largest races in the country? Another Party has been using religion as the main platform. Surely in the year 1955, the people have advanced far enough to accept the principle of religious tolerance. Yet another Party has been using purely local matters which only concern municipalities and towns as their main appeal to the voters. If the voters were to elect such candidates they would elect persons whose vision cannot see beyond the limits of their parish. This coming election is a Federal Election. The electorate will elect their representatives to sit in the Federal Legislative Council which decides policies for the Federation as a whole. Any parochial outlook would only serve to show that the person cannot see the wood for the trees.

Regarding independent candidates, it only shows that they cannot obtain the support of any Party. They are responsible to nobody except themselves. They appear to be persons of individualism. Individuality can never hope to achieve cohesion in policies which will affect the daily life of everyone in the Federation of Malaya.[69]

THE MERDEKA COMPACT

The Alliance formula turned out clearly to be the one favoured by the Federation's diverse population at this time. On Election Day, 27 July 1955, the coalition swept all the 52 seats on offer except one which went to the Islamist PMIP. Furthermore, the turnout averaged an impressive 80 per cent.[70]

With this strong mandate, the Alliance's leaders could now prepare for, and to gain independence for the Federation without undue delay. After being Member for Railways and Ports in the Executive Council since 1953, Hau-Shik now became Minister of Transport under Chief Minister cum Home Affairs Minister Tunku Abdul Rahman. The important portfolios of Economic Affairs and of Defence were still reserved for nominated members. The others in Tunku's Cabinet were Ismail Abdul Rahman (Natural Resources), Abdul Razak Hussein (Education), Leong Yew Koh (Health and Social Welfare), V.T Sambanthan (Labour), Suleiman Abdul Rahman (Local Government, Housing and Town Planning), Sardon Jubir (Works), and Ong Yoke Lin (Posts and Telecommunications).

At UMNO's general assembly held in mid-December that year, it was decided just a week before the Tunku was to meet the leader of the Malayan communists, Chin Peng, in Baling in Perak State, that independence be achieved by 31 August 1957. There was no need to wait till the next election was almost due.

The Baling Talks were held on the afternoon of 28 December and finalized the next morning. No agreement could be reached. In fact, Chin Peng himself would later suggest that the Tunku was merely using the meeting with him to gain further legitimacy in the eyes of the British.[71] The Tunku also admitted that the talk "gave my campaign to end the Emergency a real boost".[72]

At this critical stage in the process, trouble was brewing for Hau-Shik in his home base. The Selangor Branch Working Committee had asked for the party's Central Working Committee to decide on the constitutionality of the selection on 3 September 1955 of the 43 members of the Kuala Lumpur District Sub-Branch Committee. The Central Working Committee held an emergency meeting at the Chinese Assembly Hall in Kuala Lumpur to discuss the matter. The extremely heated meeting, from which the major interested parties, namely Yong Pung How, Ong Yoke Lin, Lee Hau-Shik and Leung Cheung Ling (president of the Federation of Selangor Guilds and Associations), were after some time asked to withdraw, ended with a vote for the Chairman, Tan Cheng Lock, to decide on the matter, after private meetings with Hau-Shik and Ong Yoke Lin.[73]

On 14 October 1955, the matter was resolved. After discussions with the two men, Tan Cheng Lock made the decision that the "only possible solution" to the grievances between the two men was to enlarge the district sub-branch committee from 43 to 50 members.[74]

At a meeting of the MCA Selangor Branch Association Committee (4th Term) held at the Chinese Assembly Hall on 18 December 1955, Hau-Shik, who was chairman, could not attend due to his "absence from Malaya", and instead asked for a speech of his to be read out. However, a motion to deny him this courtesy was made by Ng Ek Teong and seconded by Yong Pung How, *and carried unanimously*. Yong Pung How then proposed for a Working Committee to be formed to which would be delegated "all the power for the management and conduct of the Branch Association's business". The motion was seconded by Gary Wang, and carried out. Ong Yoke Lin, being the only name proposed by the assembly for the chairmanship, was chosen by default to succeed Hau-Shik. It was also decided that nominations for election as representatives to the General Committee of the MCA Headquarters be done in writing to be handed in seven days before the next meeting, which was duly decided to be held two weeks hence, i.e. on 2 January 1956.[75] Eighteen names were forwarded in this manner, 16 by Yong Pung How and two by Gary Wang. This being equal to the number of positions to be filled, no balloting was needed for all the 18 to become representatives to HQ. All the 32 members present at this second meeting agreed, and the whole process was over within 15 minutes.[76]

The loss of his chairmanship over Selangor MCA would have upset Hau-Shik a great deal, but he would not have had time to deal with it immediately, being in the midst of planning for his long trip with the Alliance delegation to London to negotiate on the conditions and the timing for independence. On New Year's Day 1956, a group of ten—four Alliance men and four representatives of the sultans, and one secretary for each of the two groups—left by boat for Karachi from whence they flew on to London. The Alliance men were Tunku Abdul Rahman himself, Ismail Abdul Rahman, Abdul Razak Hussein and Lee Hau-Shik.

The negotiations with the British were concluded to the delegation's satisfaction on 8 February, incidentally the Tunku's birthday.[77] It was agreed that 31 August 1957 would be Merdeka Day—"if possible", the final words being added by the Tunku to seal the deal with their counterparts. Along the way, self-government for the Federation was to be granted. This took place in April, and with that Hau-Shik became Minister of Finance.[78]

But a month before Merdeka, Selangor MCA, in what turned out to be a rowdy scenario, elected members to the general committee of its sub-branch. Through the adoption of a bloc voting system, Ong Yoke Lin's people—70 of them, known as the "young blood"—were elected while all 61 "old guards" nominees led among others by Douglas Lee, Hau-Shik's eldest son, were rejected. It appeared that what was clearly an attempt by Lee's camp to regain control had failed.[79]

The next step in the vital process of gaining independence was the creation of a Constitution. For this purpose, the Reid Commission was formed in March 1955. Such a body had been asked for by the Alliance, who had put forth the idea already in 1953. A petition sent to the Rulers on 31 August 1954 for a Special Independent Commission to be appointed to review the Constitution, had met with their approval.[80] Consisting of Lord Reid as chairman, Sir Ivor Jennings from the United Kingdom, Sir William McKell from Australia, Justice B. Malik from India and Justice Abdul Hamid from Pakistan, the Commission's job was to work out a Constitution befitting the unique political dynamics of Malaya. Canada was to have participated as well, but apparently its government felt that it did not have a competent enough representative to send for the job. Between June and October of 1956, the Commission held 118 sessions throughout the length of the peninsula, and collected 131 written memoranda from Malayan organizations and individuals.[81] It then withdrew to Rome to prepare its report. This was published in February 1957.[82]

It was to be expected that the Commission would lay its emphasis somewhat differently from the consociational position that the Alliance had developed by this time. It was quite clear that the MCA did not cohere the Chinese community as strongly as UMNO represented the Malay community; and it was also obvious that the wishes of the Malay community and of the Rulers were often at odds with those of the minorities. Most significantly, the Reid Report considered the country from a multiracial aspect while the Alliance Compact, steered by UMNO, "emphasized the symbolic and substantive Malay character of independent Malaya".[83] This meant differences in how issues of languages and schools, Malay special position, the status of the Rulers and of Islam, Malay land reservations and the granting of citizenship were approached.

New compromises had to be made—within the member parties of the Alliance, within the Alliance Party itself, and between the Alliance and the British colonialists. Much has been written about the compromises that were reached at this point in time to allow for Merdeka to be achieved by the set date, and there is no real need to repeat them here.

And so, Merdeka was achieved, to great pomp and promise, on 31 August 1957. The first Cabinet retained Hau-Shik as Minister of Finance, while his UMNO partner in the Executive Council, Ismal Abdul Rahman, was sent to New York and Washington D.C. to represent the new country as its Ambassador to the United States and its first Permanent Representative to the United Nations.

But to reach an understanding of how wise the compromises made to attain Merdeka were, and how well they succeeded, one would have to consider how this new nation developed over the coming decades. The 1960s, especially, with the expansion from Malaya to Malaysia, first with Singapore and then without, while being threatened by Indonesia, and ending with the racial riots of 13 May 1969, were to a substantive extent, consequences of the hurried compromises made in the 1950s. The new political formula constructed between 1969 and 1974, which included the extension of the Alliance to include as many as 14 parties in the shape of the Barisan Nasional; the carving out of Kuala Lumpur into a federal territory; the heavy amendments made to the Constitution in 1971, and to parliamentary practices; the adopting of draconian laws to control the mass media and student and other civil society movements; and the initiation of the comprehensive New Economic Policy (NEP), in many ways may be used to pass judgement on the Merdeka Compact and to highlight its limitations and naiveté. But then, that would be grossly ungenerous and unfair. The history of a nation does not move like an arrow, in a straight and predictable trajectory; and politics is nothing if not strategic responses to the pressing expediencies and unique challenges of the day. In Malaysia's case, history would appear to be dialectical in its path dependence more than anything else. In any case, the Constitution and the Merdeka Compact did achieve its immediate goals, and did provide sufficient stability to the nation, if not as much individual liberty and economic prosperity as the founding fathers may have hoped for.

But a simple comparison of the election results between 1955, when the Alliance did so well on their Merdeka ticket, and 1959, does show that much was not right with the Alliance. It was true that the MCA was not pulling its weight and, as had been suspected, did not enjoy the support of large segments of the Chinese Malayan population; but it was equally true that Malay support for UMNO was not as solid as had been claimed. Too many key issues were still unresolved.

State legislature elections held over five weeks in July 1959 had no doubt seen the Alliance winning 207 of the 282 seats, but its share of the popular vote amounted only to 55 per cent. In the east-coast states of Kelantan and Trengganu, the Alliance lost heavily, dropping in support from 78.1 per cent to 31.4 per cent of the votes in Kelantan, and from 84.9 per cent to 37.4 per cent in Trengganu.[84] This was probably a post-Merdeka honest reaction in these states—and elsewhere—to the compromises made in the west-coast states. Most clearly, in the 1955 elections, while the federal electorate was estimated to include only 16 per cent non-Malays, as much as 33 per cent of Alliance candidates were non-Malays, i.e. 17 of 52. There were good reasons for this to have been the case, although the arguments would not have concerned grassroots voters too much. For example, the Alliance was aiming "to increase Chinese participation and to overcome their reluctance to accept citizenship on minority terms"; and "the Chinese were contributing most of the campaign funds".[85]

The MCA, now under the Penang-based Dr Lim Chong Eu who had in March 1958 surprisingly taken over the party presidency from the ageing Tan Cheng Lock, was under pressure to defend the education policy. There were now 104 federal seats being contested. The Alliance National Council planned to allocate 30 or 31 of these to the MCA, but Chong Eu called for 35 to be kept for the party. His arguments were mainly that the MCA having a chance at holding one-third of the seats would be a guarantee against attempts to change the Constitution, and that the Chinese electorate had since 1955 grown from 11.2 per cent to 35.6 per cent and should therefore be represented accordingly. The demands also included one on the Chinese language as medium of instruction and examination to be fully recognized in the schools.

The public release of Chong Eu's demands five days before nomination day on 15 July angered the Tunku, who in retaliation threatened to move ahead without the MCA. To avoid such a crisis, the MCA backed down and settled for 31 seats. Also, the MCA candidates were to be chosen by the Tunku and the issue of Chinese education would not be included in the manifesto. This damaged MCA morale and cohesion tremendously and it went on to win only 19 of these 31 seats in the elections.[86] A large group, led by Yong Pung How, resigned from the party, some in order to contest as independent candidates.[87] As a whole, the Alliance did retain a two-thirds majority by winning 74 of the 104 seats in the election, albeit with popular support of only 51.7 per cent.

ECONOMICS AND STABILITY

Notably, while the allocation of seats within the Alliance and the choice of issues for inclusion in the manifesto were points of contention, economic policy did not appear to be on the forefront of debate. As T.H. Silcock said of the 1959 election:

> Economic policy is not generally a matter of disagreement. Since one of the main avowed aims of policy is the raising of the

relative economic position of the Malays, this is, superficially at least, surprising. It suggests that the non-Malays do not take very seriously the risk of major institutional changes—internal discrimination and preferences such as have been introduced in Indonesia and the Philippines, and are content to allow such money as the finance minister agrees to spare to be spent on rural development and Malay business projects.[88]

What this also suggests is that economic thinking in the initial period of Malayan nationhood was a conservative and cautious one. In fact, a comparison of the 1947 census with that from 1957 shows that the rural Malay population had actually been growing while the non-Malays were urbanizing to the same extent. This made a progressive programme based on urban development all the harder to propose. As E.K. Fisk put it when studying the Malayan economy in the early 1960s:

[In] so far as the opportunities for transfer to the advanced sectors of the economy are in the urban areas—and this is very largely true, due to the limitation on expansion of the estate and mining sectors—the Malay section of the rural population has been very much less affected by them than the non-Malays. [...] Despite the general prosperity of the Malayan economy and the general rise in the level of the GNP, the trend of productivity in the backward peasant sector has been downwards rather than upwards.

Add to this the fact that Malaya now has a responsible elected government, and that the rural Malays are the dominant factor in the majority of the electorates, so that they in effect determine who shall govern the country, and there is a very strong limiting factor in the range of economic policy that is politically practicable. Concentration of government resources on the promotion of the advanced sectors of the economy, however attractive from the point of view of its effect on the growth of the GNP, could not be undertaken by a responsible government with an eye to future elections unless the trend of distribution of the offtake from the backward sectors to the advanced sectors could be dramatically changed in favour of the rural Malays. [...] The result is that all current planning is coloured by the necessity for a clear and rapid improvement in the lot of the rural Malays, with a consequent heavy emphasis on the development of the backward sectors of the economy, rather than on the bouyant and advanced sectors.[89]

Politically, the economic-policy options were clear to the Alliance. There was little choice. In fact, under the second five-year plan initiated in 1960, Deputy Prime Minister Razak announced that 50 per cent of public investment would be spent on rural development. But be that as it may, it should be noted that the 1957 census also revealed that as much as 9.6 per cent of the working population in the Federation was employed in secondary industries, exceeded in Asia at that time only by Japan and India.[90]

Hau-Shik's role from 1955 to 1959 was as Minister of Finance. To grasp his thoughts and his state of mind, we should turn to some of his key speeches made at this point, and to the budget statements delivered in the two years during which he was in charge of the finances of independent Malaya. These texts also reflect the stances and the hopes of the first Alliance government.

During the November 1956 assembly of the Legislative Council, Hau-Shik introduced the federal budget for the following year. He announced that the budget was formulated for the achieving of economic goals enunciated in the Alliance manifesto of 1955, and called it "an act of faith", given uncertainties in the primary product markets. However, despite the election promise to maintain a balanced budget while expanding the economy, it was now clear that this first budget would show a deficit. There were three major challenges that had had to be considered: instability of the revenue; a constantly increasing trend of expenditure; and a need for new capital investment on a vast scale. Plans were afoot, he said, to raise financing, and this in turn would required the Federation to maintain a "reputation for financial stability in world opinion". The first depended on external factors, and revenue from the primary product sector was expected to fall. Hau-Shik was also in the process of negotiating for further aid from the United Kingdom to finance Emergency expenditure.

Successive deficits in 1956 and 1957 resulting from rising expenditure and falling revenue also called for the taxation structure to be reviewed. This involved direct taxation, a registration fee on car imports, and the withdrawal of tax exemptions on lotteries. Export duties would not be increased while import duties and excise duties (on local products) would be. Lastly, Hau-Shik pointed out that the financial situation of the State and Settlement governments was bad.[91]

A year later, on 4–14 December 1957, the Minister presented a somewhat more optimistic and upbeat economic future: "… the point I wish to make is that, in considering the general level of expenditure and revenue proposed for 1958, our financial foundations are stronger in terms of reserves than they were two years ago".

The government's sources of revenue had three sources, namely, income tax; import duty in tobacco and cigarettes; and export duty on rubber; followed by import duty on petrol and export duty on tin and tin-in-ore. Hau-Shik argued against taxes being raised this time, be these direct or indirect ones:

> 1958 may be a year of consolidation rather than rapid expansion of economic activity and emergency expenditure may be substantially reduced in 1959. Let us have a little time

to settle down to our newly accomplished independence before taking important steps to ask our people to tighten their belts which were probably fairly loosened during the celebrations of Merdeka.[92]

Costs to be incurred for maintaining the armed forces and the police, as well as for education would not be deferred due to the central importance of the functions involved. Where federal expenditures were concerned, despite support in kind by the United Kingdom, the Emergency had since 1948 cost the federal government a billion Straits dollars.

Hau-Shik also revealed that the government had started seeking advice on the establishing of a central bank. Malaya had also applied for membership in the International Monetary Fund (IMF), the International Bank for Reconstruction and Development (IBRD), and the International Finance Corporation (IFC). All the three applications had been accepted, subject to compliance with the terms and conditions of acceptance. Inflation was a serious worry, and domestic spending had been increasing and bank deposits falling despite exports payments being in decline. He warned:

> It has been accepted by experts in economics that the rise in wages can never catch up with the rise in inflation. Once the game commences it would be like a vicious circle going round and round, fast and fast, until, like a sputnik rocket, it crashes, to disaster.[93]

Hau-Shik ended his speech in eloquent manner, and his concluding and poignant words from that occasion are worth repeating here.

> In conclusion, Sir, may I say that throughout this survey I have made no attempt to gloss over unpalatable facts or to draw a

rosier picture than the facts warrant, taking into consideration our present and future financial circumstances. It is my considered view that the facts give solid grounds for confidence in our budgetary proposals and in the future generally provided we do not rush to spend our reserves to finance ambitious capital projects in the public sector, and to allow major increases in domestic expenditure until various factors which will enlarge our available resources begin to operate. Those factors are: a change in market conditions to facilitate a load flotation, a reduction in emergency expenditure, and the maintenance of prices and production of our main export commodities. The Federation has made enormous advances in the field of social services during the past two years and we are determined to make further advances. To do so, though, we must demonstrate to all who are willing to share in our long-term prosperity that we are not going to jeopardise our stability by running before we walk. We want to climb steadily upwards and not up and down. The foundations of a building are more important than the superstructure. The Alliance Government is determined that the foundation of the independent Federation shall be so well and truly laid so that the rising generation will be able to build as high as they wish and, perhaps, to look back on us as statesmen rather than politicians.[94]

Bank Negara Tanah Melayu (Central Bank of Malaya) would in fact come into being on 24 January 1959.[95] Hau-Shik, who had been "closely associated ever since the matter first came to public attention in the Report of 1954 by the International Bank Mission", spoke at the launch, attended by some of the Rulers, Cabinet Ministers, Ambassadors from several Commonwealth and other countries. He made it a point to thank Commonwealth Bank of Australia for "making available members of its own staff to plan and work in the Bank Negara Tanah Melayu during its formative years".

> The establishment of the Central Bank is the most important step that we have taken in the field of finance and economics since Independence Day. It marks the beginning of a new era in the development of the Federation's financial and banking system. It means that we assume the full financial responsibilities that flow from political independence and that we are determined to make provision to manage our financial affairs on a sound and solid basis. [...] In the last resort, it must be the Government, rather than the Central Bank, which carries responsibility for determining the nation's financial policies, but we have provided that there shall be, as there should be in a true democracy, public ventilation in the unlikely event of any serious disagreement arising between the Government of the day and the Board of the Central Bank on matters of financial policy.⁹⁶

Despite certain inherited limitations due to the currency system, the Central Bank succeeded very well in what it was meant to do at that point in time, i.e. in raising capital investments from the domestic market. As a later evaluation by economist John Drabble would show:

> Initially, the Bank was not empowered to issue a separate Malayan currency as this would have involved withdrawal from the Currency Board which covered Malaya, Singapore and the British Borneo territories. The Board was not finally dissolved until June 1967, by which time Singapore had left the Federation.
> The Central Bank's early focus was on regulating and encouraging the activities of commercial banks in Malaya, in particular to expand their role as lenders to domestic borrowers. This it did so successfully that total loans and advances grew by nearly 84 per cent from 1960 to 1963.

> [...] Looking overall at the sources of economic growth, increase in capital stock emerges as by far the most important, accounting, in Malaya, for 70 per cent of the growth of GDP, followed at a great distance by additional labour inputs (17 per cent), and the balance (13 per cent) from improvements to technology, education and organisation.[97]

Perhaps it is appropriate to end this narration of Malaya's first Minister of Finance by highlighting a couple of points he made on 7 May 1957, when tabling the Industrial Development Policy, and which appeared to be central to his strategic thinking where the economic well-being of the country was concerned.

> [...] There is a need to secure a rapid increase in the productivity of this country to provide adequate employment opportunities for a growing population; that this expansion is required not only in primary production but also more particularly in secondary industry, that this expansion is likely to require larger industrial units than the traditional industrial structure in the Federation has developed; and that Government promotion and protection of secondary industry is a necessary condition of the development on the scale required.

But most poignantly, Hau-Shik stated—and it was a point that he had long reiterated—that whatever the plans for development may be, their success depended "above all other considerations, on [the government's] ability to maintain confidence, domestically and abroad, in the financial and economic stability of this country".[98]

NOTES

1. Yao Souchou, *The Malayan Emergency: Essays on a Small Distant War* (Copenhagen: NIAS Press, 2016), p. 11.

2. H.S. Lee papers 3(c)/3/48. Major-General Ralph Hone was the Chief Civil Affairs Officer Malaya (CCAO (M)) under the British Military Administration that ran British Malaya immediately after the war. He was thus the man responsible for the civil administration of the newly re-acquired colony.
3. H.S. Lee papers 9(a)/9/22.
4. H.S. Lee papers 121/6/38. Thomas Lee disclosed privately to the author in June 2019: "My mother had a hard time looking after all of us during the war years as refugees in India."
5. K.G. Tregonning, "Tan Cheng Lock: A Malayan Nationalist", *Journal of Southeast Asian Studies* 10, no. 1 (March 1979): 49.
6. Tan Cheng Lock, "Letter from the President of the Association to the Secretary of State for the Colonies, London", in *Malayan Problems from a Chinese Point of View by Tan Cheng Lock*, by C.Q. Lee (Singapore: Tannsco, 1947a), p. 23.
7. Tregonning (1979), p. 50.
8. Leong Yee Fong, "Chinese Politics and Political Parties in Colonial Malaya, 1920–1940: A Study of the Kuomintang and the Malayan Communist Party", Masters thesis, Universiti Sains Malaysia, Penang, 1977, p. 195.
9. H.S. Lee papers 9(a) 9.9/2.
10. Ibid.
11. Lee Kam Hing, "Lee Hau Shik: His Life and Times", in *Chinese Diaspora since Admiral Zheng He: With Special Reference to Maritime Asia*, by Leo Suryadinata (Singapore: Chinese Heritage Centre, 2007), pp. 155–56.
12. Leong (1977), p. 195.
13. Paul H. Kratoska, *The Japanese Occupation of Malaya: A Social and Economic History* (London: Allen & Unwin, 1998), p. 318.
14. Veena Sikri, *India and Malaysia: Intertwined Strands* (Singapore and India: Institute of Southeast Asian Studies and Manohar, 2013), pp. 307–8.
15. Victor Purcell, *The Position of the Chinese in Southeast Asia*, Secretariat Paper no. 3, Eleventh Conference, Institute of Pacific Relations,

Lucknow, India, 3–15 October 1950 (New York: International Secretariat, Institute of Pacific Relations, 1950), p. 49.
16. Kratoska (1998), p. 292.
17. Zainah Anwar, *Legacy of Honour* (Kuala Lumpur: Yayasan Mohamed Noah, 2011), pp. 108–17.
18. Barbara Watson Andaya and Leonard Y. Andaya, *A History of Malaysia* (London: Macmillan Press, 1982), p. 254.
19. Zainah (2011), pp. 118–19.
20. Donna J. Amoroso, *Traditionalism and the Ascendancy of the Malay Ruling Class in Colonial Malaya* (Petaling Jaya and Singapore: SIRD and NUS Press, 2014), pp. 136–39.
21. Zainah (2011), p. 119.
22. Amoroso (2014), p. 164.
23. A.J. Stockwell, *British Policy and Malay Politics During the Malayan Union Experiment 1945–1948*, The Malaysian Branch of the Royal Asiatic Society Monograph No. 8 (Kuala Lumpur: MBRAS, 1979), p. 179.
24. K.J. Ratnam, *Communalism and the Political Process in Malaya* (Singapore and Kuala Lumpur: University of Malaya Press, 1965), pp. 52–53.
25. Mohamed Noordin Sopiee, *From Malayan Union to Singapore Separation: Political Unification in the Malaysia Region 1945–65* (Kuala Lumpur: University of Malaya Press, 2005 (1976)), pp. 38–49.
26. Ibid., pp. 41–43.
27. C.F. Yong and R.B. McKenna, *The Kuomintang Movement in British Malaya, 1912–1949* (Singapore: Singapore University Press, National University of Singapore, 1990), pp. 204–6.
28. Ibid., p. 213.
29. Ibid., p. 215.
30. Tang Eng Teik, "Malaysian Literature in Chinese: A Survey", in *The Chinese in Malaysia*, edited by Lee Kam Hing and Tan Chee-Beng (Shah Alam: Oxford University Press, 2000), p. 345.
31. Yong and McKenna (1990), pp. 216–18. See also Goh Jing Pei, "'Chineseness' in Malaysian Chinese Education Discourse: The Case

of Chung Ling High School", Master of Arts thesis, Graduate School of the University of Oregon, 2012, https://scholarsbank.uoregon.edu/xmlui/bitstream/handle/1794/12443/Goh_oregon_0171N_10437.pdf;sequence=1.
32. C.F. Yong, *Tan Kah-Kee: The Making of an Overseas Chinese Legend* (Singapore: Oxford University Press, 1987), pp. 330–33.
33. Yao Souchou, *The Malayan Emergency: Essays on a Small Distant War* (Copenhagen: NIAS Press, 2016), p. 18.
34. Lee Kam Hing and Heng Pek Koon, "The Chinese in the Malaysian Political System", in *The Chinese in Malaysia*, edited by Lee Kam Hing and Tan Chee-Beng (Shah Alam: Oxford University Press, 2000), p. 200.
35. Yong Shook Lin (1898–1955) was a lawyer, whose family were Hakka tin mine owners in Selangor. He was Chairman of the Bar Council of Malaya. See http://shooklin.com.my/history-milestones/yong-shook-lin/. His son, Yong Pung How, also a lawyer trained in Cambridge, was Chief Justice of Singapore (1990–2006), after working 20 years in finance. See http://www.straitstimes.com/politics/how-i-became-chief-justice.
36. Khoo Teck Ee (1902–1953), born in Penang, was a lawyer and banker, and president of the Malayan Estate Owners' Association. Before the war, he served on the Sanitary Advisory Council and the Selangor State Council.
37. Tan Cheng Lock passed away on 13 December 1960 at the age of 77. Lau Pak Khuan (1894–1971) was a Hakka who worked as a labourer on coming to Malaya at the age of 17, and ended up owning and managing many tin mines in the state of Perak. Lau was co-founder of the Chung Khiaw Bank and the Overseas Union Bank. He was the first chairman of Perak MCA. On 10 April 1949, at a meeting of the Perak MCA, a grenade was thrown at the stage. Tan Cheng Lock was badly injured, along with four others: "He lost two pints of blood, his shoulder was broken and he was severely shocked" (Tregonning 1979, p. 61). Lau left the MCA in 1956 on the eve of Malayan independence over disagreements on citizenship rights and

the status of the Chinese language. See Ho Tak Ming, *Ipoh: When Tin was King* (Ipoh: Perak Academy, 2009), pp. 623–624, 699.
38. H.S. Lee papers 3(c) 3.48.
39. K.J. Ratnam, *Communalism and the Political Process in Malaya* (Singapore and Kuala Lumpur: University of Malaya Press, 1965), p. 154.
40. K.G. Tregonning, "Tan Cheng Lock: A Malayan Nationalist", *Journal of Southeast Asian Studies* 10, no. 1 (March 1979): 58.
41. Ibid., p. 59.
42. Ibid., p. 60.
43. Ibid., p. 61. Leong Yew Koh (1888–1963) was a lawyer, born in Sungei Siput, Perak. He was the first Secretary-General of the MCA, and still holds the distinction of being the only non-Malay to have served as Yang di-Pertua Negeri in a Malay majority state. He held that position in Malacca from 1957 to 1959.
44. Tan Miau Ing, "The Formation of the Malayan Chinese Association (MCA) Revisited", *Journal of the Malaysian Branch of the Royal Asiatic Society* 88, part 2, no. 309 (December 2015a): 124.
45. P.B.G. Waller, *Notes on the Malayan Emergency: Strategies and Organization of the Opposing Forces*, Operations Analysis Department Research Memorandum OAD-RM 4923-8, Prepared for U.S. Army Research Office, Durham, North Carolina 27706 (Menlo Park, California: Stanford Research Institute, 1967), p. 7.
46. Ibid., p. 49.
47. Although repealed in 1960 when the Emergency ended, the post-colonial government replaced it with the Internal Security Act. This stayed in place for over 50 years and was in its turn repealed and replaced by the Security Offences (Special Measures) Act in 2012. Detention without trial, however, remains the defining feature.
48. Waller (1967), p. 76.
49. Ray Nyce, *Chinese New Villages in Malaya: A Community Study* (Singapore: Malaysian Sociological Research Institute, 1973), p. 51.
50. Ibid., pp. 48 and 61.
51. Ibid., pp. 174–76.

52. *Monthly Review of Chinese Affairs*, FCO141-7626/43-48, Secretary of Chinese Affairs, Federation of Malaya, October 1950, p. 10.
53. Waller (1967), p. 76.
54. *Monthly Review of Chinese Affairs*, FCO141-7628-59, Secretary of Chinese Affairs, Federation of Malaya, January 1952, p. 12.
55. Leon Comber, *Malaya's Secret Police 1945–60: The Role of the Special Branch in the Malayan Emergency* (Clayton and Singapore: Monash University Press and ISEAS, 2008), p. 177.
56. *Monthly Review of Chinese Affairs*, FCO141-7628-59, Secretary of Chinese Affairs, Federation of Malaya, January 1952, pp. 12–13.
57. Tregonning (1979), p. 68.
58. Ibid.
59. Ooi Kee Beng, *The Reluctant Politician: Tun Dr Ismail and His Time* (Singapore: Institute of Southeast Asian Studies, 2006), pp. 57–58.
60. Tregonning (1979), pp. 68–69.
61. Ooi (2006), p. 64.
62. Tregonning (1979), p. 71.
63. Ibid., p. 72.
64. H.S. Lee papers 73.5/17.
65. Ooi (2006), pp. 66–67.
66. H.S. Lee papers 73.5/20.
67. The Alliance Manifesto for the 4th Kuala Lumpur municipal elections to be held on 4 December 1954, for example, declared that the MIC KL Branch, had joined the Alliance. See H.S. Lee papers 1.676b.
68. See, for example, Heng Pek Koon, *Chinese Politics in Malaysia: A History of the Malaysian Chinese Association* (Singapore: Oxford University Press, 1988), pp. 200–19, for a good summary of this.
69. H.S. Lee papers 2.56/1–4. This speech was recorded two days in advance, on 11 July.
70. Ooi (2006), pp. 69–70.
71. Ibid., pp. 71–74.
72. Tunku Abdul Rahman Putra Al-Haj, *Political Awakenings* (Petaling Jaya: Pelanduk Publications, 1986), p. 67.
73. H.S. Lee papers 698.1/2–17.

74. "MCA Row: A Happy Ending", *Straits Times*, 14 October 1965, p. 4.
75. H.S. Lee papers 74.3/31–36.
76. H.S. Lee papers 74.3/37–39.
77. See details of issues discussed in Ooi (2006), pp. 75–81.
78. The cost to the family, especially for his wife and the younger children, was a heavy one. As Thomas Lee recalls it to the author in June 2019: "After the war, when my father was very busy in Malaya, my mother spent most time with her friends and her side of the family playing mahjong. My younger brother (Alex) and I hardly saw her or father because when they got home, we were asleep as we went early to school the next day."
79. "Ong and Young Blood Defeat Old Guard", *Straits Times*, 29 July 1959.
80. H.S. Lee papers 16.68/1–9.
81. Gordon P. Means, *Malaysian Politics* (London: Hodder and Stoughton, 1999), pp. 173–92. A good rendering of the significance and achievement of the Reid Commission can be found in Joseph M. Fernando, *The Making of the Malayan Constitution*, MBRAS Monograph no. 31 (Kuala Lumpur: Malaysian Branch of the Royal Asiatic Society, 2007 (2002)). For a thorough study of the subject, see Fernando's doctoral thesis, "The Emergence of the Alliance and the Making of Malaya's Independence Constitution, 1948–1957", PhD thesis, Royal Holloway, University of London, The British Library, British Thesis Service, 1995.
82. *Report of the Federation of Malaya Constitutional Commission 1957*, Colonial no. 330 (London: Colonial Office, 1957).
83. Heng (1988), p. 228.
84. T.H. Silcock, "Communal and Party Structure", in *The Political Ecocomy of Independent Malaya: A Case-Study in Development*, edited by T.H. Silcock and E.K. Fisk (Canberra: Australian National University, 1963), pp. 18–19. Silcock points out that the triumph of the Islamist PMIP in Kelantan and Trengganu influenced the direction of the government's economic policy, stimulating "a strong emphasis on rural development in the second five-year plan".

85. Ibid., p. 15.
86. Ooi (2006), pp. 125–27.
87. Margaret Roff, "The Malaysian Chinese Association, 1948–65", *Journal of Southeast Asian History* 6, no. 2, Modern Malaysia (September 1965): 40–53.
88. Silcock (1963), pp. 14–15.
89. E.K. Fisk, "Features of the Rural Economy", in *The Political Economy of Independent Malaya: A Case-Study in Development*, edited by T.H. Silcock and E.K. Fisk (Canberra: Australian National University, 1963), p. 164.
90. E.L. Wheelwright, "Industrialization in Malaya", in *The Political Economy of Independent Malaya: A Case-Study in Development*, edited by T.H. Silcock and E.K. Fisk (Canberra: Australian National University, 1963), p. 210.
91. H.S. Lee papers 2.28/1–11.
92. H.S. Lee papers 2.22/1–9.
93. H.S. Lee papers 2.122/1–9.
94. Ibid.
95. Don McKenna, "Financial Developments since Independence", in *The Political Economy of Independent Malaya: A Case-Study in Development*, edited by T.H. Silcock and E.K. Fisk (Canberra: Australian National University, 1963), p. 196.
96. H.S. Lee papers 2.103.
97. John H. Drabble, *An Economic History of Malaysia, c. 1800–1990: The Transition to Modern Economic Growth* (Canberra: Australian National University, 2000), pp. 174–75.
98. H.S. Lee papers 2.108/1–9.

EPILOGUE

AFTER 1959

> Undeterred by such complicating factors, the UMNO-dominated Alliance government decided that the basis for creating a future citizenry would be Malaya's traditional culture and heritage, meaning Malay language and culture. Non-Malays, however, argued that a more appropriate path was to work towards a Malaysian identity that would reflect the country's multi-ethnic background.
>
> —Barbara and Leonard Andaya[1]

In July 1959, just before elections took place, it was announced by the respected New York publication *Pick's Currency Year* that Malaya was Asia's wealthiest nation. That conclusion was drawn based on "circulation of currency per head of population". Coming at 24th spot after 23 western countries, Malaya was classed as "moderately wealthy", just a nose ahead of Hong Kong, and far ahead of Japan, Siam and Ceylon.[2] While such a ranking may not say very much about the socioeconomic situation experienced by the population at large, it does commend Malaya's new government for carrying out a smooth transition in the finances of the country.

Much credit should be given to its finance minister for the achievement. In fact, for this and other contributions to the new nation, Hau-Shik was granted the KBE (Knight Commander of the British Empire) in 1957, for which he was entitled to use "Sir" before his name, and then at the second anniversary of Merdeka, in 1959, just before he left politics, he was awarded the SMN (Sri Maharaja Mangku Negara), which carried the title of "Tun". Indeed, one could say that the conferment of the latter title signalled the end of his career as a politician, a career he was drawn into more by circumstances than by choice.

The ranking by *Pick's* also suggests that Malaya was in a healthy enough economic state as it entered the turbulent 1960s, although the election results of 1959 did show that there was much unrest and that the Alliance did not stand on as solid foundations as might have been assumed by the British.

But then, despite the political rhetoric, the founding of Malaya should not be seen as an endgame, neither for the retreating colonialist nor for the leaders of the new nation. The problem of Singapore and the northern Borneo territories still had to be solved, and any solution would require the Federation of Malaya to function as a pillar for it.

This transitional nature of politics and of nation building in the region, it can be said, was poignantly expressed in the various transitions in Lee Hau-Shik's life. His time as a politician was almost over once independence was gained in 1957, and his loss of control over the Malayan Chinese Association (MCA) in Selangor in 1955 was already a sign that his interests and talents lay more in the corporate world of dealings between elites rather than in the daily rough-and-tumble dirty world of politics.

In his first press interview, given a month after leaving office in August 1959, Hau-Shik told the *Straits Times* that he was "fully satisfied that the country's finances were sound".

This was because the Federation's currency was backed by 110 per cent security, and the country was only partly developed, meaning "there is such a lot of potentialities". Hau-Shik informed the public that he would have stood for the parliamentary election if his health had permitted it. He had been suffering from laryngitis that whole year: "I was advised by medical specialists that I would lose my voice completely if I took part in electioneering." He denied that his decision resulted from the crisis triggered earlier in the year by Lim Chong Eu's demands for more seats for the MCA.

> I remained as a minister during and after the MCA crisis because I agreed with the Alliance. I would have resigned if I had disagreed. This is a clear indication of my stand.

Still convinced that the MCA was the only party that could represent the Chinese, Hau-Shik said that the party was not "a dead horse" as claimed by those who had resigned from it following the crisis—and this included his son, Douglas Lee: "If the association was no good, they should stay behind and try and improve it. No organisaton is perfect and it is up to the members to try to make it as perfect as possible."[3]

Fading from the political scene after his term as finance minister, his influence continued in the world of big business and finance as had been the case when he first came to Malaya over three decades earlier. Two of his sons—Douglas Lee and Alex Lee—continued to have a considerable impact on Malaysian politics, while his bank, the Development & Commercial (D&C) Bank, which began with a paid-up capital of $5 million and was registered on 4 October 1965, became a major financial institution in the country before being absorbed into the RHB Banking Group.

The tin market was in fact in a bad state in the late 1950s when he left politics, and Hau-Shik moved into property development by forming a company called On Tai. Apparently, it was the Tunku who, knowing as much as he did about Hau-Shik, suggested that his retiring companion should set up a bank, and requested that Tan Siew Sin, Hau-Shik's successor as finance minister, issue him a banking license.

By the time Hau-Shik stepped down in 1984, D&C was the fifth largest commercial bank in Malaysia, represented by 28 branches. But by 1990, the Lee family had divested all its major corporate holdings. As Lee Kam Hing notes: "It could be said that except for some small, private companies held by various members of the family, the business which Lee Kwai-Lim and Lee Hau-Shik created did not survive."[4]

The newspaper that Hau-Shik started in 1946 on his return from India, *China Press*, of which he was chairman for 42 years, ran into difficulties on several occasions, and it was eventually sold off. Today, it is Malaysia's second largest newspaper, and has since 2001 been owned by the MCA's investment arm, Huaren.

As his son Thomas Lee remembers him, Hau-Shik was "scrupulously honest, maybe to a fault". A workaholic, he had very little time left over for his seven sons and two daughters. During the handing over of his father's papers to ISEAS Library on 5 May 2010, Thomas Lee shared a few of his memories with the audience.[5]

> I saw more of him after his political life had ended and in fact served on the boards of *China Press* and D&C Bank with him as Chairman. My directorship of *China Press* ended abruptly. The Company needed a loan from HSBC, and the bank wanted all the directors to guarantee the loan. I objected and said it was unreasonable to expect me to do so. He replied that any director refusing to guarantee should resign. He got a letter of

resignation on the same day, which he accepted without saying a word. That was the way he was.

My father and I shared the same passion for golf, and I must say some of the happiest times we had with him were the family reunions at Cameron Highlands. There, family and friends played golf with him and he entertained the family and all the many friends to champagne and drinks at his Cameron Highlands house. A very organised person. We were all told, Breakfast at 7, Golf at 8, Lunch at 1, Tea at 4, Cocktails at 7 and Dinner at 8. [...] Even in his old age, he enjoyed his drinks. The secret, he told me is to alternate your drinks. Whisky one day, brandy the next.

Although golf was his favourite sport, Hau-Shik practised riding, rowing and taijiquan, convinced that a bad spine was the cause of all illnesses. One of his greatest social contributions was in aiding the setting up of the Lady Templer Hospital in Kuala Lumpur, where he, in 1960, became the Chairman of its Board of Governors.

Tun Sir Colonel (twice over) Henry Lee Hau-Shik, a man of many and varied achievements, and one of the signitories of the Declaration of Independence—in fact his is the only Chinese name on the document—passed away on 22 June 1988 at the age of 87, after failing to recover from a gall bladder operation. A month-long exhibition was staged at Muzium Negara after his demise, as the country's show of appreciation for its only foreign-born founding father. As Thomas Lee remembers it:

His funeral took place at the Cheras Crematorium on Sunday 26 June 1988, attended by his family, his close friends and people from many sections of Malaysian Society. Many condolence messages were received. Hundreds of people attended his wake which lasted a few days, and the Government allowed his funeral procession to go past his favourite places in Kuala Lumpur. A main street in Kuala Lumpur, the High Street, was renamed after him in his honour.[6]

* * *

As pointed out in Barbara and Leonard Andaya's third edition of *A History of Malaysia*, the years between 1942 and 1969 were an extended period during which a new nation was being negotiated into being from among the British colonies in Southeast Asia. The Japanese occupation was no doubt a short one, but its significance was profound, and out of those 2½ years were unleashed forces that elbowed for space and recognition until the violent rioting in May 1969 in Kuala Lumpur led to a deep restructuring of the country and changed the nature—and aims—of inter-ethnic interactions. The stability of the system constructed under the Second Malaysia Plan (1970–75) kept the UMNO-dominated Barisan Nasional as the ruling party until 9 May 2018.

The wish to establish a New Malaysia after that date will need many revisits by scholars and politicians to the period before 1969—and definitely to the period before 1959—to mine for understandings, not so much about what went wrong, for that would be an unfair and unscholarly disregard of the multi-dimensionality of history and the endless expediencies of politics, but for the broader reasons why things happened the way they did and for deeper insights into the consequences.

Knowing the stories and motivations of key players is a fruitful asset in such an exploration, for ingrained official histories and their counteracting narratives cannot be relied upon to provide new answers and new inspiration the way the telling of contextualized individual lives do—and cannot help doing. In that sense, the life of Hau-Shik will continue to provide much material to inspire future Malaysians with.

NOTES

1. Barbara Watson Andaya and Leonard Y. Andaya, *A History of Malaysia*, 3rd ed. (London: Palgrave Macmillan, 2017 (1982)), p. 295.
2. "Malaya is Wealthiest Asian Nation", *Straits Times*, 30 July 1959.
3. "Tun Lee Confident of Malaya's Financial Future", *Straits Times*, 4 September 1959, p. 5.
4. Lee Kam Hing, "Lee Hau Shik: His Life and Times", in *Chinese Diaspora since Admiral Zheng He: With Special Reference to Maritime Asia*, by Leo Suryadinata (Singapore: Chinese Heritage Centre, 2007), pp. 161–64.
5. I am most grateful to Thomas Lee for permission to use these comments in this book.
6. From private notes made by Thomas Lee, and shared with the author.

APPENDIX

LEE HAU SHIK—POSITIONS HELD BEFORE THE SECOND WORLD WAR

YEAR	POSITION	ORGANIZATION
1933–36	President	Selangor Miners' Association
1933–41	Member	Federated Malay States Mines Chamber of Commerce
1936–41	President	Selangor Chinese Chamber of Commerce
1937–41	President	Selangor China Relief Fund Association
1938–39	Member	Federation of China Relief Fund of the South Seas
1939–41	Vice President	Kwangtung Overseas Chinese Relief Fund Association
1939–41	President	Selangor Kwangtung Association
1939–41	Vice President	Selangor Chinese Assembly Hall
1933–36, 1940–41	Member	Kuala Lumpur Sanitary Board
1939–41	Member	Malayan Patriotic Fund Selangor Branch

| 1941 | Chinese representative | Information and Publicity Bureau, Air Raid Precaution |
| 1941 | Chief | Air Raid Warden, Kuala Lumpur |

Source: Tan Miau Ing, "Tun Sir Henry Lee Hau Shik and [the] Anti-Japanese Movement", unpublished, 2009.

BIBLIOGRAPHY

Akashi, Yoji. 1970. *The Nanyang Chinese National Salvation Movement, 1937–1941*. International Studies, East Asian Series Research Publication, no. 5. Center for East Asian Studies, University of Kansas. New York: Paragon Book Gallery.

Amoroso, Donna J. 2014. *Traditionalism and the Ascendancy of the Malaya Ruling Class in Colonial Malaya*. Petaling Jaya and Singapore: SIRD and NUS Press.

Andaya, Barbara Watson and Leonard Y. Andaya. 1982. *A History of Malaysia*. London: Macmillan Press.

———. 2017 (1982). *A History of Malaysia*, 3rd ed. London: Palgrave Macmillan.

Bauer, P.T. 1944. "Some Aspects of the Malayan Rubber Slump 1929–1933". *Economica* 11, no. 44 (November): 190–98.

Booth, Anne E. 2007. *Colonial Legacies: Economic and Social Development in East and Southeast Asia*. Honolulu: University of Hawai'i Press.

Chaphekar, S.G. 1955. *A Brief Study of the Burma Campaign 1943–45*. Poona: Maharashtra Militarisation Board.

Cheah Boon Kheng. 1977. "Some Aspects of the Interregnum in Malaya (14 August–3 September 1945)". *Journal of Southeast Asian Studies* 8, no. 1 (March): 48–74.

———. 1980. "The Social Impact of the Japanese Occupation of Malaya (1942–1945)". In *Southeast Asia under Japanese Occupation*, edited by Alfred W. McCoy. New Haven: Yale University Southeast Asia Studies, pp. 91–117.

———. 1992. *From PKI to the Comintern, 1924–1941: The Apprenticeship of the Malayan Communist Party. Selected Documents and Discussion Compiled and Edited with Introductions by Cheah Boon Kheng.* New York: Southeast Asia Program, Cornell University.

———. 2012 (1983). *Red Star over Malaya: Resistance and Social Conflict During and After the Japanese Occupation of Malaya, 1941–46*, 4th ed. Singapore: NUS Press.

Chin Peng. 2003. *My Side of History (as told to Ian Ward and Norma Miraflor).* Singapore: Media Masters.

Comber, Leon. 2008. *Malaya's Secret Police 1945–60: The Role of the Special Branch in the Malayan Emergency.* Clayton and Singapore: Monash University Press and ISEAS.

Cooper, Eunice. 1951. "Urbanization in Malaya". *Population Studies* 5, no. 2: 117–31.

Dillard, J.L. 1973. *Perspectives on Black English.* The Hague: Mouton & Co.

Donnison, F.S.V. 1956. *British Military Administration in the Far East 1943–46.* History of the Second World War (United Kingdom Military Series), edited by J.R.M. Butler. London: Her Majesty's Stationery Office.

Drabble, John H. 2000. *An Economic History of Malaysia, c. 1800–1990: The Transition to Modern Economic Growth.* Canberra: Australian National University.

Emerson, Rupert. (1970) 1937. *Malaysia: A Study of Direct and Indirect Rule.* Kuala Lumpur: University of Malaya Press. Original publisher: The Macmillan Company.

Fernando, Joseph M. 1995. "The Emergence of the Alliance and the Making of Malaya's Independence Constitution, 1948–1957". PhD thesis, Royal Holloway, University of London. The British Library. British Thesis Service.

———. 2007 (2002). *The Making of the Malayan Constitution.* MBRAS Monograph no. 31. Kuala Lumpur: Malaysian Branch of the Royal Asiatic Society.

Fifield, H. Russell. 1958. *The Diplomacy of Southeast Asia: 1945–1958.* New York: Harper & Brothers.

Fisk, E.K. 1963. "Features of the Rural Economy". In *The Political Economy of Independent Malaya: A Case-Study in Development*, edited by T.H. Silcock and E.K. Fisk. Canberra: Australian National University, pp. 163–75.

Ford, Douglas. 2006. *Britain's Secret War Against Japan, 1937–1945*. Oxford: Routledge.

Frey, Marc, Ronald W. Pruessen, and Tan Tai Yong, eds. 2003. *The Transformation of Southeast Asia: International Perspectives on Decolonization*. New York and London: M.E. Sharpe.

Fujio, Hara. 2003. *Malayan Chinese & China: Conversion in Identity Consciousness 1945–1957*. Singapore: Singapore University Press, National University of Singapore.

———. 2013. "An Alternative View of Tun Sir H.S. Lee: The Anti-Japanese Movement and His Dedication to China". *Journal of Asia-Pacific Studies* (Waseda University) 20 (February): 53–63.

Glover, Patrick. 1939. "Low Malayan Tin Quota Leads to Chinese Unemployment". *Far Eastern Survey* 8, no. 13 (21 June).

Goh Jing Pei. 2012. "'Chineseness' in Malaysian Chinese Education Discourse: The Case of Chung Ling High School". Master of Arts thesis, Graduate School of the University of Oregon. https://scholarsbank.uoregon.edu/xmlui/bitstream/handle/1794/12443/Goh_oregon_0171N_10437.pdf;sequence=1.

Goh Keng Swee. 1940. *The Economic Front from a Malayan Point of View*. Singapore: Singapore Authority.

Heng Pek Koon. 1988. *Chinese Politics in Malaysia: A History of the Malaysian Chinese Association*. Singapore: Oxford University Press.

Ho Tak Ming. 2009. *Ipoh: When Tin was King*. Ipoh: Perak Academy.

Itagaki, Yoichi. 1962. "Some Aspects of the Japanese Policy for Malaya under the Occupation, with Special Reference to Nationalism". In *Papers on Malayan History*, edited by K.G. Tregonning. Singapore: Journal South-East Asian History, pp. 256–267.

James, Lawrence. 1998 (1994). *The Rise and Fall of the British Empire*. London: Abacus.

Kahin, George McTurnan. 2003. *Nationalism and Revolution in Indonesia*. New York: SEAP Publications.

Kam, Samuel W.S. 2011. *Through Wars and Peace: From the Gunfire of the Sino-Japanese War to the Golden Oil of Malaya. A Memoir by Samuel S.W. Kam at 96*. Hong Kong: Peace Book Company.

Kaur, Amarjit. 1980. "The Impact of Railroads on the Malayan Economy, 1874–1941". *Journal of Asian Studies* 39, no. 4 (August): 693–710.

Khor Jin Keong, Neil and Khoo Keat Siew. 2004. *The Penang Po Leung Kuk: Chinese Women, Prostitution and a Welfare Organisation*. Malayan Branch of the Royal Asiatic Society. Monograph no. 37.

King, Arthur W. 1940. "Changes in the Tin Mining Industry of Malaya". *Geography* 25, no. 3 (September): pp. 130–34.

King, Sam. 1992. *Tiger Balm King: The Life and Times of Aw Boon Haw*. Singapore and Kuala Lumpur: Times Books International.

Kratoska, Paul H. 1998. *The Japanese Occupation of Malaya: A Social and Economic History*. London: Allen & Unwin.

Lai Ah Eng. 1986. *Peasants, Proletarians and Prostitutes: A Preliminary Investigation into the Work of Chinese Women in Colonial Malaya*. Research Notes and Discussion Paper no. 59. Singapore: Institute of Southeast Asian Studies.

Lee C.Q. 1947. *Malayan Problems from a Chinese Point of View by Tan Cheng Lock*. Singapore: Tannsco.

Lee Kam Hing. 2007. "Lee Hau Shik: His Life and Times". In *Chinese Diaspora since Admiral Zheng He: With Special Reference to Maritime Asia*, by Leo Suryadinata. Singapore: Chinese Heritage Centre, pp. 151–67.

Lee Kam Hing and Heng Pek Koon. 2000. "The Chinese in the Malaysian Political System". In *The Chinese in Malaysia*, edited by Lee Kam Hing and Tan Chee-Beng. Shah Alam: Oxford University Press, pp. 194–227.

Lee Kam Hing and Tan Chee-Beng, eds. 2000. *The Chinese in Malaysia*. Shah Alam: Oxford University Press.

Lee Kuok Tiung and Mohd Safar Hasim. 2015. "Peranan Akhbar Cina dalam Artikulasi Isu-isu Sejarah dan Pembentukan Negara-Bangsa" [The Role of Chinese Newspapers in the Articulation of Historical Issues and the Formation of the Nation-State]. *Jurnal Komunikasi* [Malaysian Journal of Communication] 31, no. 1: 257–80.

Lee, Sharon M. 1989. "Female Immigrants and Labor in Colonial Malaya: 1860–1947". *International Migration Review* 23, no. 2 (Summer): 309–31.

Leong, Stephen Mun Yoon. 1977. "Sources, Agencies and Manifestations of Overseas Chinese Nationalism in Malaya, 1937–1941". PhD thesis, University of California, Los Angeles.

Leong Yee Fong. 1977. "Chinese Politics and Political Parties in Colonial Malaya, 1920–1940: A Study of the Kuomintang and the Malayan Communist Party". Masters thesis, Universiti Sains Malaysia, Penang. [Microfilm at ISEAS Library].

———. 1999. *Labour and Trade Unionism in Colonial Malaya: A Study of the Socio-Economic and Political Bases of the Malayan Labour Movement, 1930–1957*. Penang: Penerbit Universiti Sains Malaysia.

Loh Fook Seng, Philip. 1975. *Seeds of Separatism: Educational Policy in Malaya 1874–1940*. East Asian Social Science Monographs. Kuala Lumpur: Oxford University Press.

Loh Wei Leng. 2002. "The Colonial State and Business: The Policy Environment in Malaya in the Inter-War Years". *Journal of Southeast Asian Studies* 33, no. 2 (June): 243–56.

Manderson, Lenore. 2002. *Sickness and the State: Health and Illness in Colonial Malaya 1870–1940*. Cambridge: Cambridge University Press.

McKenna, Don. 1963. "Financial Developments since Independence". In *The Political Economy of Independent Malaya: A Case-Study in Development*, edited by T.H. Silcock and E.K. Fisk. Canberra: Australian National University.

Means, Gordon P. 1999. *Malaysian Politics*. London: Hodder and Stoughton.

Mohamed Amin and Malcolm Caldwell. 1977. *Malaya: The Making of a Neo-Colony*. Nottingham: Bertrand Russell Peace Foundation for Spokesman Books.

Mohamed Noordin Sopiee. 2005 (1976). *From Malayan Union to Singapore Separation: Political Unification in the Malaysia Region 1945–65*. Kuala Lumpur: University of Malaya Press.

Naoki, Soda. 2008. "Indigenizing Colonial Knowledge: The Formation of Pan-Malay Identity in British Malaya". PhD thesis, Graduate School of Asian and African Area Studies, Kyoto University.

Netherlands Information Bureau. 1947(?). *The Political Events in the Republic of Indonesia: A Review of the Developments in the Indonesian Republic (Java and Sumatra) since the Japanese Surrender.*

Nyce, Ray. 1973. *Chinese New Villages in Malaya: A Community Study.* Singapore: Malaysian Sociological Research Institute.

Ooi Keat Gin. 2013. *Post-War Borneo, 1945–1950: Nationalism, Empire and State-Building.* London and New York: Routledge.

Ooi Kee Beng. 2006. *The Reluctant Politician: Tun Dr Ismail and His Time.* Singapore: Institute of Southeast Asian Studies.

Parmer, J. Norman. 1957. "Trade Unions in Malaya". *Annals of the American Academy of Political and Social Science* 310. Current Issues in International Labour Relations (March): 142–50.

———. 1960. *Colonial Labor Policy and Administration: A History of Labor in the Rubber Plantation Industry in Malaya, c. 1910–1941.* New York: Association of Asian Studies.

Purcell, Victor. 1945. "Malaya under the British". *World Affairs* 108, no. 1 (March): 33–38.

———. 1949. "Malaya's Problems Today". *World Affairs* 112, no. 2 (Summer): 46–48.

———. 1950. *The Position of the Chinese in Southeast Asia.* Secretariat Paper no. 3. Eleventh Conference, Institute of Pacific Relations, Lucknow, India, 3–15 October 1950. New York: International Secretariat, Institute of Pacific Relations.

Puthucheary, Dominic and Jomo K.S. 2010 (1998). *No Cowardly Past. James Puthucheary: Writings, Poems, Commentaries.* Kuala Lumpur: Insan and SIRD.

Puthucheary, James Joseph. 1960 (2004). *Ownership and Control in the Malayan Economy.* Petaling Jaya: SIRD.

Ratnam, K.J. 1965. *Communalism and the Political Process in Malaya.* Singapore and Kuala Lumpur: University of Malaya Press.

Reid, Anthony. 1971. "The Birth of the Republic of Sumatra". *Indonesia* 12 (October): 21–46.

———. 1979. *The Blood of the People: Revolution and the End of Traditional Rule in Northern Sumatra.* Kuala Lumpur: Oxford University Press.

Ricklefs, M.C., Bruce Lockhart, Albert Lau, Portia Reyes, and Maitrii Aung-Thwin. 2010. *A New History of Southeast Asia*. New York: Palgrave Macmillan.

Roberts, Jayde Lin. 2016. *Mapping Chinese Rangoon: Place and Nation among the Sino-Burmese*. Seattle and London: University of Washington Press.

Roff, Margaret. 1965. "The Malaysian Chinese Association, 1948–65". *Journal of Southeast Asian History* 6, no. 2, Modern Malaysia (September): 40–53.

Sikri, Veena. 2013. *India and Malaysia: Intertwined Strands*. Singapore and India: Institute of Southeast Asian Studies and Manohar.

Silcock, T.H. 1963. "Communal and Party Structure". In *The Political Economy of Independent Malaya: A Case-Study in Development*, edited by T.H. Silcock and E.K. Fisk. Canberra: Australian National University, pp. 1–27.

Silcock, T.H. and E.K. Fisk, eds. 1963. *The Political Economy of Independent Malaya: A Case-Study in Development*. Canberra: Australian National University.

Silverstein, Josef. 1966. "The Importance of the Japanese Occupation of Southeast Asia to the Political Scientist". In *Southeast Asia in World War II: Four Essays*, edited by Josef Silverstein. New Haven: Yale University Southeast Asia Studies, pp. 1–11.

———, ed. 1966. *Southeast Asia in World War II: Four Essays*. New Haven: Yale University Southeast Asia Studies.

Smith, Simon C. 1995. *British Relations with the Malay Rulers from Decentralization to Malayan Independence 1930–1957*. Kuala Lumpur: Oxford University Press.

Stockwell, A.J. 1979. *British Policy and Malay Politics During the Malayan Union Experiment 1945–1948*. The Malaysian Branch of the Royal Asiatic Society Monograph No. 8. Kuala Lumpur: MBRAS.

Stubbs, Richard. 1976. *The UMNO, MCA and the Early Years of the Malayan Emergency, 1948–1955*. Department of Political Science, St. Francis Xavier University, Antigonish, Nova Scotia, Canada.

Tan Cheng Lock. 1947a. "Letter from the President of the Association to the Secretary of State for the Colonies, London". In *Malayan*

Problems from a Chinese Point of View by Tan Cheng Lock, by C.Q. Lee. Singapore: Tannsco, pp. 4–41.

———. 1947b. "Memorandum on the 'Quisling' Resolution passed by the Malayan Association, Bombay, on 16th November 1942". In *Malayan Problems from a Chinese Point of View by Tan Cheng Lock*, by C.Q. Lee. Singapore: Tannsco.

———. 1947c. "The Oversea-Chinese Association, India. President's Speech at Inaugural Meeting, Bombay, 24th September 1943". In *Malayan Problems from a Chinese Point of View by Tan Cheng Lock*, by C.Q. Lee. Singapore: Tannsco, pp. 1–3.

Tan Chong Tee. 1995. *Force 136: Story of a WWII Resistance Fighter*, translated by Lee Watt Sim and Clara Show. (Original title: *Wo yu 136 budiu*). Singapore: Asiapac Publication.

Tan Miau Ing. 2009. "Tun Sir Henry Lee Hau Shik and [the] Anti-Japanese Movement". Unpublished.

———. 2015a. "The Formation of the Malayan Chinese Association (MCA) Revisited". *Journal of the Malaysian Branch of the Royal Asiatic Society* 88, part 2, no. 309 (December): 107–26.

———. 2015b. "Perjuangan seorang pelarian perang: Lee Hau Shik semasa pendudukan tentera jepun, 1941–1945". *Jurnal Jabatan Sejarah Universiti Malaya* 24, no. 2: 31–50. http://www.myjurnal.my/filebank/published_article/42830/3_Lee_Hau_Shik_semasa_Pendudukan_Jepun.pdf (accessed 8 July 2016).

———. 2018. *Tun Sir Henry Lee Hau Shik: Ahli Perniagaan dan Tokoh Politik*. Kuala Lumpur: UM Press.

Tan Pek Leng. 2008. *Land to Till: The Chinese in the Agricultural Economy of Malaysia*. Kuala Lumpur: Centre for Malaysian Studies.

Tang Eng Teik. 2000. "Malaysian Literature in Chinese: A Survey". In *The Chinese in Malaysia*, edited by Lee Kam Hing and Tan Chee-Beng. Shah Alam: Oxford University Press, pp. 342–69.

Tawfik Tun Dr Ismail and Ooi Kee Beng. 2015. *Drifting into Politics: The Unfinished Memoirs of Tun Dr Ismail Abdul Rahman*. Singapore: ISEAS – Yusof Ishak Institute.

Tertrais, Hugues. 2003. "France and the Associated States of Indochina, 1945–1955". In *The Transformation of Southeast Asia: International Perspectives on Decolonization*, edited by Marc Frey, Ronald W. Pruessen, and Tan Tai Yong. New York and London: M.E. Sharpe, pp. 72–82.

Tregonning, K.G., ed. 1962. "Papers on Malayan History". Papers submitted to the First International Conference of South-East Asian Historians, Singapore, January 1961. Singapore: *Journal Southeast Asian History*.

———. 1963. "Straits Tin: A Brief Account of the First Seventy-five Years of The Straits Trading Company, Limited". *Journal of the Malayan Branch of the Royal Asiatic Society* 36, no. 1 (May): 79–152.

———. 1964. *A History of Modern Malaysia and Singapore*. Singapore: Eastern Universities Press.

———. 1979. "Tan Cheng Lock: A Malayan Nationalist". *Journal of Southeast Asian Studies* 10, no. 1 (March): 25–76.

Tsuji, Masanobu. 1988. *Singapore 1941–1942: The Japanese Version of the Malayan Campaign of World War II*. Singapore: Oxford University Press.

Tully, John. 2011. *The Devil's Milk: A Social History of Rubber*. New York: Monthly Review Press.

Tunku Abdul Rahman Putra Al-Haj. 1986. *Political Awakenings*. Petaling Jaya: Pelanduk Publications.

Turnbull, C.M. 1974. "British Planning for Post-war Malaya". *Journal of Southeast Asia Studies* 5, no. 2, The Centenary of British Intervention in Malaya (September): 239–54.

Vinacke, Harold M. 1959. *A History of the Far East in Modern Times*. 6th ed. New York: Appleton-Century-Crofts.

Waller, P.B.G. 1967. *Notes on the Malayan Emergency: Strategies and Organization of the Opposing Forces*. Operations Analysis Department Research Memorandum OAD-RM 4923-8. Prepared for U.S. Army Research Office, Durham, North Carolina 27706. Menlo Park, California: Stanford Research Institute.

Wang Gungwu. 2000. "Political Heritage and Nation Building". *Journal of the Malaysian Branch of the Royal Asiatic Society* 73, no. 2: 5–30.

Ward, A.H.C., Raymond W. Chu, and Janet Salaff. 1994. *The Memoirs of Tan Kah-Kee*. Singapore: Singapore University Press.

Wheelwright, E.L. 1963. "Industrialization in Malaya". In *The Political Economy of Independent Malaya: A Case-Study in Development*, edited by T.H. Silcock and E.K. Fisk. Canberra: Australian National University, pp. 211–41.

Winstedt, R.O. 1935. *A History of Malaya*. Singapore and Kuala Lumpur: Maricans & Sons, pp. 222–36.

Wu Xiao An. 2010. *Chinese Business in the Making of a Malay State, 1882–1941: Kedah and Penang*. Singapore: NUS Press.

Yao Souchou. 2016. *The Malayan Emergency: Essays on a Small Distant War*. Copenhagen: NIAS Press.

Yong, C.F. 1987. *Tan Kah-Kee: The Making of an Overseas Chinese Legend*. Singapore: Oxford University Press.

Yong, C.F. and R.B. McKenna. 1990. *The Kuomintang Movement in British Malaya, 1912–1949*. Singapore: Singapore University Press, National University of Singapore.

Zainah Anwar. 2011. *Legacy of Honour*. Kuala Lumpur: Yayasan Mohamed Noah.

Zheng, Victor, Wong Siu-lun, and Sun Wen-bin. 2004. "Beyond Family Enterprise: The Early Phase of H.S. Lee's Business and Political Career". Conference paper of *The 5th Conference of the International Society for the Study of Chinese Overseas*, 10 May 2004. http://hub.hku.hk/handle/10722/93554.

WEBSITES

ASIAWEEK. Undated. "Newsmakers". http://edition.cnn.com/ASIANOW/asiaweek/96/0906/feat7.html (accessed 6 September 1996).

Business Circle. Undated. "Pioneer in the Palm Oil Industry". https://www.businesscircle.com.my/pioneer-in-the-palm-oil-industry-2/.

Document Cloud. 1943. "Cairo Communiqué". Records of the Department of State Relating to World War II, 1939–1945 "740.0011 European War 1939/32623", 1 December 1943. http://www.documentcloud.org/documents/1341677-cairo-declaration-1943.html.

Goh Jing Pei. 2012. "'Chineseness' in Malaysian Chinese Education Discourse: The Case of Chung Ling High School". Master of Arts thesis, Graduate School of the University of Oregon. https://scholarsbank.uoregon.edu/xmlui/bitstream/handle/1794/12443/Goh_oregon_0171N_10437.pdf;sequence=1.

National Archives. Undated. "Statistical Information about Casualties of the Vietnam War". https://www.archives.gov/research/military/vietnam-war/casualty-statistics.html.

Proclamation Defining Terms of Japanese Surrender issued, at Potsdam, 26 July 1945. https://www.documentcloud.org/documents/1341676-potsdam-declaration-1945.html#search/p1/Potsdam.

Roodo (樂多閱讀): 蔣緯國口述自傳 [Chiang Wei-kuo's oral history]. http://reader.roodo.com/dh4733/archives/14989829.html (accessed 23 January 2011).

Shook Lin & Bok. Undated. "Yong Shook Lin". http://shooklin.com.my/history-milestones/yong-shook-lin/.

Straits Times, The. 1959. "Malaya is the Wealthiest Asian Nation", 3 July 1959. http://eresources.nlb.gov.sg/newspapers/Digitised/Article/straitstimes19590730-1.2.12 (accessed 30 July 1959).

United Nations. 2006. United Nations Member States, 3 July 2006. http://www.un.org/press/en/2006/org1469.doc.htm.

White. Theodore H. 1942. "Chiang Kai-Shek: The Leader of Fighting China Plays a Commanding Role in the Allied War Effort and the Destiny of All Asia". *Life* magazine, 2 March 1942. http://www.cbi-theater.com/life030242/life030242.html.

Yong Pung How. 2016. "How I became Chief Justice". *Straits Times*, 20 March 2016. http://www.straitstimes.com/politics/how-i-became-chief-justice.

PRIMARY SOURCES

Private papers (accessed at ISEAS Library, ISEAS – Yusof Ishak Institute, Singapore)
  Tun Dr Ismail Abdul Rahman Private Papers
  H.S. Lee Private Papers

Tan Cheng Lock Private Papers
K.G. Tregonning Private Papers

Colonial Office/Foreign Office despatches
Report of the Federation of Malaya Constitutional Commission 1957. Colonial No. 330. London: Colonial Office.
"Activities of the *Kuomintang* in Malaya", 17 March 1930; FO Memorandum by Sir John Pratt, 3 April 1930. FCO 371/14728/1489.
Monthly Review of Chinese Affairs. Secret reports from the Secretary of Chinese Affairs, Federation of Malaya. FCO141-7622 to 7631.

Interviews
Douglas Lee
George Lee
Thomas Lee

INDEX

Note: Page numbers followed by "n" refer to endnotes.

A

Abdul Razak Hussein, 172, 179, 181
A History of Malaysia (Barbara and Leonard Andaya), 205
Albert, Prince. *See* George, King
Alliance National Council, 185
All Malaya Chinese Mining Association, 145
All-Malayan Indian Independence League, 62
Amendment of the Malay Reservations Act of 1933, 16
American Civil War, 11
America's Vietnam War, 123
Ang Cheng Chong, 45, 72
anti-communist law, 121
Anti-Enemy Backing-Up Society, 10
Anti-Fascist People's Freedom League, 130
anti-Japanese activities, 49
anti-Japanese sentiments, 44
Associated Chinese Chambers of Commerce, 145
Associated States of Indochina, 122
Aw Boon Haw, 47, 102
Axis powers, 121

B

Baba-Nyonya culture, 103
Baling Talks, 179
Bandung Conference, 25
Bank Negara Tanah Melayu (Central Bank of Malaya), 190
Barisan Nasional, 183, 205
Battle of Imphal in India, 63
Beijing, 39, 43, 120, 154
Bell, Martin, 81, 91, 92
Bolshevik propaganda, 68
Bombay, Lee Hau-Shik living in, 107–9
Bose, Subhas Chandra, 62, 63

Boxer Rebellion, 39
Briggs, Harold, 165
Britain's Special Operations
   Executive (SOE), 105, 106
British
   state of emergency, 164
   support for MCA, 160
   treating Chinese, 143
British Malaya, 31, 41, 51, 64, 69, 126
British Military Administration (BMA), 16, 135, 142, 143
British military rule, 132–137
British North Borneo, 129, 131
British Royal Marines, 132
British Straits Settlements, 11, 12
Broome, R.N., 106
Brunei, 129, 131
Burma, 129, 130
   Lee Hau-Shik, 75
   Malayan Communist Party, 73
   reoccupation of, 147
Burmese Chinese, 102

C
Cairo Declaration states, 138n3
Calcutta, 50, 63, 75, 81, 83–86, 90, 99, 106
Central Bank of Malaya (Bank Negara Tanah Melayu), 190
Ceylon, 70, 106, 130, 200
chaos of re-occupation, Malaya, 142

Chiang Kai-shek, 36, 60, 118, 120
China Press, 153, 203
China Relief Committees, 102
China Relief Fund Associations, 45
China's Consul in Kuala Lumpur, 84
China's May Fourth Movement of 1919, 67
Chinese Advisory Board, 20
Chinese Chamber of Commerce, 20, 21
Chinese chauvinism, 26
Chinese Communist Party (CCP), 5, 60, 67, 68, 69, 104, 105, 144, 153, 154
Chinese Consul General Kuo Ling Pak, 83
Chinese educationists, 156
Chinese labourers, 11, 16
Chinese Miners' Association, 44
Chinese nationalism, 51
Chinese politics, 26
Chinese population, 144
Chinese Protectorate, 5
Chinese school system, 26
Chinese Tin Mines Rehabilitation Loans Board, 145
Chinese Tin Mines Rehabilitation Loans Fund, 145
Chinese unemployment, 11
Chinese Unit of All India Radio, 93
Chinese vernacular education, 69

Index

Chin Peng, 179
Chungking
    Federated Malay States, 90
    Hau-Shik's plans, 85
    inflation rate, 85
    Kwangtung Provincial Bank, 86
    Martin Bell, 91, 92
    Overseas Chinese Industrial Bank, 89
    refugees of Chinese origin, 105
    South Seas Chinese Association, 95, 100
Chung Kuo Council for General Mobilization, 49
Churchill, Winston, 118
citizenship rights, 151, 195
civil society movements, 183
Civil War, 120
Clementi, Cecil, 69, 136
Cochin China, 122
Cold War, 71–74, 119, 153, 164
colonialism, 17, 18, 64, 75, 118, 150
colonial Malayan economy
    agricultural sector, Malay Peninsula, 8
    Anti-Enemy Backing-Up Society, 10
    Chinese unemployment, 11
    Colonialism's plural society, 17, 18

Communist Party of Malaya, 9, 10
contract labour system, 9
contractors, 8
employers and employees, organizations, 5
Federated Malay States, 6, 9
female migration. *See* female migration
Government of India's Indian Emigration Act of 1922, 4, 5
the Great Depression, 6, 7, 10, 11
Hainanese, 6
indentured labour system, 4
Indian workers, 5
in Kajang, 10
Labour Code, 4
labour force, 7
labour movement activities, 5
labour unions in Malaya, 5, 6
political developments, 7
rubber production and mining of tin, 4
tin in twentieth century, 11–14
tin production, 11
urbanity and unemployment, 14–16
world economy by 1931, 6
Colonial Office, 96

colonial policy, 146
Comfort Mission, 47
Comintern, 133
Communism, 123, 166
Communist Party of Malaya (CPM), 9, 10
communist rebels, 165
communist terrorists, 157, 159
Community Liaison Committee (CLC), 161, 67
contract labour system, 9
contractors, 8, 9

D
Davis, J.L.H., 106
Dawn Kathleen Glen, 40
death marches, 131
Development & Commercial (D&C) Bank, 33, 202
Devonshire House in Mussoorie, 84
Dien Bien Phu, 123
direct taxation, 188
domestic expenditure, 190
draconian laws, 183
Dutch Borneo, 131
Dutch colonialism, 64
Dutch-controlled Banda Islands, 8

E
East India Company, 31
economic policy, 185
Emergency Regulations Ordinance of 1948, 165

Emerson, Rupert, 17, 18, 27n3, 46, 51
European colonialism, 118

F
Federal Executive Council, 145
federal expenditures, 189
Federal Finance Committee, 145
Federal Legislative Council, 145, 178
Federated Malay States, 6, 9, 16, 41, 65, 69, 70, 90, 102, 129, 136
Federated Malay States Chamber of Mines, 144
Federation of China Relief Fund of the South Seas, 47, 72
Federation of Malaya Agreement, 149, 154, 155, 161
Female Domestic Servants Bill of 1925, 22, 23
female migration
    Chinese Chamber of Commerce, 20, 21
    Chinese female immigration, 19
    Chinese migration in Malaya, 24
    in Chinese schools, 25
    domestic labour, 22
    education policies in Malaya, 26
    after the First World War, 19
    government and secret societies, 20

the Great Depression, 20
Indian immigrants, 19
Kuomintang, 24, 25
Lee Hau-Shik's economic stature, 27
marriage prospects of male Chinese, 21
prostitutes, 21, 22
after the Second World War, 19
socio-economic situation, 26
squatter population, 23
Straits Settlements, 22, 23, 27
in tin and rubber industries, 23
French Vichy government, 121

G
Gandhi, Mahatma, 129
Gaozhou Association, 45
Gent, Edward, 142, 143, 148, 157
George, King, 39, 52n3, 111n30, 146
global wars
    All-Malayan Indian Independence League, 62
    British Malaya, 64
    Chinese Communist Party in 1927, 60
    Cold War, 71–74
    East Asia, 76, 77
    Greater East Asian Co-Prosperity Sphere, 61
    India's Army of Liberation, 63
    Japan's invasion of China, 74, 75
    Kesatuan Melayu Muda, 65
    liberating Asia and Asians, 62
    Masanobu Tsuji, Colonel, 61
    Military Administration in Malaya, 75
    Ownership and Control in the Malayan Economy, 63
    Pacific War, 75
    Peninsular Malays, 64
    "pro-Malay policy", 65
    "reading clubs" (*Epposho*) in Malayan cities, 75
    Shenyang, 60
    Singora (Songkhla), 62
    Sino-Japanese war. *See* Sino-Japanese war
    Tokyo's modernization, 59, 60
    Versailles Treaty of 1919, 60
Government of India's Indian Emigration Act of 1922, 4, 5
Great Depression, The, 6, 7, 10–11, 20
Greater East Asian Co-Prosperity Sphere, 61, 62
Guangdong Province, 36, 38
Guangxi Province, 36
guerrilla army, 147
guerrilla war, 15, 76, 122, 154
Gurney, Henry, 154, 156–58, 162, 164, 167

H

Hailam community, 68
Hakka Association, 47
Hamid, Abdul, 182
Hisaichi, Terauchi, 124
Ho Chi Minh, 121, 122, 133

I

immigrants, 16, 27, 147
indentured labour system, 4
independence, 163, 164, 170, 172, 174–176
Independence of Malaya Party (IMP), 152, 167, 168, 169
India, 4, 6, 31, 51, 63, 64, 129, 142, 153, 171, 182
Indian Communism party, 129
Indian customs, 90
Indian immigrants, 19, 147
Indian labourers, 5, 18
Indian National Army (INA), 62, 63, 147
India's Army of Liberation, 63
Indo-Chinese governments, 122
Indonesia, 109, 123–125, 127, 147, 183
Industrial Development Policy, 192
inflation, 189
inter-ethnic strife, 142
International Bank for Reconstruction and Development (IBRD), 189
International Finance Corporation (IFC), 189
International Monetary Fund (IMF), 189
International Tin Conference, 157, 172
Ismail Abdul Rahman, 171, 173–175, 179, 181, 183

J

Japan, 4, 32, 36, 37, 44, 60, 71, 107, 108, 118, 119, 124, 128, 138, 147
Japanese forces, 152
Japanese invaders, 131
Japanese invasion, 13, 43, 48, 74, 75, 90, 97
Japanese liberation, 123
Japanese military ambitions, 66
Japanese occupation, 76, 147
Japanese surrender, 125–132, 142, 146, 147
Japan's European Axis partner, 47
Japan's Southern Expedition Army Group, 124
Java, 124, 126
Jennings, Ivor, 182

K

Kam Gu-chan (a.k.a. Kho Chun), 34, 35
Kam Kho Chun, 34
Kam Kwok-Chun, 40, 43
Kam Lun Tai, 34, 37, 38, 42–44
Kam, Samuel, 34, 35, 51n2
Karen separatists, 130

Kekuatan Rakyat Istimewa (KRIS), 108
Kesatuan Melayu Muda (KMM), 65
Khoo Teck Ee, 158, 160, 195n36
Knight Commander of the British Empire (KBE), 201
Korean War, 119, 122–123
Kuala Lumpur, 41–44, 81, 84, 91, 93, 103, 104, 106, 109
   election, 167, 168
   electoral triumph in, 170
   United Malays National Organisation, 167
Kuala Lumpur Sanitary Board, 144
Kuan Cheng Girls School, 144
Kuomintang (KMT), 5, 6, 24, 25, 38, 144, 152–154
   branches, 68
   member, 89
   resurgence, 67
   troops, 122
Kwan Choi Lin, 41
Kwangsi Province, 34
Kwang Tung Province, 34
Kwangtung Provincial Bank, 86
Kwong Wah Yit Poh, 153

L

Labour Code, 4
Lau Pak Khuan (also Lau Pak Kwun), 46, 89, 91, 109, 110n26, 159, 195n37

leaders of guilds and associations, 156
Lee, Alex, 202
Lee Chee Lin, 36
Lee, Douglas, 181, 202
Lee Hau Mo, 34, 141
Lee Hau-Shik
   budget statements, 187, 188
   Burmese Chinese and Straits Settlements, 102
   China's Ministry of Overseas Affairs (Yuen, K.L.), 84
   in Chungking, 85
   contributions in post-war years, 146
   departure from India, 141
   economic stature, 27
   Evacuees Committee, Chairman of, 82
   federal budget, 187
   in India, 84
   loss of chairmanship over Selangor MCA, 181
   Malayan Chinese, 101
   Malayan Chinese Association, 156, 160, 167
   Malayan Communist Party, 105, 106
   "Martin" (Major J.M. Bell), 81
   Member for Railways and Ports, 171
   positions held, 144, 145
   return to Malaya, 144

Rotary Club of Dehra Dun, 84
taxes, 188
United Malays National Organisation, 164, 167
Lee Hau Wai, 34
Lee Kam Hing, 203, 206n4
Lee Kwai Lim (a.k.a. Lee Chee Lin; Li Tou Kong), 36, 203
Lee, Thomas, 203, 204
Lee Wai Sheung, 36
Leong Yew Koh, 151, 162, 173, 179
Leung Cheung Ling, 180
Lim Bo Seng, 106
Lim Chong Eu, 175, 184, 185, 202
Lim, Robert M.K., 93
local elections, 163, 166, 167, 171

M

Macdonald, Malcolm, 161
MacGillivray, Donald, 173, 174
MacMichael, Harold, 137, 148
Malaya, 64
    Abdul Razak Hussein, 172
    communists and elections, 167–178
    Community Liaison Committee, 161–167
    economics and stability, 185–192
    establishing of central bank, 189, 191
    Indian immigrant labourers, 147
    Industrial Development Policy, 192
    International Bank for Reconstruction and Development, 189
    International Finance Corporation, 189
    International Monetary Fund, 189
    Japanese occupation of, 147
    local elections, 166
    Malayan Chinese Association. *See* Malayan Chinese Association (MCA)
    Merdeka compact, 178–185
    nationalist Chinese movement in, 154
    population, 146, 186
    reoccupation of, 147
    rural development, 187
    rural population, 186
    sources of revenue, 188
    urban development, 186
Malayan Association of India, 103
Malayan Chinese, 66, 80, 81, 91, 94, 95, 98, 101, 103–105
Malayan Chinese Association (MCA), 33, 99, 104, 111, 153, 156, 158–160, 162, 169, 173, 185, 201

Index

Chinese educationists, 156
English-educated
   professionals, 156
   funds, 166
   leaders of guilds and
     associations, 156
   membership, 166
   political collaboration with
     UMNO, 164, 168, 171
   role in quiet war, 164
   Tan Cheng Lock, 163, 168
Malayan Chinese community,
   27, 100, 104, 134
Malayan Chinese population, 17
Malayan Communist Party (MCP),
   15, 49, 68, 72, 73, 74, 104–107,
   133, 147, 152–154, 164
   active or material assistance,
     164
   brutal murders, 164
   campaign of violence and
     terror, 164
Malayan Democratic Union
   (MDU), 151
Malayan evacuees, 104
Malayan General Labour Union
   (MGLU), 9
Malayan Indian Congress (MIC),
   174
Malayan Oxbridge Alumni
   Association, 35
Malayan People's Anti-Japanese
   Army (MPAJA), 49, 132, 147
Malayan race (*bangsa Malayan*), 65

Malayan society, 71
Malayan sultanates, 128
Malayan Union, 142, 143, 148,
   149
Malayan Union Advisory
   Council, 145
Malay community, 63, 158
Malay nationalism, 152
Malay Nationalist Party (MNP), 109
Malay political power, 143
Malik, B., 182
Mao Zedong, 120, 155
Marco Polo Bridge Incident, 44
McKell, William, 182
Merdeka Compact, 183, 184
migrant labourers, 4, 27, 147
migrant workers, 31, 32
Military Administration in
   Malaya, 75
Miners' Association of Negeri
   Sembilan, 144
Mountbatten, Louis, 132
Muhammad Hatta, 64, 124
mui tsai system, 22–23
municipal elections, in Penang,
   167
Mussoorie, 84, 85, 87, 88, 90, 93,
   94, 99, 101

N

Nanyang Chinese communities,
   45
Nanyang Provisional
   Commission, 73

Nanyang Siang Pau, 153
Napoleonic Wars, 8, 126
Nationalistic Party (Kuo Min Tang), 24
New Economic Policy (NEP), 183
North Borneo Chartered Company, 132, 137

O
Oi Sim, 34
Ong Yoke Lin, 169, 179, 180
Onn Ja'afar, 148, 161, 170
    Independence of Malaya Party (IMP), 152, 168
On Tai, 203
Opium Wars, 32, 59, 129
Overseas Chinese, 66, 83, 84, 87, 91, 94, 95, 100, 101
Overseas Chinese Affairs Commission, 155
Overseas Chinese Association (OCA), 98, 99, 105, 156
Overseas Chinese Industrial Bank, 89

P
Pacific War, 51, 64, 75, 96
Pan-Malaya Malay Congress, 148
Pan-Malayan Council for Joint Action (PMCJA), 151
Pan-Malayan Federation of Trade Unions, 164
Pan-Malayan Labour Party, 174

Pan-Malayan Third Representatives Conference, 73
Pan-Malaysian Islamic Party, 167
Parti Kebangsaan Melayu Malaya (PKMM), 109, 149
Penang, 8, 14, 20, 21, 31, 37, 45, 48, 132, 135, 137, 154, 174
Peninsular Malays, 64
People's Liberation Army in Shanghai, 43, 44
People's Political Consultative Conference, 155
People's Republic of China, 120
Perak, 11, 12, 14, 16
Pergerakan Melayu Semenanjung (Johor), 148
Philippines, 108, 121, 124
political agitation, 143
political consciousness, 66, 109, 124, 144
political polarization, 176
politics
    in Asia, 117, 118
    British military rule, 132–137
    European colonialism, 118
    hot war to cold war, 119–125
    Japanese surrender, 125–132
    modification and reformulation, 118
    Potsdam Declaration, 119
Port Dickson, 109, 135
Port Swettenham, 135
Potsdam Declaration, 119

Index

"pro-Malay policy" of recruitment, 65
prostitutes, 21, 22
Purcell, Victor, 93, 111n30
Pusat Tenaga Rakyat (PUTERA), 151
Puthucheary, James Joseph, 63

Q
Qing Dynasty, 33, 154
Qing government, 36

R
Rangoon Chinese, 103
Rawlings, G.S., 92, 93
Reading Rooms (Shu Po She), 24
refuge in India
   in Bombay, 107–109
   Britain's Special Operations Executive, 105, 106
   Burmese Chinese, 102
   bus terminus at Kineraig, 88, 89
   in Calcutta, 81
   China's Consul in Kuala Lumpur, 84
   Chinese Communist Party, 104, 105
   Chinese Wartime capital, 90–97
   Chungking, 85–87
   Evacuees Committee, 82
   Federated Malay States, 102
   Haiching, 82–83
   Hau-Shik's case. *See* Lee Hau-Shik
   Japanese invasion of India, 90
   Kwangtung Provincial Bank, 86
   Lim Bo Seng, 106
   Malayan Association of India, 103
   Malayan Chinese, 80, 81
   Malayan Chinese Association, 104
   Malayan Chinese community-in-exile, 100
   Malayan Communist Party, 104–107
   Malayan evacuees, 104
   "Martin", 81, 82
   in Mussoorie, 84
   Overseas Chinese Association, 98, 99, 105
   Overseas Chinese evacuation, 83, 84, 87
   Overseas Chinese Industrial Bank, 89
   Republic of China, 97
   Rotary Club members, 84
   Straits Settlements, 102, 103
   Tan Cheng Lock, 100, 101
Reid, Anthony, 127
Reid Commission, 181
"The Road of Independence", 176
Roosevelt, Franklin, 118

Royal Economics Society, 40
rubber industry, 4, 6, 14, 23
   unemployment in, 166
rural development, 186, 187
rural population, 186

S
Sarawak, 129, 131, 132
Selangor China Relief Fund
   Association, 43, 46
Selangor Chinese Assembly Hall, 104
Selangor Chinese Chamber of
   Commerce (SCCC), 41, 42, 144, 145, 151, 159
Selangor Guangdong Association, 44
Shenyang, 60
Sih, S.H., 84, 88, 89
Silcock, T.H., 185, 198n84
Sin Chew Jit Poh, 47, 153
Singapore
   Comfort Mission, 47, 48
   CPM's attention, 10
   Ee Hoe Ean Club, 45, 46
   INA recruits, 62
   Kao Ling-pai, 45
   KMT networks, 152
   Lee Hau-Shik, 50
   Lim Bo Seng, 106
   and Penang, 14, 37, 135
   Robert M.K. Lim, 93
   S.S. *Haiching*, 82, 82
   Tan Kah Kee, 102

Tung Meng Hui, Tokyo-
   based, 67
Singapore China Relief Fund
   Association, 72
Singora (Songkhla), 62
Sino-Japanese war, 45, 51, 152
   Bolshevik propaganda, 68
   Chinese Communist Party, 67, 69
   Chinese vernacular
      education, 69
   Clementi's autocratic
      temperament, 70
   cultural transformation, 66
   High Commissioner, 70
   Kuomintang's resurgence, 67
   Malayan Chinese and
      Japanese military
      ambitions, 66
   Malayan Communist Party, 68
   Malayan society, 71
   political consciousness, 66
   Sun Yat-sen, 67
   Treaty of Versailles of 1919, 66
   Unfederated Malay States, 70
   Wuchang Uprising of 1911, 67
Socialist Republic of Vietnam, 123
South East Asia Command, 147
Southeast Asian archipelago, 126
Southern Republican Party, 24

Index

South Seas Chinese Association Malayan Branch, 95
South-West Pacific Area (SWPA), 131
Sri Maharaja Mangku Negara (SMN), 201
S.S. *Haiching*, 82, 83
state legislature elections, 184
Straits Chinese, 102
Straits Chinese British Association (SCBA), 162
Straits of Malacca, 128
Straits Settlements, 22, 23, 27, 69, 83, 102, 103, 129
Straits Times, 201, 202
Sukarno, 64, 124
Sumatra, 81, 106
    East Coast Residency, 127
    Japanese surrender, 126
    and Malaya, 127
Sun Yat-sen, 34, 36, 38, 67
Swatow, 82

T
Tan Cheng Lock, 92, 97–101, 112n56, 142, 143, 144, 151, 152, 159, 160, 163, 180, 184, 193n6, 195n37
    dealings with IMP and Onn Ja'afar, 170
    Overseas Chinese Association, 156
Tan Kah Kee, 45–47, 49–51, 72, 102, 154, 155

Tan Siew Sin, 98, 170, 203
Templer, Gerald, 168, 171–173
Thuraisingham, Dato, 169
tin industry, 4, 11, 12, 23, 38, 43, 44
    unemployment in, 166
Tokyo's modernization, 59, 60
Tokyo's surrender, 131
Treaty of London, 126
Treaty of Versailles of 1919, 66
Tregonning, K.G., 76, 142, 193n5, 196n40
Tsuji, Masanobu, 61, 77n3
Tung Meng Hui, 38, 67
Tunku Abdul Rahman, 170–175, 179, 181, 185

U
UMNO-MCA alliance, 163, 170, 176
unemployment, 14
Unfederated Malay States, 70, 129
United Kingdom, 6, 171, 182, 188, 189
United Malays National Organisation (UMNO), 143, 149, 150, 152, 158, 164, 167–169, 173, 182
    general assembly, 179
United Soviet Socialist Republic, 121
United States, 6, 11, 13, 32, 119, 121, 123, 125, 183

United States of Indonesia, 125
urban development, 186
urbanity, 14

V
Versailles Treaty of 1919, 60
Viet Minh, 122, 123
Vietnam, 121–124, 147
Vietnam Independent League, 121
Vivian Leslie, 40

W
Wang Gungwu, 63, 77n6
War Damage Commission, 145

Waring, Douglas, 42, 43
wartime China, 90–97
Wedyodiningrat, Radjiman, 124
Wuchang Uprising of 1911, 67

Y
Yong Pung How, 180, 185
Yong Shook Lin, 158, 160, 162, 195n35
Yong Yung Tai, 40
Yue Wai, 34

ABOUT THE AUTHOR

Dato' Dr **OOI Kee Beng** is Executive Director of Penang Institute, before which he was Deputy Director of ISEAS – Yusof Ishak Institute (2011–17). He is founder-editor of the popular magazine *Penang Monthly*, and the policy briefs *ISSUES* (at Penang Institute) and *ISEAS Perspective* (at ISEAS). He is also the long-time editor of *Trends in Southeast Asia* (at ISEAS), and a regular columnist for *The Edge Malaysia*.

His bestselling book, *The Reluctant Politician: Tun Dr Ismail and His Time* (2006), won the "Award of Excellence for Best Writing Published in Book Form on Any Aspect of Asia (Non-Fiction)". *Continent, Coast, Ocean: Dynamics of Regionalism in Eastern Asia*, a co-edited volume with Ding Choo Ming, was named "Top Academic Work" in 2008 by the ASEAN Book Publishers Association (ABPA).

Other noted works include *Yusof Ishak: A Man of Many Firsts* (2017); *The Eurasian Core and Its Edges: Dialogues with Wang Gungwu on the History of the World* (2015); *Young and Malay: Growing Up in Multicultural Malaysia* (2015); *Lim Kit Siang: Defying the Odds* (2015); *The Right to Differ: A Biographical Sketch of Lim Kit Siang* (2011); and *In Lieu of Ideology: An Intellectual Biography of Goh Keng Swee* (2010).

His translations of Chinese war strategy such as *Sunzi's Art of War*, *Wuzi's Art of War* and *Weiliaozi's Art of War* are the first from classical Chinese into Swedish, and are used in leadership training courses at the Stockholm Military College. He represented Sweden in the First Wushu World Championship held in Beijing in 1991, and was the silver medallist in the Taijiquan Form Competition at the 1991 European Wushu Championship held in London.

In 2017, he was awarded the *Darjah Setia Pangkuan Negeri (DSPN)* by the Governor of Penang State, for services rendered to his home state of Penang, which carries the title of "Dato".

He is Adjunct Professor (2019–) at Taylor's University, Malaysia, and was Visiting Associate Professor at the Department of Public and Social Administration, City University of Hong Kong (2009–12) and Adjunct Associate Professor for the Southeast Asian Studies Programme at the National University of Singapore (2009–11).

His most recent books include *Catharsis: A Second Chance for Democracy in Malaysia* (2018), his seventh compilation of commentaries and analyses on Malaysia and the Southeast Asian region, and *Month by Month: A Compilation of Editorials by Ooi Kee Beng* (2019).

Homepage: wikibeng.com

Lee Kwai Lim (1877–1936), Hau-Shik's father.

Lee Joy Weng (1849–95), Hau-Shik's grandfather.

The tomb of Lee Kwai Lim, Hau-Shik's father, taken in 1984.

The young Hau-Shik

Horse-riding at Cambridge

Hau-Shik and his favourite mode of transport during his time at Cambridge University.

Hau-Shik (front row, far left) was at St John's College, Cambridge University, from 1921 to 1924.

Hau-Shik (front row, centre) with other officers of the South Division, Air Raid Precaution (ARP) Kuala Lumpur, 12 November 1941.

Hau-Shik spent the war years in India. Here, Hau-Shik (fifth from right, second row) at the Baroda Open Golf Tournament 1945.

Hau-Shik and his wife Kwan Choi Lin, both in traditional Chinese dress.

A family portrait taken during the war years, which the family spent in India, 1942–45.

Kwan Choi Lin, Hau-Shik's wife.

Hau-Shik in ceremonial dress to receive his knighthood.

A family portrait of the Lee family, taken in 1960.

Hau-Shik with British High Commissioner in Malaya, Field Marshal Sir Gerald Templer. Clough Thuraisingham, Member for Education in the Legislative Council, is second from right. Hau-Shik was Member for Railways and Ports.

Hau-Shik with Tunku Abdul Rahman, Malaya's first Prime Minister.

Hau-Shik speaking at a Malayan Chinese Association general assembly.

Prime Minister Tunku Abdul Rahman, Deputy Prime Minister and Minister of Education Abdul Razak Hussein and Minister of Finance Lee Hau-Shik.

Hau-Shik with Mohamed Khir Johari, Malaya's first Minister of Education, on the occasion of a donation from his bank to the World Wide Fund for Nature of Malaysia (WWF) of which Khir Johari was the president.

Hau-Shik with Tan Siew Sin, his successor as Minister of Finance.

From left, Abdul Razak Hussein, Lee Hau-Shik, Ismail Abdul Rahman, V.T. Sambanthan, Sulaiman Abdul Rahman and Ong Yoke Lin. Hau-Shik was conferred a Tunship in 1957.

Hau-Shik wearing his Tunship medallion.

Hau-Shik receiving the award of Tunship from the Yang di-Pertuan Agong in 1957.

Golf was Hau-Shik's favourite pastime activity.

A rare picture of a smiling Hau-Shik. Here, he was about to board an MSA flight.

The Lee Clan Association was founded in 1948, with Hau-Shik as its first president. This picture was taken at the 1955 launching of the association's new building.

Hau-Shik and his delegation to an International Tin Council meeting in Washington.

Hau-Shik represented Malayan interests fervently at International Tin Council meetings until 1960.

Hau-Shik (centre, front row), president of the Malayan Olympic Council, with council members, 1958.

Hau-Shik was the Chief of Mission at the Asian Games in 1958.

Hau-Shik went into banking after his retirement from politics, and founded the Development & Commercial Bank. The picture is from the official opening of the bank, in 1966.

Hau-Shik and his wife Kwan Choi Lin, with England's Queen Elizabeth II and Prince Philip, and Princess Anne, during the Queen's visit to Malaysia in 1972.

Hau-Shik and his wife Kwan Choi Lin with England's Princess Margaret during her visit to Malaysia in 1980.

Hau-Shik celebrating his 82nd birthday

Prime Minister Dr Mahathir Mohamed, with Alex Lee at Hau-Shik's wake. Hau-Shik's funeral took place on Sunday, 26 June 1988.

Three of Hau-Shik's sons at his wake, in June 1988 (from left to right: Douglas, Thomas and Alex).

www.ingramcontent.com/pod-product-compliance
Lightning Source LLC
Chambersburg PA
CBHW051806230426
43672CB00012B/2650